CultureShock!
A Survival Guide to Customs and Etiquette

Berlin

Agnes Sachsenroeder

Marshall Cavendish Editions

This edition published in 2009 by:
Marshall Cavendish Corporation
99 White Plains Road
Tarrytown NY 10591-9001
www.marshallcavendish.us

Other Marshall Cavendish Offices:
Marshall Cavendish International (Asia) Pte Ltd. 1 New Industrial Road,
Singapore 536196 ■ Marshall Cavendish Ltd. 5th Floor, 32-38 Saffron Hill,
London EC1N 8FH, UK ■ Marshall Cavendish International (Thailand) Co Ltd.
253 Asoke, 12th Flr, Sukhumvit 21 Road, Klongtoey Nua, Wattana, Bangkok
10110, Thailand ■ Marshall Cavendish (Malaysia) Sdn Bhd, Times Subang,
Lot 46, Subang Hi-Tech Industrial Park, Batu Tiga, 40000 Shah Alam, Selangor
Darul Ehsan, Malaysia

Marshall Cavendish is a trademark of Times Publishing Limited

ISBN: 978-0-7614-5681-0

Please contact the publisher for the Library of Congress catalogue number

Printed in Singapore by Times Printers Pte Ltd

Photo Credits:
All black and white photos from the author. All colour images from Photolibrary.
■ Cover photo: Corbis.

All illustrations by TRIGG

ABOUT THE SERIES

Culture shock is a state of disorientation that can come over anyone who has been thrust into unknown surroundings, away from one's comfort zone. *CultureShock!* is a series of trusted and reputed guides which has, for decades, been helping expatriates and long-term visitors to cushion the impact of culture shock whenever they move to a new country.

Written by people who have lived in the country and experienced culture shock themselves, the authors share all the information necessary for anyone to cope with these feelings of disorientation more effectively. The guides are written in a style that is easy to read and covers a range of topics that will arm readers with enough advice, hints and tips to make their lives as normal as possible again.

Each book is structured in the same manner. It begins with the first impressions that visitors will have of that city or country. To understand a culture, one must first understand the people—where they came from, who they are, the values and traditions they live by, as well as their customs and etiquette. This is covered in the first half of the book

Then on with the practical aspects—how to settle in with the greatest of ease. Authors walk readers through how to find accommodation, get the utilities and telecommunications up and running, enrol the children in school and keep in the pink of health. But that's not all. Once the essentials are out of the way, venture out and try the food, enjoy more of the culture and travel to other areas. Then be immersed in the language of the country before discovering more about the business side of things.

To round off, snippets of basic information are offered before readers are 'tested' on customs and etiquette of the country. Useful words and phrases, a comprehensive resource guide and list of books for further research are also included for easy reference.

CONTENTS

Introduction vi

Acknowledgements vii

Map of Berlin viii

Chapter 1
First Impressions 1

Chapter 2
An Overview 6

The Geography 7

The Weather 9

The History 9

The Administrative Set-Up 37

Chapter 3
The Berliners 43

Who is a Berliner? 44

What are Berliners Like? 46

The Teutonic People 46

The Foreigners 62

Are Berliners Atheists? 67

The Demography 76

Not the Fashion Capital 76

Chapter 4
Hobnobbing with the Berliners 78

The General Public 80

The Neighbours 83

Family and Friends 85

Special Occasions 87

Berlin Vis A Vis the EU 91

How Berliners View Foreigners 92

Prostitution 97

Chapter 5
Settling In 99

What to Bring 100

Visas 102

Registrations and Residence Permits 104

Accommodation 107

Shopping 124

Communications 133

Banking 135

Debit and Credit Cards 136

Postal Services 136

Knowing the Quality of a Product 137

Transport 138

Media 153

Time 155

Health Matters 155

Places of Learning 159

Beggars, Buskers and the Homeless 160

Chapter 6
Food 163

Typical German and Berlin Food 165

What Berliners Drink 171

Foreign Influences 173

The Different Meals of the Day 174

The Different Types of Eateries 175

Watering Holes 182

Chapter 7
Enjoying Freizeit in Berlin 184

Public Holidays 187

Other Events 195

Leisure Pursuits 198

Sports and Fitness 207

Green Oases 213

For the Young and Young at Heart 217

Bird's Eye View of Berlin 219

Chapter 8
Language 221

How Easy or Hard? 222

Where to Learn German 225

The German Alphabet 225

Colloquialism and
Imported Words 227

Berlinerisch 228

Punctuation 228

Non-verbal Communication 229

Chapter 9
Business in Berlin 230

The Economy 231

Germany 232

The Job Market 234

Work Attitude 235

Time at and off Work 236

Women at Work 236

Business Etiquette 237

Clash of the Classes 243

Different Types of
Organisations 244

Unions and Works Councils 246

Chapter 10
Berlin at a Glance 248

Famous Berliners 252

Places of Interest 259

Acronyms and Abbreviations 278

Culture Quiz 282

Do's and Don'ts 288

Glossary 289

Resource Guide 293

Further Reading 306

About the Author 309

Index 310

INTRODUCTION

One might think that foreigners would have no cultural problems to contend with when living in Berlin, as it is a modern and cosmopolitan city. Yet, the reality is that even a German from another state would still be a little stumped as a newbie in Berlin. What more for a Briton, or an American from across the Pond.

This book is a road map for expatriates and long-term visitors on how Berliners tick, and how to get on and along in the city, down to how to separate rubbish for recycling, which, in Germany, is something for which you need an instruction manual.

Observations about the city and its people are as unbiased as is humanly possible, taking into account the views of a cross-section of expatriates and visitors. But when describing a group of people, there's always an element of generalisation involved. Readers of this book may find observations that they agree or disagree with, since we all have our own way of looking at things. The aim of this book is to alert you to certain characteristics of the city and its dwellers, but ultimately, this exciting city is for you to discover for yourself.

One other *caveat*: dynamic cities always change rather quickly, so between the time of writing this book and its coming off the press, prices may have changed, some shops closed or new ones opened. But that makes the city vibrant and fun for your exploring.

Viel Spaß in Berlin.

ACKNOWLEDGEMENTS

Many grateful thanks must go to my husband, who obligingly answered my questions about Germany through the years. More importantly, although he inwardly cringed over a few less complimentary observations of his fellow Germans, he never once tried to persuade me to change anything in this book, accepting the fact that such a book is written from foreigners' perspectives.

My exploration and understanding of the city were also made much easier and interesting by the many good guide books, websites, newspapers and magazines which I have mentioned in this book.

All the Berliners who I came to know personally or met in passing provided the canvas on which to work on. They have my thanks, too, including those who only growled at me, as they all helped in my compilation of the Berliner characteristics.

Carol King-Reed played a significant role in introducing me to the science of crossing cultures way back in 1998, and I thank her sincerely for that.

BERLIN DISTRICTS

MAP OF GERMANY

FIRST IMPRESSIONS

'One's destination is never a place,
but a new way of looking at things.'
-—Henry Valentine Miller (American author, 1891–1980)

I<small>T WAS THE SUMMER OF</small> 1998 when I first flew to Berlin. This was just eight years after German reunification and seven years after the German Bundestag (parliament) made the decision to move the capital of Germany from Bonn to Berlin, some 500 km north-eastwards.

My husband and I were in Berlin to check out our future accommodation and the city, like many other Germans affected by their employers' move to Berlin. Acutely aware that this wasn't just any city, but *the* city which was once the Prussian capital, where Hitler and his National Socialists planned their heinous crimes, and where an infamous 155 km (96.2 miles) long wall divided family and friends for 28 years.

With such a history, first-time visitors to Berlin, myself included, could be forgiven for having high expectations about the city, especially when it's the capital of Germany. Imagine, then, my surprise when I landed at Tegel Airport. I was dumb-struck by the relatively small and almost provincial Tegel. It wasn't lacking in efficiency, but it was certainly not what one imagines the capital of Germany's international airport should be. I mean, I was thinking Amsterdam-Schiphol, or Germany's Frankfurt airport, so the modest-sized Tegel was unexpected, to say the least.

In the city centre, I was also a tad disappointed that there was no old city centre, like say, the Grand Place in Brussels. Neither was it a pulsating, financial city with skyscrapers like

Frankfurt. Friedrichstrasse, a designated business district in the heart of the city (albeit formerly East Berlin) had more punks with spiked orange, green and red hair defying gravity with the help of a good strong gel than business people in sharp suits. Large plots of abandoned land stood forlornly in between buildings that had seen better days or were in the midst of being renovated. Granted, the city as a new capital was still in its diapers, but I was (unfairly perhaps) expecting more, having been awed by many other European capitals. Even signs of recent history were missing. We didn't see any remnants of the Wall or obvious signs of where the Wall might have stood. East and West Berlin merged seamlessly into one another.

More surprises were to come. We had decided on an apartment in the former East Berlin. No, it wasn't because my husband is an *Ossi* (East German), nor was it for any practical reason such as cheaper rent or being near his office either. No, nothing of that sort. It was purely because this *Wessi* (West German) was seized by nostalgia of childhood summer holidays spent in that area. He had fallen in love with the green surroundings. Now we were here in Berlin to sign the papers.

We set off to see, or should I say imagine, our future apartment, as at that time it was still under construction. As we made our way eastwards, all I could see was endless characterless buildings, neither old enough to give off an Old Europe charm nor modern enough for one to feel vibrancy and promise. As we moved into what was former East Berlin, the boring buildings were replaced by decrepit public housing blocks or dilapidated buildings, the only decoration of which were the graffiti on the walls. Oh dear. The people also seemed to have been frozen in time in terms of how they looked: denim shorts and those multi-coloured shirts which were so 'groovy' at the time when that adjective was still fashionable. Many had haircuts which were short in front and at the sides but left long behind. Like how the male members of the pop group ABBA looked during their heydays, only that this was a whole generation ago.

After we'd parked the car in front of the signboard that declared that the plot of unfinished business behind was where our intended apartment would be, I got out, and if truth be told, filled with scepticism. Then suddenly, from the corner of my eyes, I spotted a body of water. It turned out that the apartment-to-be was next to a lake. My scepticism went down a few notches (much to the relief of my husband) as we went towards the lake. It was as the advertisement had trumpeted. A huge natural lake with curious ducks and swans hoping for a snack from us as we stood on the edge. We went round the back of the site and were met by a forested area, much to our delight.

And that was how our relationship with Berlin developed over the next decade. A city which initially did not seem very appealing turned out to be one with a great potential waiting to be discovered. A city which did have historic buildings, a wealth of museums, fabulous lakes and forests and reminders of the Nazi era and the divided city, once you know where to look for them. After the initial letdown, I realised that what made Berlin special is its whole traumatic history, and that to see and feel this chequered history, one needs to work one's way to various different sites to take the different bits in.

I was to discover that not only did the city have different faces, but it was also developing at a gallop. The changes taking place in Berlin within a decade were all the more obvious to us, as between 1997 and 2003, we lived overseas due to my husband's postings, coming back to Berlin for home leave to be amazed at the rate that Berlin was growing. From dilapidated ruins to the largest construction site in Europe to a modern city centre with spanking new office blocks and shopping arcades, the city just grew and grew. It felt as if each trip back to Berlin was a first-time visit.

Visitors coming to Berlin these days will find new office buildings and shopping malls, lovingly renovated old buildings, a vairety of eating places to suit all tastes and budgets, a quirky nightlife drawing an international crowd and so many memorials that it is causing a lot of hand-wringing as to where the next memorial should be located. Many of the old communist apartment blocks have also been

Berlin Hauptbahnhof is the main railway station in Berlin, and the largest crossing station in Europe.

given new clothes, and they are now dressed in cheerful colours. Friedrichstrasse is no longer the hang-out of punks, but home to elegant offices, restaurants, apartments and luxury shopping temples, such as the Friedrichstadtpassagen-corridors of posh tenants like Galeries Lafayette, Gucci and Versace. Tegel Airport is full of new shops and frankly, overcrowded. It will, anyhow, be closed when the Berlin-Brandenburg International Airport at Schönefeld is completed around 2011.

Whenever I think back on my first introduction to Berlin, I never fail to marvel at how the city has changed in a short decade. I feel almost like a proud parent looking at a previously troubled teen who has grown into a fine young person, with a promising future ahead.

AN OVERVIEW

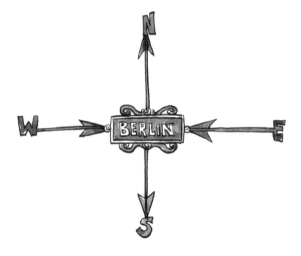

CHAPTER 2

'Berlin is definitely the most exciting city in Germany.
My overall impression is that people from the outside
perceive Berlin as young and dynamic......Berlin is multi-
faceted. I like the rich history one can experience, be it
buildings or streets one sees when simply walking or cycling
around ......It is fascinating and unique to experience the
integration of a city that had been divided for decades.'
—Associate Professor Jörg Rocholl, who joined the faculty
of the European School of Management and Technology in
Berlin, after eight years in the US

THE GEOGRAPHY

Berlin is located at 52° 31' 12'' N, roughly as far north of the equator as Birmingham, UK and Calgary, Alberta, Canada. It is tucked away at the north-eastern corner of Germany, just 80 km (49.7 miles) from the border with Poland.

Approximately 3.4 million people live in an area of 892 sq km (344 sq miles) with the widest expanse of the city standing at a distance of 45 km (27.9 miles) from east to west and 38 km ((23.6 miles) from north to south. It is slightly smaller than Washington and about half the size of London.

Berlin at a Glance

Area: 892 sq km (344 sq miles)

Population: 3.4 million

Coordinates: 52° 31'N, 13° 24' E

Location in Germany: North-east

Highest natural point: Müggelberg (115 m/379 ft)

The name 'Berlin' is widely thought to have Slavish roots; from 'Brl' which means 'marsh', giving you an idea of the city's foundation. A fairly flat and swampy city with a mean elevation above sea level of 35 m (114.8 feet), its highest natural elevation is the Müggelberg at a puny 115 m (377 ft).

Bridges over Untroubled Waters

Berlin has more bridges than even Venice—1662 in all.

Another hill, the Teufelsberg is also about 115 m (377 ft) high, but this hill in western Berlin is made from the rubble of the city after being subjected to carpet-bombing in World War II. During the Cold War, this hill served as an observation post for the Americans to spy on East Germany.

Yet, the landscape is not rendered bland by its flatness; the city has numerous lakes, and rivers and canals that worm their way around the city. The largest lake, the Müggelsee, is about 743 hectares with a depth of about 8 m (26 ft) at its deepest point. A total of 197 km (122 miles) of navigable waterways wind their way around the city. The longest river, the Spree is 45 km (27.9 miles) long and the longest canal, the Teltowcanal, extends to about 29.1 km (18 miles). In spite of the rather poor quality soil, Berlin is considerably green, with 18 per cent forests and woodlands, home to wild boars, foxes and hedgehogs.

Outside of the green areas, the city is not bare concrete or asphalt either. Some 416,300 trees line the streets, a legacy of Rudolf Virchow (1821–1902), medical professor and Berlin city councillor, who had trees planted along the streets to improve the air quality.

THE WEATHER

Berlin's location means it has hot summers and harsh winters. The average summer temperatures (June, July and August) can be anywhere between 23°C (73.4°F) to 30°C (86°F), although it has reached a record 37°C (98.6°F) before. In summer, the days are very long and it doesn't get really dark until at least 9 pm or so, making al fresco dining very popular in summer. However, summer is also the wettest time of the year, and can ruin all plans for activities in the open.

Winter temperatures usually drop to around minus 2°C (36°F), but can go far lower to minus 12°C (10°F). Not only are the months of December, January and February the coldest, but they are also the ones with the shortest hours of daylight (usually three to four hours of weak sunlight), leaving many Berlin residents often looking extra grim over the winter period. When snow falls, the landscape becomes rather magical, although making your way to work or school can be a nightmare. With global warming, the past few years have seen lighter snowfall. Once the temperatures fall below 0°C (32°F), the roads and paths ice over, and can become treacherously slippery.

THE HISTORY

> 'A people not willing to embrace it's past,
> ultimately forfeits it's future'
> —Alexander von Humboldt,
> German scientist & humanist

If Berlin were an actor, it would have surely won an Oscar for having played such a compelling role in so many historical epics that impacted on world politics. It is a city that will always remain tied to world history. Berlin of today and of the future is and will be a product of its growing up pains, especially those of the 20th century. To understand the city and its people, and some aspects of the architectural landscape as well, its history has to be looked at a little more closely.

Early Beginnings

Archeological finds suggest that there were people living around the area that is Berlin today as long ago as 8000 BC. In the middle of the 6th century, Slavic tribes started moving into the area. Two important settlements with significant economic activity developed during this time: one in Spandau and the other in Köpenick.

The Slavs continued to rule the area right up to the 10th century when Emperor Otto I brought all the Slav tribes under the jurisdiction of the German Empire. But the expansion plans of the German electors were short-lived and was ended in 983 AD by the Slav uprising.

In 1134, the German Emperor, Lothar III, appointed Albrecht the Bear (an Askanian prince) as Count of the North March (an area around Brandenburg). Albrecht's good relationship with the childless Prince of Brandenburg led to his being named as his heir. From 1157, Albrecht and his heirs called themselves the Margraves of Brandenburg. In order to keep a hold on power, Albrecht made sure the North March continued to expand, which led to the growth of two market towns, Berlin and Cölln (the area around present-day Museumsinsel and Nikolaiviertel). The first written record of Berlin/Cölln dates back to 1237. Even in those days of the original Berlin and Cölln, the population was made up largely of immigrants from other parts of present day Germany.

By the end of the 13th century, the two towns of Berlin and Cölln had superceded Köpenick and Spandau in importance. In 1432, the two towns on opposite banks of the Spree were formally united. Askanian rule ended, however, in 1320, after the death of the childless last Askanian, Heinrich. A bloody power struggle ensued between rival noble houses, leading the people to beg the Holy Roman Emperor for help.

Under the Hohenzollerns

The Emperor sent Friedrich I of Hohenzollern as a special protector, and in 1415, he was proclaimed Elector of Brandenburg. With that, the Hohenzollerns not only brought some order to the city, but would continue to rule for the next 500 years. The locals were not exactly welcoming in

the beginning, and attempts by the Elector to appropriate land from the people to build his royal residence met with the famed Berliner toughness. The Electors also had a brush with the toughness when they at first remained loyal to the Catholic faith after Martin Luther's reformation started spreading across Germany. In 1539, the Councils of Berlin and Cölln demanded for Evangelical rites and the Electors had to accede.

By the late 16th century, the population of Berlin and Cölln had reached some 12,000, but this was considered small compared to London and Paris then. However, by the end of the Thirty Years War in 1648, the combined ravages of war and bubonic plague had almost annihilated the population.

After the war, Berlin was to see many improvements under Friedrich Wilhelm (1620–1688), better known as the Great Elector. The palace was extended, private buildings encouraged, the local garrison strengthened, roads were cobbled and new districts developed. The Great Elector also opened up the Mark of Brandenburg to immigration. In 1671, exiled Jews from Vienna arrived and in 1685, 20,000 Huguenots expelled from Catholic France came; the Jews focused on finance and credit and the Huguenots in business and trade.

By the end of the Great Elector's reign, Berlin's total area had almost doubled.

In 1701, the Great Elector's son, Friedrich III, had himself crowned as King Friedrich I of Prussia. The architect, Andreas Schlüter, was tasked by the King to renovate the Palace and build the Zeughaus (today the Deutsches Historisches Museum). The Queen, Sophie Charlotte also played a hand in promoting culture and academic life.

It was during the reign of Friedrich I that the twin towns of Berlin/Cölln were merged into one administrative unit.

His son, King Friedrich Wilhelm I, was the polar opposite of his father. Instead of culture and grandeur, he invested in the military, earning himself the nickname of 'The Soldier King'. The standing army was increased to 80,000 men. The focus on military build-up resulted in the growth of the population and the rifle industry. Under his rule, parade grounds sprung up, such as the areas known today as Mehringplatz, Leipziger Platz and Pariser Platz.

His successor, King Friedrich II, better known as Frederick the Great, was revered for his turning Prussia into a military power (having entered into numerous protracted wars) and developing Berlin into an intellectual and cultural centre. The French philosopher, Voltaire, was invited to stay at the court in Potsdam, and this was also the time when people like the publisher Friedrich Nicolai, the philosopher Moses Mendelssohn and the writer Ephraim Lessing drew a fascinated intellectual crowd to Berlin. Theatre also started to flourish, a starting point of thespian Berlin.

Frederick the Great often promoted tolerance and open-mindedness, but the irony was that the Jews, including the renowned Moses Mendelssohn, continued to endure taunts and stone-throwing by hostile Berliners and had restrictions on the professions they could practise imposed on them.

'Religions must all be tolerated and the state must just be vigilant that no-one does anyone harm because here everyone must be allowed to be spiritual after their own fashion' —Frederick the Great, Prussian King (1712-1786)

Frederick the Great was also responsible for improving the architectural landscape, and some of these are still standing today: the Staatsoper (State Opera House) and the main building of the Humboldt

University (previously Prinz-Heinrich-Palais), both on Unter den Linden, and the Französischer Dom and Deutscher Dom on Gendarmenmarkt.

On the commerce side, many manufacturing companies came under state control, including the porcelain manufacturer, Gotzkowsky, which became the famous KPM (Königlich-Preussische Porzellanmanufaktur). Trade barriers of those days were set up; what could be produced in Prussia were banned or heavily taxed.

Frederick the Great was succeeded by Friedrich Wilhelm II. One of his most (if not the only) important contribution to the city was the Brandenburger Tor (Brandenburg Gate) with the Quadriga (the triumphal chariot driven by the Goddess of Victory) on top, which would later become the centre stage for many dramatic moments of the city's history. Under his rule, Prussia started to decline and the once powerful Prussian army was defeated by Napolean's troops in 1806 in the battle near Jena and Auerstedt. On 27 October 1806, the French marched through the Brandenburg Gate, Berlin was occupied and the Quadriga was taken to Paris.

Some political reforms which paved the way for a stronger Prussia came about during this time; a new directive was introduced to let towns and cities be responsible for their own administration, and a Town Council was elected by the citizens in secret ballots, although the voting was restricted to only a small percentage of the population with an annual income of over 200 Talers. The Friedrich-Wilhelms-Universität was founded in 1810, which went on to draw many top German academics who contributed to significant scientific achievements.

In 1814, after Napolean was defeated, the Quadriga returned to her rightful position atop the Brandenburg Gate.

The years after saw no positive political development. The promise of a Prussian constitution by King Friedrich Wilhelm III was not kept, and there was heavy censorship and persecution of opposition. The people channelled their energies into commerce and the textile, engineering and metal industries grew. The modest workshop of August Borsig was founded in 1837, which would later become a successful

locomotive factory. The first railway line between Berlin and
Potsdam was up and running in 1838, and a bustling city
life developed. Blocks of flats sprung up, the first of them
around Potsdamer Platz. As immigrants poured into Berlin
in search of job opportunities, the social problems also grew.
From a population of 170,000 in 1800, it was a bursting-at-
the-seams 412,154 by 1849.

In spite of the lack of political freedom and the many
social problems, cultural life developed during this time. This
was the era of the famous architect, Karl Friedrich Schinkel
(think Altes Museum, Neue Wache and Schlossbrücke),
the famous sculptor, Gottfried Schadow (most well-known
for the Quadriga), and a very active opera and theatre
scene. It was also the time when salons (places where the
intellectual members of society met to exchange ideas)
and *Lesekonditoreien* (reading cafés, where people went to
read newspapers and discuss hot topics of the day)
mushroomed. Those with less loose change in their pockets
were not left out; there were pubs in tents where they could
go to for socialising. The reading cafes and pubs were also
where unhappiness with the political situation in Prussia
was aired.

As prices increased and poor harvests left many hungry,
the tension mounted. The Berliners decided to petition the
King on 17 March 1848 for more democratic development.
The next day, two shots were fired at the crowd in front of
the palace, and 200 people were killed in the ensuing riot.
The King withdrew the army, and came out to honour the
victims of the riot. Freedom of assembly and of the press
were promised, giving Berliners hope that their petition
had been successful after all. However, further unrest and
suppression followed.

A person who contributed to the improvement of Berlin's
infrastructure at this stage was the Chief of Police, Carl Ludwig
Friedrich von Hinckeldey. His duties included crushing
anyone with overly liberal ideas and modernising the city's
infrastructure. He had the first water pipes built, founded
a professional fire brigade and passed building regulations
which gave birth to the famous Berliner *Mietskasernen*

(tenement houses) with *Hinterhöfe* (courtyards). By 1865, there was a horse-drawn railway, joining the horse-drawn buses that were plying the city since the 1840s. The Rotes Rathaus (the Red Town Hall) was also built between 1861 and 1869.

In 1862, Otto von Bismarck was appointed chancellor and he successfully manoeuvred the unification of all German states. The German Empire was proclaimed on 18 January 1871, with Berlin as the imperial capital. King Wilhelm I became Kaiser.

The Rotes Rathaus is the town hall of Berlin, located on Rathausstraße in Berlin-Mitte.

An important improvement to Berlin's infrastructure at this time was the new sewerage system installed in 1873, turning effluents into fertiliser. The first electric tramline started running in 1881. AEG-Allgemeine Elektrizitäts Gesellschaft (General Electric Company) was founded in 1887. In 1902, the first underground railway was opened. The famous department stores of Wertheim and KaDeWe (short for Kaufhaus des Westens) were opened in 1904 and 1907 respectively. Smaller but well-known retailers which still exist today such as Peek & Cloppenburg (clothes) and Leiser (shoes) also started up around this time.

Berlin was also the newspaper capital of Germany and the Berliner Morgenpost, founded in 1898 by Leopold Ullstein, still exists today, although it is now owned by Axel Springer AG.

These developments attracted more immigrants, and by 1910, the population had reached 3.7 million.

This was all to change abruptly with the start of World War I when the German Empire went to war against England, France, Italy and Russia after the heir to the Austrian throne was assassinated in 1914 in Sarajevo. Although the people were enthusiastic and filled with patriotic pride in the beginning, the mood soon changed when the casualty count rose. Planning and production of war essentials were based in Berlin and it took its toil on the city. A large swathe of the population was left starving, and ordinary people and politicians soon started protesting. By the autumn of 1918, defeat seemed only a matter of time. Ordinary citizens and soldiers revolted in the so-called November Revolution and on 9 November 1918, the then German chancellor, Prince Max von Baden announced the end of Hohenzollern monarchy.

The Weimar Republic

After Kaiser Wilhelm II abdicated, all gloves came off. Confusion reigned as to which political faction would govern. Friedrich Ebert of the Social Democratic Party of Germany (SPD) became president, but the leader of the Spartacists (a breakaway pacifist faction of the SPD which later became the German communist party), Karl Liebknecht, and Independent German Social Democratic Party (USPD—*Unabhängige Sozialdemokratische Partei Deutschlands*) called for the overthrow of Ebert's government. In January 1919, the Spartacists led angry battles which ended only when the *Freikorps* (a group of right-wing officers) murdered the two main leaders, Karl Liebknecht and Rosa Luxemburg.

On 19 January 1919, the elections for the National Assembly were held. This was the first time that women were allowed to vote. The elections confirmed the SPD as the party to lead the government. On 6 February, the first sitting of the new Assembly took place in Weimar, instead of Berlin, for security reasons. Six months later, Germany received its first post-war democratic constitution. The Weimar Republic (so named as the constitution was developed in that town) was born.

This constitution was, on paper, almost beyond reproach as an extremely progressive one for its time. However, putting it into practice on a population still so new to democratic notions was another matter altogether. The system of electing Reichstag deputies based on proportional representation from party lists seemed much fairer compared to a first-past-the-post system, especially for smaller parties, but the effect was a government cobbled together from numerous parties, often with stridently opposite views. Decision-making was a nightmare.

In reality, the Weimar Republic was plagued by opposition from left-wingers, right-wingers and ordinary Germans not enamoured with democracy. It was burdened by reparations it had to make under the Peace Treaty of Versailles and further weighed down by high unemployment and inflation.

There were constant revolutionary threats, culminating in the biggest uprising led by the right-winger Wolfgang Kapp in March 1920. The president and other government officials fled Berlin, but thanks to the unwillingness of the ordinary citizens to accept the putsch leaders, Kapp's attempt at purging the government failed.

On 27 April 1920, a law was passed which created a new Berlin which took in other towns and country communities and had a total population of 3.8 million under one municipal authority.

The situation continued to be tense, as the reparations imposed on Germany was a stranglehold. Right-wingers used this as a ground for sowing discontent and Walther Rathenau, the Foreign Secretary, was murdered on his way to work from his home in Grunewald.

In spite of the difficult times, Berlin saw development in some areas. Traffic volume increased as more people had their own vehicles. Potsdamer Platz became so busy that Germany's first traffic signal tower was installed there in 1924. Modelled on the one on Fifth Avenue, New York of 1922, the tower was demolished in 1936 (although a reconstructed tower was installed in 1997 on the same spot). The then City Councillor for Transport, Ernst Reuter, spearheaded the merging of the various companies providing public transport, and so the Berliner Verkehrs-Gesellschaft (BVG-Berlin Transport Company) was born. Air traffic was also on the rise with the founding of Lufthansa on 6 January 1926 (then known as Deutsche Luft Hansa Aktiengesellschaft, a result of the merger of Deutsche Aero Lloyd and Junkers Luftverkehr) based at Tempelhof Airport.

Refrigerators, vacuum cleaners and radios made their debut during the twenties, although these could only be afforded by a small percentage of the population.

On the cultural side of life, Berlin of the twenties was home to a creative crowd. It was a film capital and one of the most famous products of the thriving film industry of the 'Golden Twenties' was perhaps the Berliner, Marlene Dietrich. Writers, poets, dramatists, cartoonists and artists such as Thomas and Heinrich Mann, Bertolt Brecht, Alfred Döblin, Erich Kästner, Käthe Kollwitz, Max Liebermann and Heinrich Zille were the backbone of creativity during the Weimar Republic. Many of them immortalised society under the Weimar Republic in their works.

Berlin during this time also experienced an upsurge of sexual emancipation, or in the eyes of conservatives, decadence and debauchery. Cabarets with topless revues provided as much entertainment as did theatres and cinemas. But this image of Berlin was not one that applied to the entire society; many ordinary Berliners could hardly make ends meet.

Under the Nazis

How someone who was granted German citizenship only in 1932 could go on to become German chancellor a year later and wreak so much death and destruction will remain an agonising question forever. Historians have and will continue to debate the factors that opened the way for Adolf Hitler and his evil regime. Was it the miscalculation of some individuals, or the wish by some Germans to destroy parliamentary democracy, or the effects of the turmoil after World War I, or Hitler's charisma or a combination of different factors?

Politically, Berlin in the twenties was firmly 'red' and Hilter's National Socialist German Workers' Party (*National Sozialistische Deutsche Arbeiter Partei*—NSDAP) at first made no gains with Berliners. Starting from their base in Bavaria, NSDAP spent much of the twenties trying to broaden their appeal throughout Germany.

In 1926, Joseph Goebbels was appointed *Gauleiter* (Head of a Nazi administration district). Goebbels opted for head-on clash with the communists. He rented the Pharus Rooms in Müllerstrasse, Wedding, a place where the communists had always held their meetings, to the outrage of the latter. This provocation led to successive street battles between the left-wing and right-wing groups. While the working class remained loyal to the left, the middle-class began to see the NSDAP as a way to prevent the city being seized by the communists or even to get rid of parliamentary democracy. Many industralists started contributing financially to the NSDAP. A staunch right-wing newspaper baron, Alfred Hugenberg, with considerable influence over the media, contributed to Hitler's rise. The economic meltdown in the world also helped the NSDAP, as did Hitler's adroit use of the radio for propaganda.

The first sign of success for the NSDAP was the elections of 1930 where it became the second largest party in the Reichstag with 130 seats. Attacks on Jews and Jewish interests began.

In the 1932 elections, NSDAP did even better, winning 230 seats. Intrigues followed, whereby General Schleicher (then defence minister) first eased himself into the position of Chancellor after removing Franz von Papen. Von Papen retaliated by convincing President Paul von Hindenburg that Schleicher was incompetent and to appoint Hitler in his stead. On 30 January 1933, Hitler became Chancellor. Berliners were especially stunned, as in contrast to the rest of Germany, they had voted decisively against the Nazis at the last elections.

Hermann Göring, then Prussian minister for the interior, was the chief architect for the suppression of political opponents. Police officers were replaced by members of the SA (*Sturmabteilung*—stormtroopers) and SS (*Schutzstaffel*—protection squadron), both paramilitary organisations tasked to protect Hitler. Attacks against Social Democrats, Communists, Jews and intellectuals who did not conform with Nazi ideology took place. Göring also built up the much feared Gestapo (short for *Geheime Staatspolizei*—Secret State Police).

The Reichstag fire on 27 February 1933 was used by the Nazis as an excuse to impose a state of emergency. Thousands of opposition politicians were also rounded up and taken to concentration camps.

In spite of the Nazi terror, they still failed to achieve an absolute majority in the Reichstag elections on 5 March 1933. In Berlin, they only managed 34.6 per cent of the votes. However, together with their coalition partner, German National People's Party (DNVP—*Deutschnationale Volkspartei*), they had 51.9 per cent of the nation-wide votes.

On 23 March 1933, the Enabling Law (*Ermächtigungsgesetz*) was passed, after skillfully preventing the communists and a substantial number of Social Democrats from attending. Only the remaining Social Democrats bravely voted against it. The Enabling Law wiped out whatever parliamentary democracy that was left and dictatorship was shooed in.

A Prescient Line from Heinrich Heine

'Where they have burned books, they will end up burning human beings, too.' (*Dort, wo man Bücher verbrennt, verbrennt man am Ende auch Menschen*) —Heinrich Heine, German essayist and poet, from his play Almansor (1821)

What followed was a step up of persecution against Jews, political opponents, homosexuals, church members and other 'undesirables'. On May 11, the burning of thousands of books which contradicted Nazi ideology took place on Bebelplatz on Unter den Linden.

Nazi brutality was not directed only at these 'undesirables'; by 1934, the SA troops had fallen out of favour with Hitler, who was convinced that they were conspiring against him. On 30 June, the Night of the Long Knives as it has come to be known, many SA leaders were executed.

On 2 August 1934, President Hindenburg died. Hitler merged the offices of president and chancellor and made himself the head of the combined positions—the *Führer*.

Throughout Germany, all aspects of life came under Nazi control after that. Newspapers and radio programmes were full of Nazi propaganda, trade unions were replaced by the Nazi's 'German Labour Front', craftsmen and traders were brought under umbrella organisations and even leisure clubs became Nazi-organised ones. This was the stage of the *Gleichschaltung*—putting into the same gear—a euphemism for making sure everyone toed the line. The Nüremberg Laws were passed in 1935, effectively depriving the Jews of citizenship rights and imposing many other restrictions on them.

Berlin, being the capital of the Reich, became a showcase for Nazism. The 1936 Olympics in Berlin, although planned long before the Nazis came to power, was cleverly used by them as the ultimate propaganda opportunity for Germany and Nazi ideology. In the streets, the gypsies were all interned and later sent to extermination camps as a major 'clean up'. Unfortunately for the Nazis, the Aryan supremacy idea was dashed by 22-year-old black American athlete Jesse Owens winning four gold medals.

Hitler's plan for Berlin was for it to become the centre of power of a great German world empire, and be named 'Germania'. Albert Speer was the chief architect for the grand plans of transformation, who, in getting Berlin ready for his grand masterpiece, demolished many apartment blocks along the way.

The next spell of brutality that caught world attention was the *Kristallnacht* (Crystal night—referring to the broken glass) on 9 November 1938. Organised attacks on Jewish interests took place all over Germany. Jews were beaten up and almost all of the synagogues in Berlin were destroyed.

Hitler also put into gear his empire building. After swallowing up Austria and regaining control of the Rhineland with hardly a murmur from the other powers, he was emboldened to invade Poland on 1 September 1939. But this time Britain and France declared war, and World War II began.

World War II

Weary of wars which they knew too well brought only hardships, Berliners did not show any patriotic enthusiasm as they did when World War I started.

The Jews started facing intensified persecution. From 1941, Berlin Jews were deported to concentration and extermination camps.

During this time, there were many resistance groups in Berlin, such as the Red Band (*Rote Kapelle*) led by Arvid Harnack and Harro Schulze-Boysen; the Confessional Church (*Bekennende Kirche*) led by the priest, Martin Niemöller; and the Saefkow-Jacob Group with Anton Saefkow and Franz Jacob as its leaders. The odds were unfortunately stacked up against them; many were arrested and executed. Attempts on Hitler's life were also plotted by some, but were never successful. The most well-known attempt is of course the one by Claus Schenk von Stauffenberg on 20 July 1944, not least because of the Hollywood film portrayal by Tom Cruise. The bomb went off, but Hitler was only slightly injured. The ring leaders were rounded up and executed.

Conditions in Berlin worsened with the allied air raids, which reached its peak in 1943. All in all, the air raids on densely populated residential areas, government buildings and industrial centres killed between 20,000 to 50,000 Berliners. Many more were injured. The city was reduced to rubble, leaving survivors without homes or any infrastructure to speak of.

Claus Schenk Graf von Stauffenberg

Born in the Stauffenberg castle of Jettingen on 15 November 1907, von Stauffenberg was a Catholic aristocrat and German army officer. He played a major role in the failed 20 July 1944 plot to assassinate Adolf Hitler.

Although he initially believed that Hitler's National Socialist policy offered Germany favorable opportunities, he soon became alienated by the regime's racial ideology.

While recovering from serious wounds sustained while fighting in Tunisia, von Stauffenberg became convinced that Hitler had to be assassinated, once he realised the negative consequences of Hitler's policy in Eastern Europe and was shaken by the damage that Hitler's war had brought upon Germany and Europe.

His assassination attempt was unsuccessful and he was executed.

By January 1945, the Russians were advancing dangerously close to Berlin. Every Berliner was roped in to defend the city and there was no question of surrender as far as the Nazi leadership was concerned. By April, they were practically just outside the city. Hitler retreated to his bunker (the area around Wilhelmstrasse and Voßstrasse), joined by his girlfriend, Eva Braun and his loyal propaganda minister, Joseph Goebbels and his family.

As the Allied troops continued their advance, Hitler married Eva Braun on April 29, and both committed suicide one day later. To prevent the Allies gloating over his body, he gave instructions for both their bodies to be burned.

On May 1, Goebbels and his wife killed their six children before committing suicide. A number of Hitler's deputies and staff committed suicide, while others tried to escape, with about 100 of them succeeding. A day later, the Military Governor of Berlin, Helmuth Weidling surrendered. The Russian troops celebrated their victory with frenzied looting and raping in Berlin.

The Carving Up of Berlin

The official surrender of the German troops took place at Karlshorst on 8 May 1945 after hundreds of thousands had died in the Battle of Berlin. But for those who survived, life was a miserable one of meagre rations, poor health conditions and increasing crime rates.

In July, the Western Allies moved into their pre-arranged occupation sectors: the Americans occupied Kreuzberg, Neukölln, Tempelhof, Schöneberg, Steglitz and Zehlendorf, the British took Tiergarten, Wilmersdorf, Charlottenburg and Spandau, and the French Wedding and Reinickendorf. At the 17 July to 3 August 1945 Potsdam Conference in Schloss Cecilienhof, the leaders of the three big powers, USSR, USA and Great Britain, met to discuss the political and economic set-up of the future Germany.

The relationship between the Western powers and the Soviet Union disintegrated over the economic reforms in the sectors occupied by the Western powers. In June, the representatives of the Soviet Union flounced out of the Allied Control Council, and shortly after, on 23 June 1948, the Western powers introduced the Deutsche Mark in West Germany. The Soviet authorities of the eastern sector were outraged at this unilateral move and punishment came swiftly; that very night, electricity in the western sector supplied by stations located in the eastern sector was cut off. Transport links between the east and west were also stopped.

The isolation of West Berlin had begun, in an attempt to drive out the Western powers. As food and fuel supplies started running low, the Western allies started the Berlin airlift, with planes delivering supplies round the clock. At its height, planes were landing and taking off in 30-second intervals. By 12 May 1949, the Soviets had given up the blockade, but to be on the safe side, the allies continued their airlift till October. By the time the airlift ended, 277,000 flights had flown 2.3 million tons of supplies into West Berlin. There were sadly also casualties; in the 120 serious accidents, 31 US and 39 British aircrew members, and 8 German helpers lost their lives.

The airlifts by the *Rosinenbomber* (literally 'raisins bombers') which delivered crucial supplies to West Berlin had not only helped the West Berliners survive, but turned the Western allied troops from occupiers to allies in the eyes of West Berliners.

Heroes of the Berlin Airlift

When the Soviet blockade of West Berlin started, American and British pilots flew in supplies to the West Berliners, even in inclement weather. This lasted from July 1948 to May 1949. The Berlin airlift is a moving and heartwarming tale, but there was an even more touching tale within. Retired Col. Gail Halvorsen (then 28 years old) from the US Air Force happened to talk to some Berlin children watching the flights coming in one day in July 1948. He was as much moved by their plight as taken by their politeness. He shared his last chewing gum with them, and sorry that it wasn't enough for the 30 plus children standing around him, he promised to return with more, and said they would recognise his plane as he would wiggle the wings as a signal. Col. Halvorsen started making parachutes from handkerchiefs, and begged candy rations to tie to the chutes from his squadron mates, who obliged. These were then parachuted down to the children waiting below in Berlin Tegel airport. When word got out about the 'candy bomber', American companies (such as Hershey's and Mars) donated tons of candy and chocolate bars, and other companies donated linen cloth for candy parachutes. American school children helped to tie the candy to parachutes, which Col. Halvorsen and his squadron colleagues dropped to the children in Berlin. The result was a deep affection between Berliners and Americans. In 2008, the 60th anniversary was celebrated with the veterans coming to Berlin for an airshow, and being warmly received by the Chancellor, Angela Merkel.

This was truly a case of not only winning the war, but also winning the hearts and minds of the locals.

The blockade was the straw that broke the camel's back. Berlin was on its way to being divided. The Basic Law (the constitution) came into force in the Federal Republic of Germany on 24 May 1949, and the German Democratic Republic was founded on 7 October of the same year. For the Federal Republic of Germany, Berlin was a federal state; for the German Democratic Republic, Berlin was the capital.

Another result of the Berlin blockade was the stocking up of supplies in West Berlin, financed by both Berlin and Federal reserves. The stocks included fuel, food, clothing and even toilet rolls. When the canned food neared their expiry date, they were sold on the market for a low price, to recoup some of the expenditure. These 'sales' were eagerly snapped up by the Berlin housewives. A rather nostalgic dish in Berlin, *Moppelkotze* (green beans and pieces of beef out of a can), was one of the items that were eagerly snapped up when the Berlin Senate offloaded these canned beans and beef onto the market.

In the earlier years of the division, Berliners could still move about relatively freely between east and west. An estimated 2.5 million people fled from the GDR during the 1950s. On the political level, there were espionages and counter espionages.

Economically, West Berlin was better off than East Berlin. When the communists decreed a rise in the 'quotas' (the work output fixed by the authorities) on 16 June 1953, the workers downed tools. Workers at the Friedrichshain Hospital and Stalinallee construction project were the first to strike, but soon workers in around 250 towns had joined in. Although most images of this protest were of Leipzigerstrasse as the media could get good images and footages from the western side of Potsdamer Platz, the protest was in reality widespread across the GDR. The demonstrations were eventually violently crushed by Soviet tanks rolling in and declaring martial law. In East Berlin alone, 12 protestors were killed and some 400 others injured. This was East Germans' 'Tiananmen Square'.

Berlin became like a child torn between two bitter, divorced parents—one communist and extolling socialism, the other democratic and fervently capitalistic. Economically, West Berlin was progressing by leaps and bounds, with financial support from West Germany and the Marshall Plan aid, while East Germany remained in a rather sorry state. The differences led to many East Germans going over to West Germany

To stem the flow, the ultimate nightmare happened. In the early hours of 13 August 1961, barbed wire went up and S and U-Bahn lines into West Berlin were closed. The 'anti-fascist protection barrier' (as the Wall was called by East German authorities) was put up. Before the cement wall went up, some East Berliners managed to flee to the West with just the shirt on their back. People swam across the Spree, crashed through barriers, jumped out of buildings if it happened to be West Berlin outside the windows and climbed over fences to escape. One of the most enduring picture is possibly the one of border guard, Conrad Schumann (then only 19), making his leap to freedom on 15 August over the barbed wire at Bernauer Strasse in full uniform. The barbed wire was quickly reinforced by a concrete wall, separating Berliners from families and friends, and preventing East Berliners going to work in the West. The wall continued to be 'improved' upon, and eventually the Wall became in effect two walls with a no-man's land in-between, with border guards standing watch in towers. They didn't hesitate to shoot anyone trying to escape; but ingenuity born out of desperation led many East Berliners to come up with the most novel (and risky) methods of fleeing to the West; 239 persons in all lost their lives trying to escape to the West.

The Allies, meanwhile, protested through diplomatic channels but feared that any drastic action could mean a nuclear war. All they could do was pussy-foot around the situation. Visits to the Wall by leaders of both East and West were made, including US President John F. Kennedy in 1963.

West Berlin during this time became very attractive to young men who were looking to avoid conscription due to the special rules of demilitarisation in Berlin. Once they got permanent residency in West Berlin, they could avoid being enlisted. Another side effect of the Wall was the loss of many workers which included East Berliners who could no longer travel to the West and others who left West Berlin for other parts of Germany. The shortage was made up by the influx of foreigners: Turks, Yugoslavs and Poles, laying down the foundation for the high percentage of immigrants in Berlin today.

Both East and West Berlin continued to develop architecturally. In the West, the Philharmonie (Philharmonic Concert Hall) and the Neue Nationalgalerie (New National Gallery), and in the East, the Fernsehturm (TV Tower) and the Palast der Republik (parliament of East Berlin) were all built during this time.

The political tension started to lessen, but restlessness surfaced with the younger generation. The student movement developed and in 1966, West Berlin saw the first anti-American demonstration because of the Vietnam War, something which was sacrilegious to the Berliners who had experienced the kindness of the 'candy bombers' and heroes of the airlift. A demonstration against the visit of the Shah of Persia in 1969 resulted in the police shooting dead a student, which gave birth to the *Ausserparlamentarische Opposition* (APO-extra parliamentary opposition), an influential movement. The APO in West Berlin later split into moderate and radical wings; the latter giving Germans their first taste of terrorism with their violence.

By the seventies, West Berlin was a magnet for those seeking alternative lifestyles and communal living. By the eighties, squatting was the trend, caused mainly by the shortage of cheap housing.

In 1987, Berlin's 750th anniversary, *Nikolaiviertel*, a reconstructed medieval area in East Berlin, was built. In the West, an international building competition was organised, inviting international architects to build houses in inner-city districts.

The *glastnost* and *perestroika* campaigns of then Russian president Mikhail Gorbachev which started in 1985 had little impact on Berlin. The GDR authorities resisted the wave of reforms that was sweeping through the Soviet Union, Hungary and Poland. The future for the East Berliners seemed depressingly bleak. Yet, the Wall was to fall sooner than anyone dared hope.

The hole in the Wall started with Hungarian authorities removing the barbed wire fence at their border with Austria. Alert East Germans knew that here was their chance. Many went on holiday to Hungary in order to slip through the border to Austria. Those who didn't manage to get through sought refuge in the West German embassy there. Other East Germans surged towards the West German embassies in Prague and Warsaw. On 30 September 1989, Hans-Dietrich Genscher (the then foreign minister of West Germany) appeared on the balcony of the Praque embassy to promise the East Germans huddling there that they would be brought to West Germany.

In East Berlin, the discontent reached boiling point. Opposition became more daring. For the 40th anniversary of the GDR on 7 October 1989, Erich Honecker and his SED laid out the typically communist type of celebrations-parades of weaponry and troops in starched uniforms. The East Germans were, however, more interested in welcoming Gorbachev, who had been invited to the celebrations. Demonstrations were harshly put down, but it could not hold back the seething rage of most East Berliners. On 9 October, another bout of demonstrations took place, with some 700,000 people marching through Leipzig. Thankfully, the security forces did not resort to violence. On 18 October, the SED leadership passed from Erich Honecker to Egon Krenz, although no one was expecting any easing of the iron grip under the similarly hawkish new leader. The Berliners knew their fate now laid in their own hands, and on 4 November, the biggest demonstration in GDR history took place; a million Berliners gathered at Alexanderplatz to demand for more freedom in their lives.

The Wall Falls

On 9 November, the unimaginable happened. Günther Schabowski, a member of the SED cabinet, annnounced at a press conference that it was no longer necessary to get a visa to leave the GDR. The press conference was being aired live in the GDR, and East Germans set off to the check-points to test the truth of the announcement. The border guards were no match for the swell of people demanding to be let out, and the first border to open was the one at Prenzlauer Berg at 10:30 pm. Shortly after midnight, all the checkpoints were open.

West Berliners welcomed their Eastern cousins coming through the border by popping open bottles of champagne. Strangers embraced one another. The pictures and footages captured of this historic moment are such emotional ones that few people can remain unmoved even when looking at the images today.

The days that followed were euphoric ones. East Germans were given 100 marks each as welcome money by the Federal

Republic, which could be collected from the banks. People began hacking at the much despised Wall. A provisional crossing at Potdamer Platz was set up.

In February 1990, representatives from the four allied powers and the two Germanys met in Ottawa, Canada, to thrash out the future of Germany in the 'two plus four' talks. One of the results of the talks was the agreement by the four allied powers to withdraw their troops, which they did within four years after the talks. On 15 July, the then German Chancellor, Helmut Kohl, met with Gorbachev to work out the terms of German unification. After all other political and administrative issues had been ironed out between the allies, the Soviet Union and the Federal Republic of Germany, 3 October 1990 was declared the official day of German unification.

On 2 December 1990, elections for the Berlin House of representatives were held in conjunction with the first all-Germany elections since 1933. An SPD and CDU (Christlich Demokratische Union-Christian Democratic Union) coalition was voted in for the House of Representatives. The newly elected Mayor, Eberhard Diepgen, was finally able to take his

A memorial to the victims of the Wall.

A barely visible line between the two cars marks the previous location of the Wall.

seat at the Rotes Rathaus (Red City Hall, so-called because of the building's red bricks), located in East Berlin.

Within a few years after the fall of the Wall, U and S-Bahn lines and buses were running between East and West.

Becoming a Capital City

In June 1991, the Bundestag decided by a narrow margin (just 18 votes) to move the capital of Germany from Bonn to Berlin. The 1990s was a period of construction and restoration of Berlin and the city became the largest construction site in Europe. After massive administrative planning, the Bundestag finally had its first meeting in the restored Reichstag in September 1999.

Although Berlin was now united politically, unification in people's minds was harder to come by. The euphoria of the fall of the Wall didn't last very long after economic problems surfaced and bubbles burst. The Easterners were disillusioned that capitalism didn't exactly bring overnight riches to everyone and resented what they saw as a patronising attitude of the *Wessis*. The Westerners grew tired of the solidarity tax, which they saw as an endless milking of their hard-earned money. Many also saw the *Ossis* as a bunch of

The Reichstag is one of the most visited attractions in Berlin and since 1999, has become the seat of the German Bundestag again.

DEM DEUTSCHEN VOLKE

culturally backward people. They were also smarting over the withdrawal of the generous subsidies they had to prop up West Berlin during the Cold War. Countless companies in the former East were bankrupted as they were unable to cope with the new market economy, while some companies in the West also folded, as they had only managed with hefty subsidies. The cost of unification was much higher than the earlier estimates, so there was much hand-wringing with the politicians as well. The economic and social problems led to some ordinary citizens taking out their frustrations by attacking foreigners (including German-born ones).

Berlin celebrated the 10th anniversary of the fall of the Wall in November 1999 by having the trio of George Bush Sr., Mikhail Gorbachev and Helmut Kohl together in Berlin for a spell of back-slapping and a party at the Brandenburger Tor.

From 2000 to 2008

Anyone who has not been back in Berlin for the last ten years or so will be astounded at how much changes the city has undergone. Physically, the city has had a face-lift. Old buildings have been 'botoxed' and now look remarkably wrinkle-free. Spanking new buildings have been built. The

Prenzlauer Berg is now a pleasant area popular with the young and creative crowd.

major train stations and many trains themselves have now been upgraded. Areas once considered 'shabby', like Prenzlauer Berg, is now the 'in' place with the young crowd. It is also drawing tourists and a creative crowd.

But the city is still struggling with its financial problems, partly because of the massive re-building works, partly because of mismanagement of subsidies, and partly because of corruption by a previous CDU parliamentary leader which costs Berlin several billion euros. Unemployment is high and there is a lot of discontent on the ground. The social problems have bred an alarming ascend of right-wing groups and youths who resort to drink and violence.

While Germany is governed by a coalition of uncomfortable bed-fellows (the SPD and CDU) at the time of writing, a 'red-red' coalition (SPD together with the Left Party-Die Linke) have held court in Berlin since 2001. While the CDU did get over 20 per cent of the votes in both the 2001 and 2006 elections, the SPD harnessed over 30 per cent in both elections, making them the clear winners.

In spite of the problems still confronting Berlin today, one can be sure the plucky city will always rise to the challenges ahead. We only need to look at its history to know that it will.

Milestones	
1197 and 1209	First written reference to Spandau and Köpenick respectively
1237	First documented mention of Cölln
1415	Friedrich of Hohenzollern proclaimed Elector of Brandenburg
1539	Protestantism adopted
1618 to 1648	Thirty Years' War. Population of Berlin almost decimated
1671 and 1685	Jews and Huguenots immigrate respectively
1701	Friedrich III crowns himself King Friedrich I of Prussia
1740 to 1786	Military expansion and development of culture under Frederick the Great
1806 to 1809	Napoleon's troops occupy Berlin
1838	First railway line running from Berlin to Potsdam
1862	Otto von Bismarck appointed prime minister of Prussia
1871	German Empire proclaimed, with Berlin as Imperial capital
1881	World's first electric tramline starts running
1902	First underground line opens
1914 to 1918	World War I
1918	End of Hohenzollern rule
1919	Birth of the Weimar Republic
1920	Greater Berlin created. 1920s a mixture of Roaring Twenties and hyperinflation
1933	Hitler comes to power
1936	11th Olympic Games in Olympia Stadion

Milestones	
1938	Kristallnacht-Jewish properties attacked and set on fire
1939 to 1945	World War II
1948 to 1949	Soviet blockade of West Berlin. Citizens survived through Berlin Airlift
1949	Germany split into East and West. Berlin becomes capital of East Germany
1961	The Berlin Wall is built
1987	Berlin celebrates its 750th birthday
1989	The Berlin Wall falls
1990	Official reunification on 3 October
1991	German parliament votes to move the capital from Bonn to Berlin
1999	First sitting of German parliament in Reichstag, Berlin

THE ADMINISTRATIVE SET-UP

Berlin, a city state, is one of the Federal Republic of Germany's 16 relatively independent states (*Länder*). All the federal states have their own constitution and government. Berlin's political set-up is made up of the Senate and the House of Representatives.

The Senate

The Senate is the government and comprises the Governing Mayor and a maximum of eight senators. The mayor is elected by the House of Representatives, who then selects the members of the Senate. The Senate essentially sets the general governing policies of Berlin.

The current mayor (elected in 2001 and re-elected in 2006) is Klaus Wowereit, a Social Democrat. The current Berlin government (which term ends in 2011) is often referred to as a 'red-red' coalition, comprising members of the Social Democratic Party and the Left Party.

The House of Representatives

The House of Representatives, the parliament of Berlin, is elected for a five-year period by the German citizens resident in Berlin. There are at least 130 members from different political parties who have received enough votes to pass the threshold of 5 per cent.

At the time of writing, in the 16th legislative period, there are 149 members: 53 from the Social Democratic Party (SPD), 37 from the Christian Democratic Union (CDU), 23 from the Left Party (Die Linke), 23 from the Green Party (Bündnis 90/ die Grünen) and 13 from the Free Democratic Party (FDP). The next elections will be in 2011.

Berlin's Boroughs

Berlin has 12 boroughs (*Bezirke*) in all:
- Charlottenburg-Wilmersdorf
- Friedrichshain-Kreuzberg
- Lichtenberg
- Marzahn-Hellersdorf
- Mitte
- Neukölln
- Pankow
- Reinickendorf
- Spandau
- Steglitz-Zehlendorf
- Tempelhof-Schöneberg
- Treptow-Köpenick

Each district has its own district council, mayor and for Berlin residents, the all-important citizens' office (*Bürgeramt*), where all matters relating to passports, personal identification cards, registration of addresses, income tax cards and any other business in connection with the authorities are conducted.

The districts which tourists and other short-term visitors are most likely to explore are Mitte, Tiergarten and Charlottenburg. Most of the tourist must-sees are in these districts, such as the Brandenburger Tor, the Reichstag, the Museumsinsel, Fernsehturm, the park Tiergarten (which

The Berliner Dom (Berlin Cathedral) and Fernsehturm (TV Tower) are some of the must-sees in this exciting city.

is the name-sake of the district it is in), Friedrichstraße, Potsdamer Platz, Zoologischer Garten, the shopping mile Kurfürstendamm and the palace Schloss Charlottenburg.

Berlin as it is today was formed from a patchwork of different towns and villages stitched together. Hence, the 12 districts (which themselves are a consolidation in 2001 of previously 23 districts) have distinctive characters of their own. Certainly the split into East and West Berlin also had an impact on the districts. They are discussed in more detail in Chapter Five, to help you decide which district you might want to live in.

Berlin and Brandenburg

Berlin is circumscribed by another federal state, Brandenburg. A caricature of Berlin-Brandenburg might be a fried egg, sunny side up, with Berlin being the egg yolk and Brandenburg the egg white surrounding it. Often overlooked by foreigners and looked down upon by Berliners, Brandenburg is actually a vast 29,477 sq km (11,381 sq miles) of idyllic towns and villages, tree-lined streets, 3,000 lakes and over 30,000 km (18,642 miles) of waterways. There are also more than 500 castles and manor houses and 10,500 historical monuments

Potsdamer Platz was almost completely destroyed during World War II, and was bisected by the Berlin Wall during the Cold War. However, it has since risen again as a glittering new centre for the city.

in Brandenburg, making it ideal for weekend escapes. In the capital, Potsdam, are the famous Sanssouci palace and park, and the Schloss Cecilienhof (where Stalin, Truman, Churchill and later Attlee huddled to discuss Germany's future in what is called the Potsdam Conference).

With a population of only about 2.5 million, Brandenburg is sparsely populated and has unfortunately seen very little investments. There is high unemployment and pockets of dilapidated towns. The economic underdevelopment has spawned groups of disaffected youth. In recent years, this bunch of social delinquents have taken out their frustrations on mostly dark-skinned foreigners, leading some to unfairly and inaccurately label the whole of Brandenburg a 'no-go' area.

'All free men, wherever they may live, are citizens of Berlin, and, therefore, as a free man, I take pride in the words: *Ich bin ein Berliner.*'
—President John F. Kennedy, at Schöneberg Town Hall, 26 June 1963

WHO IS A BERLINER?

The speech made by the then president of the United States was essentially political grandstanding, intended as a morale booster to the West Berliners living in a divided city. But Kennedy's impassioned '*Ich bin ein Berliner*' (I am a Berliner) has become iconic.

So who are the 3.4 million people who might declare today '*Ich bin ein Berliner*'?

14 per cent of Berliners are foreigners (that is, those without German citizenship), made up of a whopping 184 nationalities. With the relatively easy naturalisation of immigrants with 'German blood' (*Spätaussiedler*—late settlers), quite a few with German citizenship also have an immigrant background, coming mostly from the former Soviet Union, Poland and Romania. New statistics released on 1 July 2008 by the Berlin-Brandenburg Statistics Office revealed that 25.7 per cent of Berliners have an immigration background, once you take into account the naturalised Germans. Most of them (44.5 per cent) live in the district Mitte, rather than the widely-held belief that immigrant families tend to congregate in Neukölln or Kreuzberg. The 2008 statistics showed that Neukölln and Friedrichshain-Kreuzberg had 38.7 per cent and 36.6 per cent respectively of Berliners with immigrant roots.

The largest foreign communities are the Turks, people from the former Yugoslavia and the Poles. There is also a significant number of Italians, French, Americans, Russians and Vietnamese. Not all the Germans in Berlin were born or bred in Berlin, either; so if you add on all the other regional accents and dialects of Germany, Berlin is quite a Tower of Babel.

Berlin has a history of immigration, as mentioned in Chapter Two. First, people from the areas around Berlin came, then the Huguenots and Jews arrived. In more recent history, Germany encouraged immigrant labour to help in the post-war reconstruction. These 'guest workers' (*Gastarbeiter*) were expected to work in Germany for a few years and then return home. Most of the Portuguese and the Greeks did exactly that.

A great number of Turks also started coming to Berlin in 1961, recruited to replace the East German workers who were suddenly prevented from travelling to West Berlin after the Wall was built. Unlike the Greeks and Portuguese, the Turks stayed on. After the recruitment of the 'guest workers' ended in 1974, many Turks continued to come to Berlin as family members of those already in Berlin. The crackdown by the Turkish military on the Kurds also sent Kurdish refugees streaming to Germany. The number of Turks in Berlin reached some 115,000 in 2007.

A large number of ex-Yugoslavs are also in Berlin, who came either as guest workers or as refugees fleeing the conflicts back home in the early 1990s. The more than 51,000 ex-Yugoslavs are now classified under the six (or seven) countries that emerged after the break-up of Yugoslavia: Bosnia and Herzegovina, Croatia, Republic of Macedonia, (Kosovo, if you recognise the self-declaration of independence), Montenegro, Serbia and Slovenia.

There are about 44,000 Poles in Berlin, making them the third largest group of foreigners in Berlin. The group is actually even much larger, as many of the Poles with German ancestry have been naturalised as German citizens.

The Vietnamese are also present in fairly large numbers in Berlin: about 12,000 in 2007. You tend to notice them more, of course, with their distinctive Asian features.

WHAT ARE BERLINERS LIKE?

Trying to pin down the common characteristics of a group of people is incredibly difficult, since everyone is different for a start. It involves a generalisation that borders on stereotyping, if not exactly that. When talking about Berliners, it becomes even harder as the large number of foreigners and immigrants make the city a kaleidoscope of cultures. Within each nationality, there are also different sects, ethnicities and regional characteristics that add even more diversity. Different generations behave differently and inter-marriages affect behavioural patterns, too.

Generalisations

'All generalisations are false, including this one.'

—Mark Twain

The description below is therefore only an aerial view of the different communities who live in Berlin, as a microscopic look is beyond the scope of this book.

THE TEUTONIC PEOPLE

When sifting out the common Teutonic denominators, there is also the regional differences to take into account. What we know as Germany today was fundamentally different principalities ruled by noble houses jealously guarding their own turfs in medieval times. The Reformation of Martin Luther which began in 1517 then split the people along religious lines. Germany didn't become united until 1871. The man responsible for this was Otto von Bismarck, chancellor of Prussia, who provoked hostilities with France to persuade the southern German states to join his North German Confederation. In the aftermath of the Franco-Prussian War, which saw the French soundly thrashed by the formidable Prussian army, the southern German states were finally convinced into joining a German Empire with Prussia at the centre of power. This history partly explains why many Germans today still identify strongly with their region, sometimes even more than with the country itself.

Berlin is itself formed from a cobbling together of towns and settlements, some joining as late as 1920 (such as Spandau and Köpenick).

Apart from the patchwork foundation of the country and the Catholic-Protestant cleavage, another event in history also contributed to the different characteristics of the Germans: the divisive Berlin Wall which split the country into communist East and capitalist West for almost three decades.

But in spite of the differences wrought fundamentally by history, there are a number of characteristics which are considered typically Teutonic.

Law-abiding and Orderly

Ask anyone who has had some encounter with Germans to name a German characteristic, and you are most likely to hear about orderliness.

In Germany, there are rules and regulations for everything, including when you can create a racket, when you have to pipe down and in which coloured container you have to throw what type of garbage in. Germans generally follow the rules to the letter, and will not hesitate to correct and chide a complete stranger for failing to follow the rules.

Some say that it must be Germany's turbulent history that has made Germans dislike uncertainty and crave orderliness. Whether it's nurture or nature (maybe it's in the genes), it's certainly '*Ordnung muss sein*' (order is a must) in Germany.

When there is an established system of doing things in place, a good German will follow it from point A to Z systematically. No short-circuits, please. Go to a supermarket and watch how Germans wait with one euro in hand, while the customer who has finished his purchases puts the supermarket trolley back in the trolley bay, locks it, collects the one euro that pops out from the lock and goes off, before the waiting German will put his/her euro in to retrieve that very same trolley. I've tried giving a customer returning the trolley a euro and taking the trolley from her, saving both the time and trouble of all these locking and unlocking, but received only a cold stare, as if I'd tried to rob her. It's true that some Germans use a special 'coin' (not real money) to get the trolley, so in these instances it cannot work as the customer would want to hang on to the special 'coin', but I've actually observed the Germans perform this ritual with religious fervour even though both customers were using euros.

But, and this is a big but: Germans do throw orderliness and system to the wind in some instances. We're not talking about the anarchists, hooligans or neo-nazis, but ordinary Germans. People coming from countries where queues and lines are an established part of life have complained with gritted teeth about Germans surging towards the doors of trains and trams, instead of forming an orderly line and boarding in turn. Many Americans and British people have been shocked by this behaviour, not least because it doesn't gel with the famed German orderliness. Germans generally do queue when they are, say, at the baker's or at an ATM—it's not total anarchy in Germany, don't worry—but somehow when they see a S-Bahn or U-Bahn approaching, the bull-sees-red flag syndrome comes to the fore. You'd think that they had just spotted Angelina Jolie and Brad Pitt on the train and are rushing for autographs.

Berliners have always been known to be tough, and you will find that on certain issues, they aren't such law-abiding Germans. When the smoking ban in certain public places came into effect in January 2008, not a few Berliners continued puffing. There were also stories of irate diners roughing up waiters who tried to stop them smoking.

Thorough, Disciplined and Hardworking

The instinct to be orderly and systematic means that Germans are thorough in executing their tasks, making them very reliable workers and business partners. But this thoroughness can drive an American used to faster decision-making nuts, as the German mulls over each step before progressing on to the next.

Germans are also famed for their discipline. An article in *Der Spiegel* online in 2008 reported that, from surveys conducted, the average German rated discipline as very important.

The image of the hardworking German has taken a slight beating in recent times. As is very often the case in developed countries, the younger generation tends to be much less anxious about working. Used to the country's economic success and a system of generous social welfare, many of those under 40 are more keen on having a 'good life', and now. It's not rare to hear of 30-somethings who are prepared to leave their well-paying jobs and take a 'gap year', just travelling the world. The generous social welfare system certainly does not encourage youngsters to think about their retirement fund, although with the aging population, the system is under strain.

Forthright and Clear
Germans mean what they say and say what they mean. They are straightforward and honest, and will speak their minds clearly. In the *Der Spiegel* article mentioned above, surveys conducted showed that Germans also rated the stating of one's opinion clearly very highly.

Germans are also not given to hyperbole. All very trustworthy and reliable; trouble is, the directness can end up sounding rather tactless, if not downright rude. Coupled with the fact that Germans are not prone to praise, their comments can make you feel like a tiny chihuahua being torn apart by a Rottweiler. In fact, the Germans are not fond of polite speak, which in some other cultures is seen as tactfulness. The Germans may see your attempts at being tactful as being unclear, or worse, wishy washy.

As the Germans like to be clear and systematic in their dealings, foreigners often feel that the Germans are telling them what to do. Germans want to be very precise in what they say for probably a good reason. Oral agreements are binding in this country, so they avoid saying things that may lead to misunderstandings.

Punctual
The much talked about German punctuality is no myth. You might have heard about how you can tell the time from the arrivals of trains in Germany and this is really the case, if the train drivers are not on strike. However, a dent to this sterling reputation occured in January 2008. The media

reported with dismay that in a survey conducted, German trains no longer ran like clockwork—there were too many delays. From the headlines, I was similarly horrified at the degeneration of German punctuality, until I read the details: most of the trains were considered late when they arrived 4 minutes past the scheduled time.

Cold and Stolid

Cheerful Californians, outgoing Latinos and ever polite Japanese are always shocked at how stern and no-nonsense the Germans (except perhaps the Rheinlanders) are, especially those from the North. The average Berliner makes (UK's prime minister) Gordon Brown look positively friendly. Performing a job efficiently means being focused and serious; smiles and chattiness are distractions and unrelated to the proper execution of a job. Newcomers to Germany are always horrified at the robotic and unsmiling service staff. Just before the FIFA World Cup 2006 held in Germany, Berlin actually launched a campaign to urge the natives to smile more.

The flip side of the coin is that the Germans find the American friendliness 'superficial'. If you need to recover

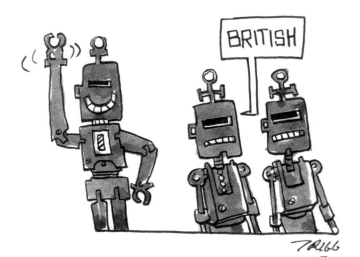

from the cold and unsmiling service, drop by a Starbucks or Mcdonald's; the staff there are often young and immersed in the American service culture before being let loose on customers, so you can get your friendly service fix there.

But these service staff might suffer from stress for all that smiling. In 2008, German psychologist Professor Dieter Zapf of Frankfurt University warned that people who had to smile professionally on their jobs were at risk of stress, depression and even heart problems.

Angst

It's not for nothing that the word *angst* is German. Meaning fear, anxiety, apprehension, insecurity or a combination of all these emotions, *angst* crept into the English language around the 1940s. History keeps getting blamed for all German peculiarities, but it's difficult not to come to this conclusion once we know what the Germans have been through.

The Germans tend to be excessive worriers, and this helps to partly explain why they are so sparing with the smiles. Newspaper articles also tend to adopt a tone of 'Germany is going to the dogs'.

Patriotism and Self Image

Does patriotism exist in Germans? Chances are, those who have known Germans decades ago would say no. Those who got to know Germans at or after the FIFA World Cup 2006 would say yes, judging by the sea of black, red and gold flags flying everywhere. Both groups are right.

Hitler (back to history books again) played on Germans' national pride to gain and remain in power. He painted himself as a patriotic saviour, who would bring glory to the country once he had built his powerful Germania.

The subsequent national guilt and shame of the Germans (bar the handful of sickos) over the atrocities committed by Hitler and Co led them to distance themselves from anything resembling patriotism and nationalism. For decades, any overt sign of national pride was taboo. To the credit of the leaders of the German nation after World War II, the Germans are not allowed to forget the Holocaust and there are reminders of

'Where in the world has one ever seen a nation that erects memorials to immortalize its own shame?'
—Avi Primor, former Israeli ambassador to Germany, praising Germany for facing up to its responsibility over its dark history.

this shameful chapter of their history everywhere, including in their education.

In spite of all these efforts, it's always much harder to impress on a generation, far removed from the event and distracted by more exciting pop culture, the guilt of their forebears. Many Germans, especially those in their teens, have not much interest in the history of a divided country, let alone the Holocaust.

So by the time the FIFA World Cup came to be hosted by Germany in 2006, the younger football fans had much less trouble waving the German flag and showing their patriotism than their parents or grandparents. The German media covered this phenomenon (till then, waving a German flag at games was hardly ever done) rather extensively, and you could almost hear the mixture of embarrassment and wonderment. By the time the handball world championships came round in 2007 (also held in Germany), there was no more hesitation about whether one should wave a flag or not. Patriotism was no longer a dirty word.

No Hang-ups about Nudity

In Germany, a Janet Jackson's 'wardrobe malfunction' won't have the nation hyperventilating. Nudity is treated in a somewhat blasé fashion.

Germans don't go to a sauna hiding modestly behind a big towel. They get down to the suits they were born in, and mind you, the saunas are often open to both sexes. Foreigners feel like Victorian prudes when they first enter a German sauna clad in a towel or swimwear. Even if you're a beautiful woman, the men in there will not glance at you; they are all extremely discreet. Germans are just, well, comfortable in their own skin. After all, a sauna is an enclosed area; they think nothing of strutting around a beach with nothing on except sun protection lotion. The *Freikörperkultur* or popularly known by its acronym FKK (literally 'free body culture', meaning naturism) has a long history in Germany.

The first FKK club was founded in Essen in 1898. FKK was apparently intended as a health regime, to expose the body to sunlight. The East Germans were particularly fond of naturism under communist rule as a way of expressing anti-establishment sentiments. After unification, FKK seems to be much less practised, but you can still find 'free bodies' on beaches.

If you look at a map of Berlin, you will see some lakeside areas (for example, Wannsee) marked 'FKK'. Here's where you can let it all hang out.

The Berliner *Schnauze*

And even as you're bracing yourself to face the naked, tactless and unsmiling Teutons you're going to meet, here's another piece of news for you: if you think the above description of the Teutonic race is scary, just note that the Berliners are held in awe by the Germans themselves as the grandmasters of directness. The *Berliner Schnauze* (the Berliner muzzle or mouth), the biting sense of 'humour' of the Berliners, is something even the Germans are wary of. Berliners have a reputation of being the toughest and rudest of all

Germans and I've heard often enough non-Berliner Germans complaining about the Berliners. The Berliners are the New Yorkers of Germany, in other words.

You might by now be filled with trepidation, but stop; don't start unpacking just yet. Before you decide against relocating to Berlin, do be assured that there are nice Berliners and Germans around. People from different generations and different backgrounds do have dissimilar attitudes and behaviour. Most of the younger Germans are often more

Rest assure that there are many nice Berliners who will make your stay pleasant and meaningful.

relaxed and un-German, for want of a better description. They are very similar to any other young person in Europe, North America, Australia and New Zealand. Pop culture and modern technology have closed many cultural gaps. The business executive with more international experiences will be quite different from a baker in a small village. The characteristics above have been highlighted so that should you come across them, you know it's a cultural thing and not an insult directed at you personally. They often also appear cold and unfriendly in the beginning, but once you get to know them better, or have an occasion to meet them in a social setting, you'll be amazed at how different they can be.

The Post Office Lady and Me

The first time I went to the post office near my home (in 1998), I found a stone-faced lady behind the counter. For the 5 minutes that my Christmas parcels were being weighed and processed, I felt like I was dealing with the Sphinx. Not a single muscle twitched on her face. I was certain she somehow disliked me.

The years went by and each time I went to the post office, the Sphinx was there to serve me efficiently, but without any facial changes. But by then, I knew that she was just being German, and appreciated her attentive and quick service.

Christmas 2007 was the year the Wall fell between us. My exotic Bulgarian Christmas card envelope was an irregular shape—it didn't fit any of the German standard shape and size (all properly set out on a plastic template). Sphinx's colleague who attended to me suggested that I trim 1 mm off the edge of the card, then it would be a German standard size and shape and offered me a pair of scissors for my impromptu surgery.

Sphinx looked from the corner of her eyes and joked 'You can write "Puzzle" on the envelope for description of contents'. I did a very un-German thing and burst into peals of laughter, while Sphinx remained true to her genes and kept a straight face.

I went home happy that I was now accepted as a *Stammkunde* (regular client), although it took all of nine years for her to venture a joke, albeit without a smile.

The Berliner Humour

"Is there such a thing?" you may well ask in incredulity. The Germans are not humourless. On the contrary, they have their Jon Stewarts, Mr. Beans and slapstick comedians. Harald

Berliner Humour

My husband didn't like the dusky pink colour that the external walls of our building was being painted with. "Looks like the colour of my grandma's underwear," he groaned to the painter. In a nanosecond, the painter shot back, "What beautiful underwear your grandma has!"

Schmidt and Oliver Pocher are examples of the German counterparts. It's just that there is a time and place for it.

The Berliner humour is spoken of in hushed tones even by the Germans. Although called humour, it's not about good-natured, knee-slapping jokes. In keeping with the Berliners' grittiness, the jokes are more acidic barbs and revered for its being *schlagfertig* (quick-witted).

East is East and West is West, and Never the Twain Shall Meet

Before we move on to the foreigners, a thought might have crossed your mind. Is the above description about West Berliners, East Berliners or both?

You would be tired of hearing about history's role in the characteristics of the Berliners by now, but the city's division into a capitalist West and a communist East for decades was bound to have its impact.

Nowadays, you can hardly tell a *Wessi* from an *Ossi* anymore from their dressing, which you still could a decade ago. But what about the mentality?

Many former East Germans have moved to West Germany, or are working comfortably with West German colleagues. But there are still tensions or at least ruffled feelings between many *Wessis* and *Ossis*, not least because West Germans have grown tired of the economic costs of unification, which amounted to €1.4 trillion of public transfers by 2008. The 'solidarity tax' they have to pay seems not to have any end in sight, and some feel that priority is given to developing the infrastructure in the East, even as those in the West are neglected. Some *Wessis* still see the *Ossis* as boors lacking in finesse.

Many *Ossis*, on the othe hand, see the Westerners as a bunch of arrogant, mercenary types. They also resent being treated as inferior relatives; East Germans earn slightly less than West Germans even if they are on the same executive level, for example. East Germans feel that they have a sense of community, non-existent in the West, and that their youngsters are more hard-working, unlike the spoilt brats *drüben* (over there).

The East Germans had expected life to improve significantly after the fall of the Wall. For some, it did, as they reached the top ranks of politics, such as Angela Merkel (Chancellor of Germany) and Wolfgang Thierse (former Speaker of Parliament), or found lucrative careers in the media or football, such as Michael Ballack (captain of the national football team). But for too many, things did not change much, or even worsened, as they failed to come to grips with the new market economy. The disillusionment has led many East Germans to feel nostalgic about life in the good old DDR (*Deutsche Demokratische Republik*—German Democratic Republic) days in a syndrome called *Ostalgie* (a play on the words *Ost* for East and *Nostalgie* for nostalgia). Suddenly, socialism was a good idea; it was only not efficiently put into practice.

2007 was an important year in Berlin's history. It was the year when the babies born when the Wall fell turned 18 (the age of majority). The leading German magazine *Der Spiegel* ran a special on some of these young adults born on 9 November 1989 and although certainly not representative across the board, it was interesting to read about their (and their parents') perceptions of life before and after the breach in the Wall. Many of the perceptions mentioned in the above paragraph were echoed by those interviewed (many of them East Berliners). *Der Spiegel* also commissioned a survey which sought the views of 1,004 East and West Germans which was conducted in October 2007. The sobering results showed that many East Germans (especially those aged between 35 to 50) felt that the social safeguards, the school system and level of security were much better in DDR times than in unified Germany. What was most startling was that 35 per cent of East Germans from ages 14 to 24 (and 37 per cent of East Germans aged between 35 to 50) would prefer to live in the East, if the Wall was to be re-built today.

Do Berliners Wear Lederhosen and Dirndls?

Whenever a caricature of a German is drawn, it's invariably a beer-swigging chap in *lederhose* (leather shorts) and a funny hat. If the figure is female, she will be a *dirndl*—the apron over a long full skirt and puffed-sleeve blouse ensemble replete with ample bosom.

The idea that these images represent all Germans is a myth. These are traditional costumes of the Bavarians (in southern Germany) and they do wear these togs proudly for festivals such as *Oktoberfest*, but they are not the national costume. Bavarians also see themselves as Bavarians first, rather than Germans, and non-Bavarians generally don't care too much for these folksy costumes.

No Berliner will be seen dead in such a gear, unless the person is a promoter for a Bavarian beer or waiter in a Bavarian restaurant. The Teutonic Berliners basically don't run around in traditional costumes, festival or not. Only the provincial types wear folk costumes, they would snort.

Berliners don't wear *dirndl*—except at a Bavarian beer market!

However, the other famous German summer 'uniform' of shorts, sandals and socks can be seen quite often in Berlin, expecially on the older generation.

Superstitions

Germans, especially the younger generation, are not excessively superstitious nowadays. But they are aware of the superstitions that have been handed down for generations and may choose to observe them, if only as a tradition.

Some of the superstitions are familiar to people from Western cultures, like the number 13 being unlucky. Black cats also feature in German superstition. If a black cat crosses your path from right to left, it's a bad omen, but if the feline crosses from left to right, you're spared any calamity.

Chimney sweeps (they still wear their traditional uniform with a black top hat) are believed to bring luck. Some Germans say you have to actually shake their hands for the luck to be activated, but others (it's certainly more convenient) believe just spotting one will do. Finding a four-leaved clover will also bring good luck.

Many Germans (especially women) have a thing about horoscopes. You'll find horoscope readings for the week in almost all of the womens' magazines.

Belief in the Supernatural

Many Germans are also fascinated by supernatural powers. A programme on a private TV channel, Pro Sieben, entitled *The Next Uri Geller*, actually drew quite an audience, who could vote for the winner by phone. And they voted for a fellow in a sort of Jedi-Knight costume, with a black raven as assistant, who allegedly could connect with the netherworld. True, there were plenty of Germans who snorted and derided the 'charlatans' but that such a programme has a place on German TV tells you that some Germans do believe in psychokinesis, telepathy and the afterlife. The TV audience certainly look wowed by the contestants. And we thought Germans only believed in cold, hard facts.

One of my neighbours is also a believer of paranormal powers. The occasions when I had to go and collect my parcel which the postman had left in her care in my absence, I would have to spend at least 10 minutes listening to her abilities to predict events and, like Prince Charles, talk plants into growing up green and strong. For full effect, she has a black cat with piercing green eyes, which Frau W. says can read a person's character. I've never really dared ask what her cat thought of me.

Neo-Nazis

Although called neo-Nazis, this bunch of unhinged people actually don't have much of an ideology. They love displaying Nazi symbols and machismo, it's true, but underlying all the aggression and bravado is just a bunch of insecure social misfits, who find strength in numbers. Being part of a neo-Nazi group gives them a sense of belonging and power they otherwise lack.

Eastern German states tend to have a larger community of far-right groups, which is often attributed to the region's woeful economy plus the communist regime's not instilling the sense of responsibility regarding Nazi crimes in them. The East German leaders, unlike their Western cousins, have never assumed any responsibility for the Holocaust. If anything, they actually played the role of victims of Nazism themselves. That's not to say, however, that all neo-Nazis are East Germans, or vice versa.

Worryingly, violence committed by neo-Nazis is on the rise. The far-right party, NPD (*Nationaldemokratische Partei Deutschlands*), has been active on the grassroots level, funding far-right youth centres for the disenchanted youth, thus attracting new recruits. In some areas, they also fund retail outlets selling Nazi paraphernalia. After much debate, it was decided that banning the NPD would not dismantle the group but only send them underground, or worse, win them more sympathy. So the NPD is allowed to exist, but watched closely by the authorities.

Apart from foreigners, the neo-Nazis have attacked German politicians as well: Giyasettin Sayan, belonging to the left-wing Party of Democratic Socialism, and Hans-Christian Ströbele, of the Green Party, were attacked in Berlin-

Lichtenberg (2006) and in the Warschauer Strasse undeground in Berlin (2002) respectively.

Much to the dismay of many Berliners, a Thor Steinar outlet, a brand of clothing associated with the neo-Nazis, opened in the city centre in February 2008. In June 2008, the NPD did relatively well in municipal elections in the Eastern state of Saxony, adding to the concerns about the rise of right-wing sympathisers.

In Berlin, Lichtenberg and Marzahn have the dubious honour of being neo-Nazi hang-outs. However, attacks against foreigners are not restricted to these two districts. In October 2007, 12 skin-heads attacked three Greeks (two male waiters and a female bartender) in Pankow.

According to a prominent anti-racism campaigner, Uwe-Karsten Heye, a record number of around 600 people were attacked by neo-Nazis in 2007.

Violent Hooligans

It's not only neo-Nazis who are violent. From late 2007 to 2008, there has been an increase in violent incidents committed by hooligans. The victims are often bus-drivers who get beaten up for telling a hooligan that his ticket isn't valid or to stop vandalising the bus windows. Sometimes stones are thrown at them for no apparent reason. Victims have also included passengers who had the courage to tell off hooligans for swearing at other innocent passengers or frightening a young child by letting off firecrackers on the platform of the train station.

Berlin has the dubious honour of being the German city with the highest number of violent offences against the police, way ahead of Frankfurt and Hamburg in positions two and three. These incidents tend to take place in some areas of Wedding, Kreuzberg, Neukölln, Moabit and Schöneberg.

A Millstone Round Their Necks

Like every nationality, there are as many pleasant Germans as there are less pleasant ones. The difference is that Germans tend to get bad press most, if not all, of the time. I have personally come across a handful of youngish, educated

Britons and Belgians who view ordinary Germans like they were Hitler re-incarnated. Germans seem to have to bear this cross for a long time to come, and they do it stoically. It bears repeating here, therefore, that Germans are not as stolid and unpleasant as they are often made out to be, and you will discover many charming Germans during your stay in Berlin.

Burden of a Negative Image

'Ignorance and hysteria too often characterise coverage of Germany in the foreign, and especially the British, press. Jonathan Carr, who from the mid-1970s to the late 1990s served as Bonn correspondent for the *Financial Times* and then *The Economist*.... brought knowledge and reason to the job....'
—*The Economist*, 21 June 2008 issue, made this observation of the negative press often suffered by Germany, in an obituary for one of their former correspondents, Jonathan Carr.

THE FOREIGNERS

There are many Berliners with immigrant backgrounds who are Berliners through and through. Born and grown up in Berlin, their behaviour and thinking are no different from a Teutonic Berliner. Others have not managed to integrate into German society and their lifestyles resemble that in their country of origin. The term 'foreigners' used here is a general term to distinguish them from Teutonic Berliners.

The Turks

Germany's citizenship law is based on *jus sanguinis* (*Abstammungsrecht* in German—the law of the blood). In practical terms, it means that someone who has a German ancestor but who cannot speak a word of German and knows nothing about German culture will find it easier to become a citizen than a non-ethnic German who was born and bred in Germany and speaks, writes and thinks in German. The law was reluctantly changed in 2001 to make it easier for a German-born foreigner to get citizenship if the parents have lived for at least eight years in Germany. But acceptance of foreigners has been slow in coming.

As mentioned earlier, the Turkish guest workers who came to Germany were not supposed to stay on and no effort was therefore made to integrate them into German society. Many Germans and politicians, including the former chancellor, Helmut Kohl, made clear their unwillingness to give non-Teutonic Germans citizenship. The Turks had their revenge when one of Kohl's sons married a Turk, but that's another story.

The Turks have always felt unwelcome in Germany, and this has fuelled a love for Turkey, even if they've never lived there. This was well demonstrated in the Euro 2008 football/soccer tournament, when Hamit Altintop and Hakan Balta, ethnic Turks who were born and grew up in Germany, opted to play for the Turkish national team.

The Turks are the largest immigrant community in Berlin; indeed, the city has the largest number of Turks outside of Turkey. The size of this community was well showcased during Euro 2008. A surprise last minute win over the Czech team that took Turkey into the quarter finals resulted in Berlin resembling Istanbul or Ankara, when the streets turned into a sea of red and white Turkish flags waved by jubilant Turks. In Berlin's famous shopping street, Ku'damm, some 25,000 Turks caused a major traffic jam as they celebrated on the streets. When Turkey ended up playing against Germany in the semi-finals, there were concerns about violence among some fans of both teams. Fortunately, the politicians, both teams and most Turkish and German media all actedly responsibly, calling for focusing on friendship, football and joint celebrations. In the predominantly Turkish neighbourhood of Kreuzberg, many Turks waved both Turkish and German flags and discussed during half-time with their Teutonic neighbours the teams' performance. When Germany won after a nail-biting game, Berlin did not descend into violence. In general, the city erupted into celebrations, with many Turks joining in, in spite of their mixed feelings. Many German-Turks took the practical view that whichever team lost, they still had a team to support in the finals.

Welcome or not, Turkish culture has insinuated itself so effectively into Germany that when a young foreign entertainer was asked what her favourite German food was at an interview, the young lady said *"Döner kebap"* in all innocence. *Döner kebap* has become one of the most popular fast-food item in Berlin.

Apart from Kreuzberg, large number of Turks also live in Neukölln and Wedding. While many Turks have moved out of the Turkish enclaves and have successful careers, a significant number of Turks have, however, found it less easy to fit into German society and the current relationship between Turks and Germans is not exactly warm and fuzzy. A fire in a building in Ludwigshafen (a city in Rhineland-Palatinate in southwest Germany) which killed nine Turks in early 2008 led quickly to tensions after the state premier declared a little too hastily after the incident that it was not a racist attack, when investigations had hardly started. The Turkish media reacted by suspecting that it was a racially motivated arson and Turkey requested that Turkish officers join in the investigations. The relationship between many Turks and Germans at that point of time was, needless to say, a tinder box.

The relationship among the Turks is also scratchy. The Turks are heterogeneous, divided by sects (e.g. Sunni or Alevi), ethnicity (Turk or Kurd) and level of secularity/religiosity. The politics in Turkey is often played out in Berlin. The Kurdistan Worker's Party (PKK) launched an armed struggle against the Turkish state in 1984, in a bid to have an independent state within Turkey. Turkey's military response was equally forceful, resulting in thousands of lost lives. When the Iraqi Kurds got their autonomous region after the first Iraqi war, the longing for self-government of the Turkish Kurds increased. The ongoing PKK's violent campaign and Turkey's equally harsh military response result in an extremely strained relationship between Turks and Kurds, which often spills over onto the streets of Berlin.

The Eastern Europeans

Berlin's proximity to Eastern Europe makes it the city of choice for Eastern Europeans migrating to West Europe.

From Bosnia and Herzegovina, Croatia, Republic of Macedonia, (Kosovo), Montenegro, Serbia and Slovenia

These communities came as guest workers or to escape the conflicts back home.

From Poland

Germany has traditionally seen waves of Poles coming to the country. In the late 19th and early 20th centuries, Poles streamed to the Ruhr area to work in the coal mines and other newly established industries; after WWII, Polish prisoners and forced labourers stayed on in Germany after Poland was taken over by the Soviet Union; and in the 1980s and 1990s, it was mainly young and well-educated Poles who came to Germany, many for economic reasons.

Unlike the Turks, many Poles have found it easy to become German citizens because of the *jus sanguinis* basis of German citizenship law. But they haven't exactly been welcomed with open arms either, especially since Poland became a member of the European Union, as many Germans feared that the Poles would steal jobs away from them.

There is also a history of a prickly relationship between the Germans and Poles. Poland had been carved up by the Prussians, Austrians and Russians and invaded by the Nazis in September 1939. The Nazis murdered not only Jews and Romas, but also Polish politicians and intellectuals, and shipped thousands of Poles to Germany as slave labourers. When Willy Brandt, the then chancellor of Germany, knelt in front of a monument in 1970 commemorating the Warsaw Ghetto Uprising, it did not, understandably, do much to heal the Polish wounds. When the Polish Kaczynski twins' Law and Justice Party came into power in 2005, the relationship with Germany dipped to its lowest in decades. It was only with Donald Tusk's becoming prime minister in 2007 that the relationship started improving again.

Still, it's a rather fragile relationship, easily erupting into nasty tabloid exchanges between the two countries.

Russians

Like the Poles, many of the Russians also came to Germany as *Spätaussiedler* (i.e. the descendants of German settlers in the Tsarist Russian Empire who were granted the right of return home because of their 'German blood') or as Jews from the former Soviet Union who were granted refugee status. The exact number of such Russians is difficult to ascertain, as they are considered Germans as soon as they receive their German passports and 'disappear' from the foreigner statistics. Their German status also qualifies them for German welfare immediately.

Many of these Russians have German names, but remain culturally Russian.

Asians

The countries covered under Asia according to the Berlin-Brandenburg Statistics Office include Central Asia, Middle East and East Asia. Of the roughly 68,000 Asians in Berlin, the Vietnamese make up the largest community.

The Vietnamese

Many Vietnamese came to Berlin through training and contract worker programmes of the former German Democratic Republic. They were invited to work in the East German industries but only for a limited period of time. Like the Turks in West Berlin, however, many Vietnamese did not go home. Another wave of Vietnamese came in the mid-seventies, the so-called 'boat people', who fled South Vietnam to escape the communists.

When the Wall fell, the Vietnamese in East Germany were left high and dry. Unlike the *Spätaussiedler*, they were not included in the welfare system, and had to find their own means of survival. Not a few resorted to smuggling cigarettes to earn a living in the collapsed East German economy. In the 1990s, gangland murders left the Vietnamese with a severely dented image.

Many who were caught committing crimes or who were simply not able to support themselves economically were repatriated. By 2000, however, many of those who could remain had moved on to more respectable businesses like groceries, eateries and flower shops.

Like the Turks, the Vietnamese are not homogeneous. There isn't much interaction between the more middle class and skilled 'boat people' from South Vietnam and the North Vietnamese who first came to the former East Germany for training or work.

Other Asians

Other East Asians such as the Chinese (about 6,000), Koreans and Japanese (about 3,000 from each community) are hardly distinguishable from the Vietnamese, as far as physical features go. So Germans and other Westerners tend to assume that they are Vietnamese. There are also some 6,000 South Asians (from Bangladesh, India, Pakistan and Sri Lanka) in Berlin.

ARE BERLINERS ATHEISTS?

There aren't any overt signs of religiosity in homes like there are in the predominantly Catholic south of Germany. On a visit to the Rheinland, I was amazed at how many privately erected religious shrines there were in front of individual homes while walking around a residential neighbourhood. It's not something you see in Berlin.

Berlin is often said to be a pretty godless place. Considering that between 1948 to 1990, half of Berlin was under communist rule, it comes as no surprise. Some religious holidays like Epiphany and All Saints' Day are not public holidays in Berlin, as they are in some German states. But Berliners aren't all atheists; in fact, there's a multitude of religions in the city given its cosmopolitan population.

German privacy laws make exact statistics on religious orientation difficult to obtain, but it can be said that Germany is broadly divided into a Catholic south and a Protestant north, with each denomination making up slightly over 30 per cent of the population. Berlin has substantially more Protestants (23.4 per cent) than Catholics. About 6 per cent of Berliners are Muslims. The approximately 11,000 Jews in Berlin may not be a large number, but because of history, Judaism and Jewish culture have a prominent position in Berlin.

There are smaller communities of other denominations and faith: Anglicans, Methodists, Presbytarians, Orthodox Christians, Latter Day Saints (or Mormons), Jehovah's Witnesses, Buddhists, Hindus, Sikhs and Scientologists, to name just a few. Berlin therefore has places of worship and centres for all the different believers, and Berlin being Berlin, for non-believers too, such as the German Freethinkers Association.

One might think that all the Russians belong to the Russian Orthodox Church or that all East Asians are Buddhists. But here in Berlin, it's inaccurate to associate nationalities with the religion of the majority in their home countries.

Main Religions in Berlin

Protestants—23.4 per cent

Catholics—9.1 per cent

Muslims—5.9 per cent

Jews—0.3 per cent

Source: *Welcome to Berlin*, a publication of the Berlin Senate (Integration and Migration)

The Christians

While the Lutheran and Catholic churches in Berlin have ethnic German members, there are foreigners in the flock as well. The Catholic Church has services in different languages to cater to their global village of believers, such as the Polish community, Latin Americans and Asians.

The Anglican church's language of worship is English, but its congregation is from all around the world. For a start, the pastor is English, but the assistant pastor is German (at the time of writing).

The Muslims

The Muslim community is made up mainly of Turks and Arabs (Algerians, Egyptians, Iraqis, Moroccans, Lebanese,

Palestinians and Tunisians). There are also Muslims from other countries such as Afghanistan, Bosnia-Herzegovina, Iran and Pakistan. Berlin now has about 80 mosques, with 20 in Neukölln, although some are simple converted factory floors, and not a specially built mosque as such. The first mosque in Berlin was constructed in 1924. Plans for the first mosque to be built in East Berlin (in Pankow) were, however, met by protests from the residents in 2006. Although the far-right were the most aggressive, the local residents were just as negative about having a mosque in their midst.

The terrorist attacks of 11 September 2001 may have made some Germans uneasy about Muslims, but a failed plot by some extremists to blow up trains outside the cities of Hamm and Koblenz in West Germany on 31 July 2006 really turned the heat up on Muslims.

A substantial number of Muslims in Berlin live in Kreuzberg, Wedding and North Neukölln. Neukölln has about 300,000 people, of which some 60,000 are Muslims. Here, especially along Sonnenallee, are Arab and Turkish halal food shops, restaurants, barbers, hairdressers, and funeral parlours. It's like a *souk* here, and you'd be forgiven for forgetting that you're in the German capital. The Turks call it 'Little Istanbul'. Some see it as exotic, others snort 'Gaza Strip' derisively. But it's not exactly a purely racist reaction; this area has a substantial number of poor and disenchanted residents. Every other resident is jobless and there is plenty of crime. Many of them cling on to traditonal ways of life. The children's problems in school run from a poor grasp of German to young girls being forbidden by their fathers to have swimming lessons and going on school trips. All these led Heinz Buschkowsky, the Neukölln mayor, to call it a 'parallel society', attracting instant criticism from some quarters for being politically incorrect.

But Buschkowsky did more than just comment, and sought to improve the situation by establishing language centres and hiring immigrant trainees to work in his administration. He also helped to launch a project called 'neighbourhood mothers' where youthful mothers of Turkish or Arabic descent visit young immigrant families to offer them advice on issues of health and raising children. In the spring of 2008, there were some 80 neighbourhood mothers in Neukölln, with plans to increase it to 200.

The Jews

The *Shoah* (Holocaust) began in Berlin. The Jews are so much a part of Berlin's history and so interwoven into the fabric of the city that a substantial part of this section must be devoted to this community.

The first document mentioning Jews in the Brandenburg region dates back to the 10th century. Although the Nazi crimes were horrific in terms of the scale of the brutality and the number of Jews murdered, that wasn't the first time that Jews in Berlin were discriminated against and persecuted. In the 13th century, Jews in Berlin were prevented from joining artisan guilds, and between 1347 to 1349, they were accused of causing the plague and expelled from Berlin and Brandenburg, just to name a few examples.

A significant influx of Jews to Berlin took place after the Thirty Years' War which had decimated the German population. The then Elector, Friedrich Wilhelm, encouraged foreigners and persecuted people to settle in Berlin, to boost the population and the economy. In 1671, the Elector approved an edict which allowed 50 well-to-do Jewish families expelled from Vienna the right of residency in Berlin, provided they paid an annual protection fee. The residency was also only for 20 years. Like the Turks and other foreigners after them, the Jews were not supposed to settle permanently in Berlin. Between 1671 and 1714, land for a Jewish cemetery was purchased and a Jewish hospital for the poor opened. Many poor Jews had also come to Berlin, but they were not granted any right of residency.

It was only in 1714 that the Edict of 1671 was confirmed giving Jews such a right. In September of the same year, the first synagogue in Berlin was dedicated. Sixteen years later, the rights confirmed in 1714 were substantially retracted. By 1737, only 120 families were allowed to settle in Berlin, and the rest expelled. In 1743, a 14-year old Jew, who would later play a central role in the Jewish Enlightenment, arrived in Berlin. This was Moses Mendelssohn, who demonstrated that it was possible for Jews to keep their faith and immerse themselves in German culture at the same time. In 1778, on the initiative of Mendelssohn, the Jewish Free School was founded by David Friedländer, Isaak Daniel Itzig and Naphtali Herz Wessely. The often hostile environment did not prevent the Jews from founding an association for culture and science for scholarly research on Judaism, a boys' school and later a girls' school. The Jewish Reform congregation (called the Society for Reform in Judaism at its founding) was founded in 1845. In 1850, the Prussian constitution was revised to grant equality to all Prussians, including Jews. In reality, though, the Jews could not take on senior posts in public offices, the military or in academia. In the 19th century, an estimated 22,000 Jews converted to Christianity because of marriage to Gentiles, or in the hope of advancement in their careers. But conversion didn't win them acceptance and they only ended up falling in between two chairs: no longer regarded as Jews, they were not regarded as Christians either, but only as 'baptised Jews'.

Jewish life continued to develop and in 1866, the New Synagogue on Oranienburger Strasse was dedicated. Three years later, the Orthodox Jewish religious society Adass Yisroel was founded.

By 1875, the Jewish community had reached 65,000, climbing to 144,000 some three decades later. Many of the Jews fought in World War I, but this was not recognised. On the contrary, there were accusations that they were not serving at the front, like the other Germans.

In spite of all the obstacles facing them, many Jews in Berlin succeeded in business or in the cultural realm, such as the Leiser family (shoe shops), the Wertheim family (shopping centre) and Max Liebermann (painter).

When Hitler's National Socialist Party came to power in 1933, the Jewish community in Berlin was 160,000-strong. The party launched a campaign against Jewish businesses as soon as they took over the rein. The screws continued to tighten, and in 1935, the Nuremberg Laws (discriminatory laws against the Jews) were passed. On 9 and 10 November

1938, the infamous *Kristallnacht* (literally Crystal Night or what is known as the Night of Broken Glass), an anti-Jew rampage, swept through Berlin in retaliation for the murder of a German diplomat in Paris by a 17-year-old Jew. 191 synagogues were destroyed, and another 76 severely damaged. More than 20,000 Jews were arrested and sent to concentration camps. Many worried Jews started emigrating. Some 90,000 fled in time, as in October 1941 the deportations from Berlin began, the start of the genocide of European Jews.

By the end of the war in May 1945, only about 6,500 Berlin Jews survived, through being married to non-Jews or having gone into hiding. A new Jewish community administration started to rebuild the community in December of the same year. The Jews who remained in Germany were sometimes ostracised by other Jews for staying on in the country of the Nazis.

During the years when Berlin was divided, there were two bodies in existence: the Jewish Community of Berlin in West Berlin and the Union of Jewish Congregations in East Berlin. The persecution of Jews continued in the GDR,

The Memorial to the Murdered Jews of Europe: an unusual memorial of concrete blocks.

causing many to flee to West Berlin. By 1989, when the Wall fell, only 200 Jews were left in East Berlin. In West Berlin, there were about 6,000 Jews. A year before, a Berlin New Synagogue-Centrum Judaicum Foundation was founded. In 1990, the two communities were united. But the increase in the Jewish community was to come from the immigration of Jews from the former Soviet Union, after the German federal government passed laws giving these Jews refugee status. Today, there are some 12,000 Jews in Berlin (out of about 100,000 in Germany). The Jews in Germany are the third-largest group in Western Europe, after France and Britain.

The present-day Jewish community in Germany, although no longer having to face state persecution, still have worries and wrinkles to iron out. Apart from the small but aggressive group of right-wing radicals who are bent on making life difficult for Jews, there are also hiccups among the Jews themselves.

Although the influx of Jews from the former Soviet Union is seen by some of the 'established' Jews who have been living in Germany for decades as a positive addition to the Jewish community, others disagree. For the naysayers, these newcomers are not *kosher* enough. The 'Russians' tend to be secular Jews who are not deeply religious and don't bother much with Jewish traditions. The orthodox Jews, in particular, are appalled that the 'Russians' don't keep *kosher* homes and many of the men are not circumcised. There is also the issue of whether they are truly Jews. According to *halakha* (religious law), a person is only a Jew if (s)he is a convert or has a Jewish mother. Although some streams of Judaism consider anyone with a Jewish parent (either mother or father), or who has converted, a Jew, many of the established Jews in Germany abide by the *halakha* definition. For them, many of the Russians are not Jews.

Apart from the debates on the definition of a Jew, there is also much frowning where the lifestyle and culture is concerned. Russian Jews are more focused on the economic and practical aspects of life in Germany, giving rise to accusations that they are interested only in the material advantages to be found in Germany. This large group of

The beautiful Neue Synagoge—built in 1857–66.

Russian-speaking Jews have also given some German Jews the feeling that the Jewish centres have become Russian cultural clubs.

Like them or not, the Jews from the former Soviet Union are the reason why the Jewish community in Berlin and Germany as a whole is growing so rapidly.

As for anti-semitism, it keeps rearing its ugly head, sad to say. In 2008, the Jewish cemetery in Berlin was desecrated at least twice, and significantly just before Holocaust Remembrance Day. The tight security needed for Jewish structures and buildings is a grim reminder that anti-semitism is not yet consigned to history. The number of crimes in Berlin with an anti-Semitic motive reportedly greatly increased in 2007. Police statistics showed that there were nine such incidents in 2007, compared to an average of four per year for the years 2003 to 2006.

The Scientologists

A 4,000 sq m (43,040 sq ft) Scientology Centre opened in Berlin in 2007, which caused the Germans to break out in a rash. In spite of its size and location in the country's capital, it isn't the headquarters, which is in Munich. Founded in 1954 in the US by science fiction author L. Ron Hubbard, The Church of Scientology has around eight million members globally including Hollywood celebrities, John Travolta and Tom Cruise. It is estimated that the organisation has 6,000 members in Germany, with about 150–200 members in Berlin.

While not a large community in Germany at present, they have been brought up for mention here as Germans are full of angst about the group. The Germans, scarred by their Nazi history, have an aversion to groups they see as outside the mainstream. Germany regards the group as dangerous and it is monitored by their Office for the Protection of the Constitution (the German couterpart of the FBI in the US and MI5 in the UK), except in Berlin itself. Court decisions prevent the state of Berlin from monitoring the group. All these lead critics to remark that such behaviour is itself Nazi-like intolerance and persecution.

Germans view Scientology as a cross between a sect and a business, not a religion. Berliners living near the centre tried to have a bus stop in front of the centre moved, as they were allegedly subjected to an onslaught of Scientology publicity materials when they waited for their bus. Their request was turned down, as it would cost too much money to move the bus stop. The most recent allegation is levied at Tom Cruise personally, who they claimed is using the publicity from the film *Valkyrie* (where Tom Cruise takes on the role of Claus von Stauffenberg, the officer who tried to assassinate Hitler), shot on location in Berlin, to raise the profile of Scientology.

Transcendental Meditation

Although the authorities are excessively wary of the Scientologists, they seem ready to accept other quirky groups. David Lynch, the Hollywood director (*Elephant Man*, *Mullholland Drive*), has plans to build a New Age university on Berlin's highest hilltop, Teufelsberg, offering among other subjects, the philosophy of Transcendental Meditation. So far, no opposition has been voiced, although at a lecture in 2007 given by Lynch, his guru, Emanuel Schiffgens, raised the hackles of his German audience when he hollered, "Invincible Germany!" a few times. It reminded them too much of Hitler and the audience made known their displeasure.

THE DEMOGRAPHY

There are slightly more females (about 51 per cent) in Berlin than males. Berliners between the ages 18–44 make up the largest group at 41 per cent.

Marital bliss seems to be in short supply in Berlin. Almost 48 per cent are singles (that is, not officially married although they might be in a partnership), and 46 per cent of Berliner families are single-parent households.

NOT THE FASHION CAPITAL

Berlin is not the fashion capital of Germany, as London and Paris are the undisputed fashion capitals of their respective countries. Berlin, Düsseldorf, Hamburg and Munich are all jostling with one another to be given that crown. In the first place, Germany is better known for producing cars than clothes. Granted Hugo Boss, Wolfgang Joop, Karl Lagerfeld and Jil Sander have made a name for themselves internationally, but people don't normally associate Germany with fashion.

Germans do dress up for a grand occasion, and actresses and other arty types do make sure they are nattily dressed. Business people also don the obligatory sharp suits. But the general public adopts a dress-down look. The average German prefers muted colours and casual clothes. You rarely see heavy make-up or loud jewellery on the women. Think Helen Mirren, rather than Sophia Loren. 'Fashion' to a German means

Fashion Week in Berlin. The Germans are becoming increasingly fashion-conscious and Berlin is working its way towards becoming a fashion capital.

'ready-to-wear' rather than haute couture. You can see this from the clean lines of Boss, Joop and Sander collections.

But all these are slowly changing. German women are becoming increasingly fashion conscious, with the influence of Hollywood stars and the success of Germans Claudia Schiffer and Heidi Klum as top international models (Klum made it to being a Victoria Secret model). Klum's *Germany's Next Top Model* casting shows drew droves of young Heidi Klum-wannabes to apply, and thousands more riveted in front of their television sets.

Berlin is also working its way towards becoming a fashion capital. There are young designers who are doing well, and there is every effort to make the city a fashion hub. The Berlin Fashion Week is an example, with international designers invited to showcase their collections.

HOBNOBBING WITH THE BERLINERS

'People nowadays like to be together not in the old-fashioned way of, say, mingling on the piazza of an Italian Renaissance city, but, instead, huddled together in traffic jams, bus queues, on escalators and so on. It's a new kind of togetherness which may seem totally alien, but it's the togetherness of modern technology.'
—James Graham Ballard, British author

'GRACIOUS,' YOU MIGHT SAY, looking at the title of this chapter, 'if the Berliners are so cold and unfriendly, how on earth can I socialise with them?'

You can because not all Berliners have that much-feared *Schnauze*. As mentioned in Chapter Three, you will find that there are some jolly types, too. Generally speaking, the younger generation is more easy-going, as are the Germans who are used to dealing with people from other corners of the globe. If you live or work for an extended length of time in Berlin, you will also get to experience the Germans in a social situation. And Claus in the office and Claus in the *Kneipe* with beer in hand are two very different persons. It's not only the alcohol that will get Claus to relax his facial muscles, but Germans do loosen up in a social setting, because there's a time and place for seriousness, and another for chilling out.

There are also all the other occasions where you will be with Berliners in a 'togetherness of modern technology', to borrow from J.G. Ballard. I won't go so far as to say people nowadays *like to be* together in traffic jams and bus queues, but we all invariably find ourselves rubbing shoulders with Markus and Hildegard on the S-Bahn and in the supermarkets, whether we like it or not. Germans and Berliners have their own way of doing some of these 'togetherness', so this chapter alerts you to them, to help you to be ready on day one.

THE GENERAL PUBLIC
Basic Social Norms

To complement their serious demeanour, Germans are very formal to boot. The German language (like many European ones) has a formal and informal form of 'you'—*Sie* and *Du* respectively. Only family members, young children or close friends are addressed with the informal *Du*. Germans can be colleagues for decades, but still stick to the *Sie* form.

People with whom you use the *Sie* form are not addressed by their first names either. They will be addressed as *Herr* (Mr.) Müller or *Frau* (Mrs.) Müller, never Helmut or Hannelore. If they have a PhD, they must be correctly addressed as *Herr* Dr. Müller, or *Frau* Dr. Müller.

A German with a *Diplom* (e.g. *Dipl.-Ing* or *Dipl.-Kfm*) means s(he) has a graduate degree from a university. It is not a diploma in the British context, which is obtained from a polytechnic or other higher education institution which isn't a university.

Introductions are accompanied by handshakes. Germans shake hands a lot more often than people from many other cultures, and they're not necessarily reserved for someone whom they haven't seen for ages. Some Germans even shake their colleagues' hands every day. When you

shake hands, make sure it's a firm grip. It shouldn't break the person's knuckles, but a limp grip might be taken by a German as weakness.

But shaking hands is the only physical contact that Germans make with acquaintances. They are not the 'pressing of flesh' type of people, so no squeezing upper arms in a friendly manner, no hugs and no arms around someone who isn't a family member or best buddy. Pecks on the cheeks are becoming fashionable with the younger generation, although it's probably best to leave it to the Germans to initiate it.

Some of us come from cultures where one smiles as a matter of courtesy and good service. In Germany, especially Berlin, you never bestow a smile on strangers, only on family members and friends. So don't get upset if the person serving you in a shop behaves like you've just walked into a funeral parlour by mistake. Germans see excessive smiling as strange, so you should remind yourself each morning before leaving home not to smile at people in the public sphere. Laughter, unless you're in a comedy theatre, is even more bizarre to the Germans. Some of us smile or even laugh to cover up an embarassing situation or to imply 'sorry, how silly of me'. Germans will think you're a mental case if you smile or laugh after, say, picking up someone else's luggage by mistake at the airport.

You would have guessed by now that you therefore do not walk into a shop and chatter to people in there about the dreary weather outside. Germans do say *Guten Tag* (Good Day) when entering a shop and *Auf wiedersehen* (Goodbye) when leaving, but 'small talk' is unusual, unless the customer and the shop assistant know each other well. Discussions about what colour and cut suit you best in a clothing shop are fine, but you don't need to go on about your buying the gown for your daughter's wedding and so on.

One other thing about the Germans when it comes to meeting and greeting is this: A German who is out with his family or friends normally does not introduce them to an acquaintance he meets by chance on the streets. He will stop to chat with that acquaintance for five minutes, while the family/friends cool their heels nearby and remain essentially transparent. The colleague will hardly acknowledge their presence too. If you're not used to this, it seems awfully rude. The Germans probably see it as a matter of privacy.

It also takes an unbelievably long time before a German decides that an acquaintance should be upgraded to the status of a friend and for *Du* to be used. And when that happens, they don't just say, 'Let's use *Du*, shall we?' No, there is an initiation ceremony into the brotherhood (or sisterhood) of friends, and you clink glasses of champagne with intertwined hands and the German declares his name 'Conrad', and you respond with 'Shaun'. Because it takes a long time before one is considered a friend, the friendship made tends to be very sincere and long-term, though.

The younger generation isn't generally so formal as people of their parents' generation, however. It's the generation in their late fifties and older who are more observant of all these formalities.

Getting Bruised Shoulders

New Yorkers, Londoners and people from other crowded cities have often complained about the Germans' seeming inability (or unwillingness?) to avoid bumping into the people coming from the opposite direction. They may even walk two or three abreast on a narrow path, instead of getting into a single file, so that people coming towards them can pass. To add insult to (physical) injury, it's unlikely anyone will murmur an apology after they crash into you. You'd begin to think the Germans invented Moshing and Slam Dancing.

Watch Your Shoulders!

Tired of being the one always to jump out of the way of German tanks, I once also squared my shoulders and walked straight on, thinking the burly male coming my way would never crash into a lady. Wham! He almost dislocated my shoulder and walked on as if nothing happened. Of course I can't be a hundred per cent sure he was a German, but many foreigners have similar complaints about being crushed when in Germany.

Phone Etiquette

When you call someone, you should identify yourself, and this applies to both business and private calls. When the person at the other end of the line picks up the phone, say 'Mark Jenkins, *Guten Tag*,' before you ask to speak to the person you're calling. Germans answer the phone by, likewise, stating their family name (and company name, where appropriate).

You shouldn't call anyone past 10:00 pm, unless you have been specifically told you can. You also shouldn't call Germans (except family members) on Christmas eve, because it's sacred family time.

Eating in Public

It's traditionally considered plebeian behaviour to eat and drink while on the S or U Bahn, or walking along the streets, although eating at one of the standing tables of an open-air snack shop or on a park bench is acceptable. Having said that, eating on public transport is becoming increasingly common, especially among the young.

THE NEIGHBOURS
Greeting Your Neighbours

Like everywhere else, it's polite to greet your neighbours with a '*Guten Tag*' (Good Day) or '*Guten Abend*' (Good Evening) when you bump into them outside your apartment /house. When you first move into the neighbourhood, your greeting may be met with a chilly silence or an imperceptible nod, though. S(he) may think you're just a stranger passing through, and therefore refrain from being 'too familiar'. Once they realise you're a neighbour, they will greet you and return greetings. Occasionally, a normally friendly neighbour may respond to your courteous '*Wie geht es Ihnen?*' (How are you?) with a curt '*Na ja*' (a non-committal comment, something like 'Oh well'). It means things are not going well, and the neighbour may just grunt that as he walks by without stopping. It has nothing to do with you or what you said, so don't be upset by the churlishness.

If you happen to have neighbours who never thaw, then just take note of the chilly ones and you can skip greeting them.

Greeting neighbours means verbally saying the 'good mornings' and 'good evenings' when you are within earshot of one another. You shouldn't flail your arms and shout cheery greetings to them when they are some distance away or across the road, as these would be too exuberant for Germans. Friendly neighbours may invite you over for coffee, bring you home-made marmalade, or chat with you for a bit when you meet in the corridor.

Quiet time

Germans observe 'quiet time' between 1:00 pm to 3:00 pm, and from 10:00 pm to 7:00 am on Mondays through Saturdays. On Sundays, it's quiet all day long. What this means is that during the quiet time, you shouldn't make a racket like mow the lawn, hammer and drill, play loud music or practise on your saxophone. My washing machine behaves like a heavy metal rock star during the spin cycle, so I refrain from operating it during these hours too.

If you live in an apartment block, the building's management is most likely to lay out the rules clearly in written form. The 'quiet time' imposed on residents in the building would generally be those times mentioned above. Otherwise, just know that that is the general rule which Germans follow, although there may be some inconsiderate ones who don't bother.

FAMILY AND FRIENDS
When Invited to a German home
Germans enjoy entertaining their family and close friends at home. So if you're invited to a German's home, it's quite an honour, and you should accept.

If you're invited to their home around 3:00 to 4:00 pm, then it's for *Kaffee und Kuchen* (coffee and cakes). Although called that, the fare on offer is not limited to coffee and cakes. There will be a variety of pastries, cakes and cookies and the host(ess) will ask if you prefer coffee or tea.

An invitation for 7:00 pm or 8:00 pm is, of course, for dinner, and you can expect a rather substantial meal awaiting you.

Do be punctual, as you would know by now that Germans keep to the stated times. Don't arrive earlier than the stated time, either. If you are going to be more than ten minutes late, due to unforeseen circumstances, do call your hosts to tell them.

Your host/hostess will greet you at the door, and in most German households, you will find that there is an ante room, separated from the rest of the house/apartment by a closed door. Here is where you will shake hands and hand over your gifts (flowers, a bottle of wine and/or chocolates are the norm). The male host will help the ladies out of their coats (if it's a chilly day) and there will be a coat stand in this ante room. You will then be invited into the main part of the home. You can keep your shoes on; Teutonic culture doesn't require the removal of shoes, unless your host specifically asks you to.

The Germans often start with a pre-dinner drink in the living room. A bottle of champagne (or *Sekt*, as the German sparkling wine is called) is usually opened for a welcome toast. The host will make a little speech of welcome and everyone clinks glasses, saying '*Zum Wohl*' (To your health). There will be some nibbles (nuts and crisps) to accompany the drinks. After about half an hour to an hour of chatting later, you will be invited to move to the dinner table for the meal proper. It's not unusual for the host to have a specific seating arrangement, so don't just plonk yourself immediately onto one of the dining chairs before being told where to sit.

The courses are the standard starters–main course–desserts routine. Wine, beer, soft drinks and water will be offered. The host will lift his glass and offer a toast, so don't start drinking before that is done. Germans are not known for small helpings, and when they have guests, they will make sure there is an oversupply of food. When everyone has been served, one should say '*Guten Appetit*' (literally 'Good Appetite') before starting to eat.

The good thing about German forthrightness is that you don't have to force yourself to take a second helping just to show how much you're enjoying the food, as in some other cultures. It's good enough if you make the necessary (but honest) compliments and enjoy your meal. The usual table manners apply and there isn't anything wildly different from American or British dining etiquette that you have to look out for, although Germans don't try to balance peas on the back of forks with tines facing downwards. Only don't cut your boiled potatoes with a knife. Germans never attack potatoes with knives, but forks.

Once the eating is over, you will move back to the comfortable sofa for coffee/tea and more chatting. You're not normally expected to help with the washing up. Germans don't expect guests to walk into the kitchen and ask, 'Can I help?'. They prefer to keep guests in the living and dining rooms, so don't wander uninvited around the house to admire it, either.

You can take your leave at around 11:00 pm. Your hosts will see you to the door and help you with your coats. It's not expected that they walk you to your car, but close family and friends do that, especially if the guests have travelled many kms to visit them.

Gift Giving

Being the straightforward people that they are, there are no rituals associated with giving gifts that may trip you up, as say in Japanese culture.

As mentioned in the preceding sub-section, it's appropriate to bring a gift when you're invited to dinner. Flowers, chocolates and a bottle of wine are safe bets. When giving flowers, more traditional Germans stick to odd number of stems (except 13), although the standard dozen of stems is acceptable. Lilies, chrysanthemums, white roses and all other white-coloured flowers are to be avoided, as they are used for funerals.

Perfume, jewellery, cosmetics and other more personal gifts are only given to family members, close friends and lovers. Should you need to bring a present for someone's birthday party, a book relating to the recipient's hobby, household items or 'fine foods' are appropriate gifts. Avoid giving knives or other sharp instruments—they are deemed to bring injury or even death to the recipient or his family. Bringing bread and salt to a housewarming party is a German tradition, but obviously you should also bring a present in addition if you don't want to be called a cheapskate.

SPECIAL OCCASIONS
Births and Birthdays

If your neighbour or colleague has a new addition to the family, it's a nice gesture to bring them a small baby gift. With colleagues, you should check with other colleagues first, as they might be planning to have a joint gift. When the parent gets back to the office, (s)he is most likely to celebrate with colleagues with champagne or *Sekt*. While we're on the point about getting back to the office after having a baby, you might be astounded at the generous maternity and paternity leave, if you're not from Scandinavia. Both the mother and father can take turns to go on 'parental leave' for up to an aggregate of 14 months.

Special Birthdays

Germans are particularly keen on celebrating certain years, such as the age of majority (18) and those rounding off a decade (40, 50, 60 etc). Usually a grander bash is laid out for these years. Your present for the birthday person should also be slightly more generous.

Baptism, if there is one, will be strictly for family and close friends.

Many of us are used to being given the royal treatment on our birthdays. In Germany, it's the person having the birthday who has to lay out the birthday bash. The birthday boy/girl is expected to bring cakes, pastries, cheese, ham, salami, rolls, juices and the all important champagne/*Sekt* to the office for colleagues. The birthday person is also likely to invite close friends over for dinner, or take them out to dinner or for drinks.

For all the effort, the birthday person will get presents from the colleagues and friends.

Starting School

On the first day of school for first-graders (primary one students), parents or grandparents give the child a *Schultüte* (also called *Zuckertüte*), a paper or plastic cone, which are often as tall as the child. The cone is stuffed with sweets and stationery. The 'School Bag' or 'Sugar Bag' is apparently to lessen the child's anxiety on the first day of school.

A tradition practised only in German-speaking countries, it apparently dates back to the 19th century.

To Love and to Cherish...Till Death Do Us Part

Previously, all marriages must be conducted in the *Standesamt* (registry office). A church wedding may follow after this for the religious, but the civil marriage must come first. Since January 2009, however, couples may marry in church without having to first undergo a civil marriage, although the marital rights prescribed by German law will not automatically apply to such a marriage.

For civil marriages, the couple would have weeks before that gone to the *Standesamt* to announce their intention to marry, and find out from the officials the documents they need to produce. A date for the ceremony will then be given and the requisite 'posting of the banns' done, in case anyone wishes to object.

The civil marriage is usually attended only by the two witnesses, family members and the closest of friends. All the attendees will sit or stand (if there are insufficient seats) behind the couple. The couple and the two witnesses will be seated opposite the officiating civil servant at a table at the front of the room. The civil servant willl go through the official business and as is befitting of a joyous occasion, they often read a poem or quote something interesting, to soften the rather unromantic atmosphere of the *Standesamt*. The whole ceremony usually takes about 45 minutes.

One important question that the civil servant will ask is the family name which the new family unit will adopt. In Germany, married couples can opt to use either the husband's or wife's surname, have a hyphenated family name joining both the husband's and the wife's, or even each retaining his and her own surnames.

In Germany, the wedding ring is worn on the right hand.

After the ceremony, usually everyone adjourns to a nearby restaurant for lunch. If there are too many friends attending, the couple may choose to have a small drinks and finger food party held on the premises of the *Standesamt*, and only the family and the best of friends go to the lunch/ dinner thereafter.

If the couple is religious, they will hold a church wedding. The husband or wife must be an officially registered member of the church (and paying church taxes), otherwise no church will marry them. After the ceremony, a lunch or dinner at a restaurant follows.

On the eve of or a few evenings before the wedding, family, relatives and friends of the couple gather under a marquee or in a restaurant and at first glance, it looks like a summit of rag-and-bone men. They all come with chipped porcelain plates, cups and vases which have obviously seen better days. Surely these are not wedding presents? Then, horror of horrors, they actually smash the porcelain they've brought on the ground, and seem to derive a sadistic pleasure in seeing the crockery break into smithereens. And they're actually laughing! Then, the soon-to-be married couple actually comes forward with a broom and dustpan and sweep up the smashed bits, and uncomplainingly, to boot. Have they all had a tad too much to drink?

Welcome to the *Polterabend*, an old German tradition to ward off evil spirits, which is still practised in Germany.

Another German tradition on the wedding day is the ceaseless horning of cars by the wedding convoy as they travel along the road. This makes quite a racket, so don't think it's a bunch of nasty Germans horning to tell you to get out of the way. You can recognise a wedding party as the cars often have white ribbons tied to their antennae.

Same-Sex Partnerships

Since August 2001, same-sex partnerships have been legally recognised in Germany by the Life Partnership Act, granting the registered partnerships some of the rights accorded in heterosexual marriages. The first couple to join in union under the new law were, of course, Berliners, Gudrun Pannier and Angelika Baldow, further confirming the city's bohemian and edgy reputation.

Ashes to Ashes, Dust to Dust

When someone passes away, the family will send out cards, with a black border round the envelopes, to family and friends informing them of the departure. Notices are also inserted in the newspapers.

Attendance at the funeral service is only for family and a close circle of friends, unless the person was a public figure. After the service in the church, the mourners will accompany the coffin to the burial ground. After prayers have been said, the mourners will file pass the coffin and drop handfuls of earth (stalks of flowers, in the case of the family members) onto the coffin.

After that, the family of the deceased will invite the mourners to lunch, or coffee and cakes, at home or in a restaurant.

Jews bury their departed relatives as soon as possible after death. The close relatives will symbolically tear at an item of clothing (necktie or ribbon) as a sign of their grief. The *Kaddish* (an Aramaic prayer) is traditionally said by the eldest son at the grave. Mourners place pebbles, not flowers, on the gravestone. All male mourners must wear a head covering (most non-Jews put on a hat or cap).

Muslims also bury the body of the deceased as soon as possible, usually within 24 hours. Before the burial, prayers are held (usually at home). Only male relatives and friends accompany the deceased to the burial ground.

Cremation is discouraged in Christianity but not unusual in secular cities like Berlin, while in traditional Judaism it's not practised. Muslims also do not cremate their dead. On the other hand, Hindus and Buddhists practise cremation.

The above is a skeleton outline of funeral practices of some major religions. If you intend to attend a funeral service where the customs are not familiar to you, it makes sense to check with someone who does before going, of course.

Richtfest

A special celebration associated with the construction of a new building (including a private home), the *Richtfest* is held when the shell is completed and before they crown it with the roof. A *Richtkranz*, a green wreath festooned with ribbons, is hoisted above the building and a party is thrown by the owner of the building for the workers on the construction site. Friends and neighbours are also invited. The owner provides plenty of drinks and finger food for the *Richtfest*, often held in the afternoon, as it would be unwise to expect the construction workers to continue working after all that booze. A short speech is traditionally given by the carpenter, or the site foreman, and the owner symbolically puts in the last nail.

If you're invited to a *Richtfest*, appropriate gifts would be a bottle of (always welcome) liquor or something inexpensive for the new home, such as a salt shaker (for luck).

BERLIN VIS A VIS THE EU

The EU has its roots in the European Coal and Steel Community founded in 1951. France and Germany were the key players of this community, whose aim was to have joint control of the coal and steel industries of the member states (the other members were Italy, Belgium, Netherlands and Luxembourg). As the community enlarged and evolved, France and Germany remained the two steering powers of the European community, although in recent times, the grip has slipped somewhat with 27 members in the current EU family. That said, the enlargement of the EU has actually put Germany, especially Berlin on its eastern border, in a rather central location of the enlarged EU, more or less midway between West and East Europe, boosting the exports of both Berlin and Germany.

HOW BERLINERS VIEW FOREIGNERS

With so many foreigners in their midst, one expects ethnic German Berliners to be rather open-minded about foreigners. To a certain extent, they are, if you're talking about 'white' foreigners. But 'non-white' foreigners may find life in Berlin (especially in East Berlin) more trying.

Germans, like most Europeans, are not too receptive about foreigners who don't look like them. The reasons for this attitude are, to me, a mixture of their laws, the irresponsible behaviour of a number of politicians and a very 'white-focused' media. As mentioned earlier on, German citizenship law is based on *jus sanguinis* (law of the blood). Since it has been drummed into the heads of Germans that people with German blood deserve priority when applying for citizenship, it must leave them with the impression that those without German blood don't deserve to live in Germany. From September 2008, German citizenship became even more elusive; new rules required prospective German citizens to sit for a test with 33 questions on German history, politics and society. To pass, they must answer at least 17 correctly.

Additionally, a number of mainstream politicians have irresponsibly sought to use the 'anti-immigrant' card to try to boost their popularity during elections. One of the most virulent is Hesse prime minister, Roland Koch (a Christian Democrat), who in late 2007 said that Germany had 'too many criminal young foreigners'. This was not his first attempt at anti-foreigner rhetoric; in 1999, he won the state election after he launched a petition against plans to introduce dual citizenship for foreigners living in Germany. That such rhetoric impresses the electorate also sends a chill down foreigners' spines. Another Christian Democrat, Jürgen Rüttgers, the premier of North-Rhine Westphalia, objected strongly in 2000 to a proposal to issue 'green cards' to Indian software engineers. He campaigned for giving precedence to German talent (which at that time Germany was actually facing a shortage) over bringing in foreign talent with a slogan *Kinder statt Inder* (Children instead of Indians). That he is still premier of the populous state tells you what impresses the electorate.

You will also notice something very quickly after zapping through the German TV channels. The TV hosts and newscasters are primarily 'white' Germans. There are a few 'non-white' TV newscasters and hosts, but they are still rare.

Few coloured actors and entertainers are resoundingly successful in Germany. While true that in TV soap operas like *Marienhof* and *Lindenstrasse* there are 'non-white' actors and actresses, they have yet to become very popular. And when there is one, the magazines never fail to inform you about his or her foreign genes with phrases like 'German with Turkish roots'. One women's magazine once even wrote of the success of an actor, Erol Sander, thus: 'Not bad, for a German with Turkish roots'. Even in the running commentary in a nail-biting *Bundesliga* (German football league) match, the commentator will helpfully tell you that a player is from Serbia, Bulgaria, Egypt, Japan etc.

'White' foreigners are also viewed with some degree of suspicion, once their immigrant background surfaces. Russians and East Europeans all have to contend with stereotyping, at the very least. The German football national team has a number of players with immigrant background. Two of the strikers, Miroslav Klose and Lukas Podolski, were born in Poland but immigrated with their families to Germany at eight and two respectively. During the FIFA World Cup 2006, when the German team had to play against Poland, questions popped up as to whether they would find it hard to score against their former home country. In case you're wondering, Germany did score against Poland. By the Euro 2008, hardly any doubts were voiced, and Podolski actually scored two winning goals against Poland.

Foreigners' sense of being discriminated against in Germany is no 'fairy tale' dreamt up by over-sensitive types. In autumn 2007, the Vienna-based European Union Agency for Fundamental Rights published a report which indicated that violent racism was on the rise in Germany, although it did acknowledge that it could be a result of actual increase as well as better data collection. But the report also criticised Germany's slow implementation of the EU's Racial Equality Directive, which was introduced in 2000 but implemented in Germany only in 2006. Other areas where Germany got its knuckles rapped were in jobs, education and housing, where incidences of discrimination were noted.

However, a number of initiatives undertaken by state authorities were lauded by the report to be promising, such as the campaign introduced in Berlin to encourage young migrants to apply for vocational training in the administration, police and fire services.

The average Teutonic Berliner's reaction to foreigners is not much different from their fellow Germans from other cities. In the city centre and tourist areas, Berliners don't bat an eyelid when they see someone who is obviously foreign, naturally, but in the remoter parts of Berlin, especially in the east, dark-skinned foreigners and Asians will often find themselves subjected to stares, if not worse. Walk into a local pub or restaurant and all the people in there will stop to look with fallen jaws at the foreigner. Often, foreigners get dissed. Ticket inspectors will scratch at bus tickets of foreign-looking passengers with their finger nails to see if it's a fake, while barely giving the tickets of 'whites' a glance. Inspectors checking stall holders in the open market to ensure that they have a permit for doing so will address the foreigner stall holders in curt tones and in the *Du* form, which is patronising and belittling. An American-Chinese tourist tried asking someone the way to Hyatt Hotel in the city centre, and the person simply walked away without a word.

Unfortunately, most ethnic Germans can't or won't see the discrimination being meted out. When a foreigner comments on a particular discriminatory act or even when a violent act has been committed by neo-Nazis, many Germans are quick to say 'yes, but maybe the foreigner was drunk and aggressive...' or 'we don't know the background....maybe they had an argument earlier.' It's not only ordinary Germans who react defensively; the Interior Minister, Wolfgang Schäuble, is prone to make such hurried excuses, too. Schäuble wasn't shy, either, to express interest in accepting Iraqi refugees into Germany, but only Christian ones, please.

On Racism: The Views of Two *Der Spiegel* Online Readers:

'.... I encountered a pleasant family whose wonderfully outgoing child asked me if I were American (I look very American in my attire) but before I could reply, the mother interceded with authoritative zeal, "No, he is African"—thus undermining her son's astute visual literacy and constructing for him an unnuanced view of otherness he will internalise.

I discovered, while procuring my residency papers, a higher benchmark was set for my documents than those of my white American friends who were kind enough to compare their experience with mine.

Prejudice operates here on several fronts—often subtle and pervasive, at other times pointed and severe.......'

—A Haitian- American in Berlin (name withheld)

* *

'I am German but have some Turkish friends (university graduates, mostly) who are discriminated against essentially every day by Germans, especially in shops and by the police.

If you don't have 'foreign' friends, you just don't know how bad the discrimination is. It's like they live in a parallel reality, the way they are treated by most people.

The big majority of Germans have no idea about this fact and most would probably say that there is not much open discrimination....'

—Robert Frahm

Sometimes, the racism is violent. There has also been many attacks by neo-Nazis on foreigners in East Berlin. On 31 December 2007, 15 right-wing youths attacked an Afghan family of five in Berlin-Lichtenberg as they came out to set off fireworks to ring in the New Year. In February 2008, a a 36-year-old Vietnamese lady was beaten up by neo-Nazis as she waited at a bus stop with her two-year-old daughter in the morning. On the same day, neo-Nazi youths robbed a Vietnamese flower shop and also caused slight injuries to the female Vietnamese shop owner. In March 2008, a 20-year-old woman pushed a 19-year-old Angolan off the rail platform as a train was pulling into the station. The victim only escaped being run over with the help of two passers-by who pulled him to safety.

If this sub-section sounds terribly daunting for 'non-whites' coming to Berlin, well, this is the city's rougher side. Some other European countries have similar problems, or even worse ones, but that cannot be an excuse for the handful of nasty Berliners. But don't run away with the idea that all Berliners are xenophobic; as in every country, there are open-minded Berliners (even in East Berlin) and some are extremely friendly.

GAY BERLIN

Berlin is the homosexual's paradise. I mean, here is a city where the mayor, Klaus Wowereit, is out since 2001 and attends Christopher Street Day, once in a T-shirt emblazoned with '*Ich bin Schwul*' (I am gay), with his partner. So no gay need hide in the closet here. Berlin has always had a devil-may-care atitude. Conservative Germans call it a 'freak capital', while others treat it like a teenager with adolescent excesses. So naturally Berlin has a thriving gay scene, including a gay museum. Schöneberg and Kreuzberg are where you can find most of the gay hang-outs.

In spring 2008, a memorial for homosexuals murdered by the Nazis was unveiled in Tiergarten park.

Same sex partnerships (they avoid the use of 'marriage' as a compromise to those who opposed the proposal) could be legally registered since 2001. Over the years, the rights granted to the registered partnerships have become more similar to heterosexual marriages, though not without obstacles along the way. Now, registered partners can adopt the children of his/her partner, though full adoption rights granted to heterosexual couples are not yet open to them. As at August 2008, there were 3,528 same-sex partnerships registered in Berlin, of which 2,513 were gay partnerships and 1,015 lesbian partnerships.

A word of caution: in spite of the tolerant attitude towards homosexuality by most Berliners, there is a high degree of homophobia among some Berliners: the neo-Nazis and many Turks and Russians. It's therefore not unusual for homosexuals to be verbally assaulted, spit on or even assaulted.

PROSTITUTION

Prostitution is legal in Germany, but where this trade can operate is restricted. In Berlin, Kurfürstenstraße and Potsdamer Straße (between Tiergarten and Schöneberg) are the hot-spots. With many poor eastern European countries joining the EU, German sex workers are complaining that the eastern Europeans are spoiling the market with their lower asking prices (€15 instead of €50) while other Berliners complain of prostitution and bordellos landing up in their residential neighbourhood.

THE ATTITUDE AND DEMEANOUR TO ADOPT

You've now heard about how tough, unfriendly, even anti-foreigner and anti-gay some Berliners can be. But Berlin should not be viewed as a city full of nasty and xenophobic people. On the contrary. I've laid out the cold facts only so that you won't be caught off guard. There are ways to deal with the less pleasant aspects of the city, and once you know it, you can go out and enjoy the many exciting features of the city.

If you're dark-skinned or East Asian, avoid Lichtenberg and Marzahn if you can, especially in the night, or at least exercise caution when going there.

When in Berlin, the best demeanour to adopt is one of confidence. Speak assertively. You don't have to run around like Rambo, but don't slouch or shuffle, looking at the ground as if searching for a lost contact lens. Berliners have no respect for those who appear weak or uncertain. Walk tall and straight, speak clearly, avoid banter and chatter, and don't smile unnecessarily. When asking for directions, or for help from a shop assistant, don't adopt a 'I'm sorry to bother you' tone or worse, smile and nod apologetically Japanese-style. Just ask in a straightforward manner and then say 'Thank you' and walk off.

SETTLING IN

CHAPTER 5

'He is the happiest, be he king or peasant,
who finds peace in his home.'
—Johann Wolfgang von Goethe, German playwright,
poet and novelist (1749–1832)

IT'S RELATIVELY EASY TO SETTLE into Berlin, as there is plenty of reasonably-priced property available and the transport network is excellent (provided the unions have not called for strikes). You might feel like a performing circus animal jumping through countless hoops when dealing with the bureaucrats, but that's about the hardest part. Otherwise, it's not too difficult to feel at home in Berlin.

WHAT TO BRING
Furniture and Household Appliances
Some expatriates like bringing their own furniture and decorations in order to re-create a feeling of home in a new country. If you don't feel a need for that, you won't have a problem buying the household items that you need in Berlin. Buying new is practical as you don't have to fit your existing furniture into a new home. Your household appliances from home may also not be suitable for use in Berlin as Germany's TV system (PAL), voltage and electrical sockets may be different from your home country's (it certainly is if you're from the US or UK). Of course you can use adaptors and transformers, but buying the equipment in Berlin means the advantage of easily finding someone who can repair the machine if it conks, and making it easier to buy disposable parts, like vacuum bags. You would, however, want to check that the operating manual has instructions in English.

Electronic Essentials

German electronic equipment

- Run on 220 V
- Use two-pin plugs
- Use PAL system

Important Documents

Some of the documents which you should bring with you are:

- Passport (making sure it's not on the verge of expiry)
- Birth certificate, including your childrens' if they're going to live in Berlin too
- Marriage certificate, if you're coming with your spouse to live in Berlin
- Driving licence, if you intend to drive
- Certificates of your professional qualifications, if applying for work
- Bank statements or a letter from your bank to prove your credit-worthiness
- European Health Insurance Card (for EU citizens)
- Insurance policies
- Your childrens' educational certificates if they're going to school in Berlin

The documents required by the German bureaucrats will need to be translated into German and notarised, and this can be done in Berlin. If you're uneasy about bringing your original certificates with you, you can have them translated, notarised and legalised back home before coming. The documents required will vary according to your nationality and what you may be applying for in Berlin.

Medical and Optical Needs

If you're on special medication, it's a good idea to bring enough stock of your medicine to last for a few months, with a certification from your doctor, in case you're checked at customs. If you're short-sighted, a spare pair of glasses will be handy as well. Berlin isn't short of medical professionals; it's just that it may take time to find a medical practitioner you're comfortable with and to get an appointment.

VISAS
Visa-free Entries
Citizens from the EU, US, Australia, Canada, Israel and New Zealand do not need visas to enter Germany, if they do not stay longer than 90 days within a six-month period. Apart from the citizens of EU countries, working in Germany is not allowed with these visa-free entries.

Citizens of a number of other countries also do not need visas. You can check with the German mission in your country or go to the website of the German Federal Foreign Office (*Auswärtiges Amt*), where you can find excellent information in English. For the full list of countries and their visa requirements, go to:

http://www.auswaertiges-amt.de/diplo/en/WillkommeninD/
EinreiseUndAufenthalt/StaatenlisteVisumpflicht.html

The German Federal Foreign Office
(Das Auswaertiges Amt)
Website: www.auswaertiges-amt.de

The site has detailed information on visas, working/ studying/ residing in Germany and forms on PDF format which you can download. Click on 'English', then 'Information Service' (top right corner), then 'FAQ'.

Types of Visas
There are basically three types of visas: national, hybrid and Schengen. The national visa (€30) is for persons staying within Germany only, the hybrid visa (€60) is for persons staying in Germany but who have to travel to another Schengen country, and the Schengen visa (also €60) is for travel to all 24 Schengen countries.

The Schengen Convention

The European countries which are signatories to this convention basically agree to abolish checks at their common borders. What this means for travellers is that once you are in a Schengen signatory country, you will not be checked at the border when crossing into another Schengen signatory country, making travel through most parts of Europe a breeze. Currently, the signatories are:

Austria, Belgium, Czech Republic, Denmark, Estonia, Finland, France, Germany, Greece, Hungary, Iceland, Italy, Latvia, Lithuania, Luxembourg, Malta, Netherlands, Norway, Poland, Portugal, Slovakia, Slovenia, Spain and Sweden

The earlier Schengen Agreement was signed by France, Germany, Belgium, Luxembourg and the Netherlands in 1985 in the town of Schengen (Luxembourg), hence its name. The Schengen Convention was signed in June 1990, which by then had more countries signing on.

The ease with which people in one Schengen signatory country can travel to other signatory states means that checks are tight at the border when you first enter a signatory state. If you'll be travelling to a number of other countries from Germany, do make it clear to the staff at the German mission when applying for a visa.

Work and Study Visas

Citizens of EU countries (except of those who joined the EU in 2004 and 2007) can live and work in Germany without too much red tape. All they need to do is register their address at the *Bürgeramt* (citizens' office) after arriving. For citizens whose country joined the EU in 2004 or 2007, transitional regulations apply.

For all the rest, the general rule is that you have to apply for a work or study visa before coming to Germany.

Since there are different regulations for different countries and purposes, the best option is to check with the German mission in your country. Start your enquiries early, as

applications often have to be sent to Germany for approval from the foreigners' authorities and that may take time.

REGISTRATIONS AND RESIDENCE PERMITS

If you intend to stay in Berlin longer than 90 days, other registrations are necessary.

Citizens of EU and EEA Countries

Citizens of EU countries, and the three European Economic Area countries (Norway, Iceland and Liechtenstein), need only to register their address at the *Bürgeramt* of their district. The list of all 12 in Berlin can be found at http://www.berlin.de/buergeramt.

Bring your passport/identification card along. You will be issued with a confirmation called a *Anmeldungsbestätigung*. Should you move, you have to re-register your new address.

It's highly recommended that while there, you apply for a *Freizügigkeitsbescheinigung* (Certificate of Freedom of Movement). This will come in handy to prove that you're an EU or EEA citizen, which cuts down a lot of bureaucratic hurdles when applying for other services.

Spouses and family members who are not themselves citizens of EU or EEA countries will need to apply for a *Aufenthaltserlaubnis* (residence permit) from the *Ausländerbehörde* (Foreigners' Authority).

Citizens of Non-EU/EEA Countries

Nationals of non-EU countries also need to first register at the *Bürgeramt*. Once you get your *Anmeldungsbestätiging*, you have to go to the *Ausländerbehörde* (Foreigners'Authority) to get the *Aufenthaltserlaubnis* (residence permit). You can in theory call or email for an appointment. There are different email addresses for different nationalities, and the list is to be found at: http://www.berlin.de/labo/auslaender/dienststelle/auslterminvereinb.html

The website of the *Ausländerbehörde* is, unfortunately and illogically, only in German.

It's best to go down personally to the Foreigners' Authority, preferably with someone who can speak German.

Ausländerbehörde (Foreigners' Authority)

Landesamt für Bürger und Ordnungsangelegenheiten

—Ausländerbehörde—

Address: Friedrich-Krause-Ufer 24

13353 Berlin

Tel: (030) 90269 0

Fax: (030) 90269 4099

Opening hours: Mon and Tues: 7:00 am to 2:00 pm; Thurs: 10:00 am to 6:00 pm; Wed and Fri: Closed

Public Transport:

Underground/Subway: U9 (Amrumer Str)

Train: S4 (Westhafen)

Bus: No. 147, M27

Documents to Bring Along

The Foreigners' Authority will tell you exactly what documents you should bring along. The usual documents will be:

- Passport
- Two passport photos

- Documents to prove why you need to stay in Berlin (e.g. marriage certificate if you've married a German, letter from employer if for work, letter from university if for studies)

It's a good idea to bring more than two photos and a few copies of every conceivable document you can think of.

If you're hoping to be employed, you need a residence permit which specifically states that work is permitted. The *Ausländerbehörde* will need the approval of the Federal Labour Agency for you to be employed. This approval is not easy to get; it is granted only if the job cannot be filled by a German, an EU citizen or a foreigner who has been living for ages in Germany.

The officers at the *Ausländerbehörde* are generally not nasty, but they're civil servants, which in Germany means they have life tenure. Tenured staff are the last to think about providing friendly service. Their job isn't exactly pleasant, either; there are enough cases of sham marriages just to get German residency or citizenship, so they tend to be very stern. If you can already speak some German, use it. My experience is that once you make an effort to engage them in German, they can be very helpful and friendly.

If the procedures sound terribly daunting (especially with the immensely long, unpronounceable German words), take comfort in the fact that the bureaucracy is there for a proper purpose, and not to squeeze bribes out from you, as in some developing countries. The officers don't deliberately set out to make life difficult for you; it's just red-tape they have to follow. If you don't sulk and sigh, they might sometimes exercise some discretion where they can, so it pays to be polite.

ACCOMMODATION
Short-term Accommodation
Chances are, when you first arrive, you will be staying in a hotel while you do your house hunting. As to be expected of a capital city, you will be spoilt for choice. Five-star international chains like Grand Hyatt, Hilton, Intercontinental, Regent,

Aldon Hotel, one of the most well known and luxurious hotel located right in the heart of Berlin.

Ritz-Carlton, Marriott and Westin Grand are present for those with deeper pockets. Single rooms start from at least €150 for most of them. There is also the famous Adlon, with prices starting at €240. There are also plenty of four and three-star hotels and hostels. Apartment hotels are also available.

Looking for a Home

The different districts of Berlin tend to have very distinctive characters, and even within each district, one area can be very different from another. It's not unusual for some districts to have both posh and working-class areas. All the districts of Berlin are pretty self-contained. Unless you're looking for something specific, there isn't really any urgent need to travel to Mitte for your basic needs, as there are supermarkets and discounters, pharmacies, doctors and dentists within each district. Many have their 'own' green lungs, either in the form of a huge park, forests or lakes or a combination of these.

Below is a general overview to help you decide where you might want to set up home.

Mitte

Mitte (as in the city centre around the Friedrichstraße area) is within the district also called Mitte (which includes the sub-districts of Gesundbrunnen, Hansaviertel, Moabit, Tiergarten and Wedding). The city centre is, as to be expected, where the business district is. If your workplace is in the city centre, living in the Mitte makes sense. Many of the interesting sights (Museumsinsel, Brandenburger Tor, Reichstag, Potsdamer Platz, Gendarmenmarkt, Neue Synagoge etc) are also conveniently located in this district. The problem with city-centre living is that it's a lot more congested and polluted, although since January 2008, it's been turned into an Environmental Zone, where only low emission vehicles are allowed in.

Note that in some areas of Wedding, Moabit and south Tiergarten, the neighbourhood is rougher.

Charlottenburg-Wilmersdorf

This district has some of the posher addresses in Berlin, including the sub-district Grunewald, which is the most expensive area of the city. Berlin's shopping district of Kurfürstendamm (which was the city centre of West Berlin), the Zoo and the Schloss Charlottenburg are in the district of Charlottenburg. It does have a more working-class neighbourhood as well in Siemensstadt.

This district also has the Grunewald woods and lakes (Halensee, Grunewaldsee and Teufelsee).

Spandau

Spandau in the extreme west is actually older than Berlin itself. It saw significant economic activity long before Berlin/Cölln did and had castles as long ago as 700 AD. Spandauers and Berliners still see each other as people from different cities.

If you like the feel of old baroque towns, Spandau has houses from the 18th century in the old city centre. Some parts of Nikolaikirche date even further back to the 15th century and the Juliusturm inside the Zitadelle is thought to be from the 12th century. Here, you'll be forgiven for expecting to turn the corner and bump into a medieval knight.

A leafy suburb in Charlottenburg, home to some of the posher addresses in Berlin.

The district has half of the lake, Tegeler See, and the Havel and Spree rivers flow through Spandau as well.

Tempelhof-Schöneberg

Schöneberg is considered one of the more edgy districts: the area around Nollendorfplatz is famously gay and lesbian territory and Kurfürstenstraße is where the ladies of the night hang out. The Bayerische Viertel is a much sought-after area, filled with creative and yuppie types.

Tauentzienstrasse (where KaDeWe is located) is within this district.

Tempelhof is the more family-oriented half of the district.

Steglitz-Zehlendorf

Zehlendorf is another very green address, being blessed with the southern part of the Grunewald woods and lakes like Wannsee, Nikolassee and Schlactensee. Dahlem is the upmarket area while Steglitz has reasonably-priced property.

Reinickendorf

This is where the Tegel airport is situated. The district has a mix of well-heeled and working-class residents. It's also

Locals and tourists enjoy the afternoon at Strandbar Mitte.

a very green area. Reinickendorf was occupied by the French when Berlin was divided up among the Allies after World War II.

Pankow

Prenzlauer Berg (affectionately called Prenzl'berg by locals) is in the district of Pankow.

What used to be the hangout for the alternative crowd of East Berlin, Prenzlauer Berg has blossomed into a cool neighbourhood for the young crowd. It has become rather upmarket and is full of cafes and bars.

Prenzlauer Berg is also the district with the highest birth rate. Nowhere else in Berlin do you see so many toddlers and babies in prams taking their young mothers for walks.

Weißensee also belongs to this district, and this is the least populated area of Berlin.

There are plenty of parks in the sub-district of Pankow, north of Prenzlauer Berg.

Friedrichshain–Kreuzberg

Friedrichshain was formerly in East Berlin and Kreuzberg in West Berlin.

When the Wall fell, Kreuzberg morphed from being an outpost of West Berlin into a district smack in the city centre of unified Berlin. Kreuzberg is home to a mainly Turkish and an alternative lifestyle community. If you choose to live here, be prepared for the possibility that your earthly possessions may get damaged every year on 1 May. Anarchists burn cars and throw rocks to commemorate May Day 1987, when the district erupted into violence as a result of anger at the difficult social and economic situation. May Day 2008 was touted as the quietest in the past decade, but there were still violent rioting and the setting on fire of cars and garbage containers.

But if you like things more Bohemian and an exciting nightlife, Kreuzberg is the place to be, although in recent times, Prenzlauer Berg and Friedrichshain have been stealing the crowds.

Friedrichshain is the Woodstock of Berlin. It boasts a throbbing nightlife, and is preferred by the hard-core beatniks and bohemians over the more yuppie Prenzl'berg.

This may yet change, as there are plans (amidst protests by some groups) to turn the area, especially the Mediaspree, into a chic upmarket creative zone. Universal and MTV have already set up shop there, and other investors have been looking the place over, much to the chagrin of leftish architects and other artists who prefer the place to remain boho.

Neukölln

North Neukölln is mainly populated with immigrants, especially Turks. The many social and economic problems of the Neuköllners in the north have given the district a rather sorry reputation. South Neukölln is less congested and quieter. The Britzer Garten here is a pretty manicured green space with a water playground, where kids can spend their energy.

Marzahn-Hellersdorf

This district is chock-a-block with *Plattenbau* (the bland communist-era apartment blocks). Unemployment here is high. Smack in the middle of the working-class environment is the very pleasant Erholungspark, which has exotic landscaped Chinese, Japanese and Balinese gardens within. Hellersdorf has a more mixed selection of *Plattenbau* and individual houses.

Lichtenberg

This district, like Marzahn, is economically weak, and both have a reputation for being the home of right-wing radicals as a minus and very affordable housing as a plus point. The very worth visiting Tierpark Friedrichsfelde is in this district.

Treptow-Köpenick

Tucked away in the south-eastern corner, Köpenick, like Spandau, is of older vintage. Already a busy settlement when

Berlin/Cölln were still in their diapers, Köpenick's old city centre has also managed to retain its 18th century charm. The famous landmarks here are the Rathaus and the Schloss Köpenick. Treptow is more populated than Köpenick.

The areas on the shores of the Dahme and Langer See (e.g. Grünau, Karolinenhof, Schmöckwitz), and Müggelsee (Friedrichshagen, Rahnsdorf), look like they're in the boondocks on the map, but they are wonderfully close to nature and yet serviced by public transport.

The Grosser Müggelsee, Berlin's largest lake, is in this district, as is Treptower Park, the second largest public park (after Tiergarten).

Also located within the district is Adlershof, where the 'City of Science, Technology and Media' was established in 2002, which employs 15,000 people. The nearby Schönefeld airport is slated to become the Berlin-Brandenburg International Airport. With these developments, Köpenick is likely to become more populated and popular.

Buying or Renting a Home

Property prices in Berlin are still considered very reasonable, when compared to London, Paris and Oslo, or even Hamburg

The Rathaus, one of the main attractions in Köpenick.

There are many restaurants and houses in Berlin which offer lovely views of lakes, such as these along the Müggelspree in Köpenick.

and Munich. To give you a rough idea of the prices in early 2008, a renovated 1,026 sq m (11,040 sq ft) flat/apartment in Mitte was selling for €1,090,000. A brand new loft apartment in Friedrichshain of 130 sq m (1,398 sq ft) was being offered for €260,000. In the outskirts of Berlin, around Reinickendorf, a 45 sq m (484 sq ft) apartment was going for €20,000.

Rentals are also low. A 2007-refurbished apartment of 88 sq m in Mitte was being rented out for €750 per month.

When the Wall fell, there was a building, refurbishing and investing frenzy in Berlin, not least because of government subsidies and tax incentives, which are gradually being phased out. Speculators expected property prices to rise with the move of the government from Bonn to Berlin, but the real increase didn't meet with expectations.

Most of the property on offer are apartments. Many of the older apartments are without lifts/elevators. Terraced houses and villas are rare, and tend to be in the outskirts of the city, or even in Brandenburg. Not too many Berliners own their homes (about 13.8 per cent).

The amount of the rent is quoted with the suffix *kalt* (cold) or *warm* (warm). '€550 *kalt*' means that the €550 does not include the costs of utilities and rubbish disposal etc, while '€800 *warm*' means these are included.

Should you decide to buy property, just note that the purchase price quoted does not include notarial and agent's fees and taxes, which can add another 12 per cent of the purchase price on the costs. The size of most apartments are indicated by floor area, and if they should mention the number of rooms, they usually don't include the kitchen and bathroom.

If you're buying to rent out as an investment, familiarise yourself with the tenancy laws. German laws are very protective of tenants and it isn't so easy to turf out a tenant, especially if (s)he has a child, becomes handicapped or meets with some other misfortune.

Finding a Home
The most advertisements for property sale or rental can be found in the Saturday edition of local newspapers, *Berliner Morgenpost*, *Berliner Zeitung*, *BZ* and *Tagesspiegel*. In this age of modern technology, property are also advertised on the internet. Alternatively, you can go through a real estate agent.

Looking for Property on the Net (in German)
- http://www.berlinonline.de/berliner-zeitung/anzeigenmarkt/ (then click on 'Immobilienmarkt')
- http://immonet.morgenpost.de
- http://immonet.bz-berlin.de
- http://www.tagesspiegel.de/magazin/immobilien

After Moving In
Unfurnished Homes
In Berlin (and throughout Germany), 'unfurnished' means not only that there are no furniture and curtains, but there usually isn't even a single lighting in the apartment/house. You will find only the wiring dangling out of the wall or ceiling. Fixing up your lights is a priority, ideally before you move in. There are usually only the toilet bowls, wash basins

and bathtub in place. There usually won't be any built-in cupboards, either.

When you're decorating your new rented home, bear in mind that when you move out, the place must revert back to the state it was in when you took it over. You have to fill in all the holes where you have drilled or nailed something, and remove even the kitchen unit, if you can't get the landlord or new tenant to take it over. Go easy, therefore, on your creativity, if you don't want to have to spend a fortune reinstating the place. You also have to give the walls a fresh coat of paint.

Incidentally, German kitchen sinks don't come with a garburator/garbage grinder. You have to buy one of those tiny sieves to put over the hole in the kitchen sink to prevent the food waste from going down (and clogging) the sink. If it does clog, you can buy 'drain opener' granules or liquid from the supermarkets which unblock sinks quite effectively.

Locating Your Apartment

The standard way of setting out an address is as follows:

Friedrich-Krause-Ufer 24
13353 Berlin

The building number always comes after the street name, and the zip code comes before 'Berlin'.

In Berlin, the numbering of buildings may increase equally on both sides of a road (one side with odd numbers, the other with even), or it may increase only on one side of the road, make a 'U-turn' at the end of the road and continue back on the other side. To know which sytem the road follows, take a look at the road sign at the corner of the road. Below the name of the road, you will find the numbers of the buildings on that road.

Americans should note that the floor numbering is different in Germany. The American first floor/story is called the ground floor (*Erdgeschoss* or EG for short), and the second floor/story is the first floor (1. *Obergeschoss* or 1.OG). Many of the Berlin apartments hailing from the 1900s are built

A road sign showing the building numbers on that stretch of road on Friedrichstraße.

around a courtyard. You will therefore see or hear references to *Vorderhaus* or VH (the block in front), *Hinterhaus* or HH (the block at the back of the courtyard) and *Seitenflügel* or SF (the side wings).

The Letter Box and the Intercom

If you live in an apartment, note that German letter boxes are not labelled according to unit numbers. For the postman to know which box to slot your mail into, you must put your surname on the letter box. The letter boxes of all tenants are located at the bottom of the building, where the postman can easily access without having to ring anyone's doorbell, unless it's registered mail or a bulky parcel.

The same goes with the intercom panel. You must put your name on the slot allocated to your unit.

Do check with your landlord which letter box and intercom button is yours. Don't forget to inform your non-German family and friends that they have to indicate your surname clearly for correspondence to reach you, as this takes the place of unit numbers. If you've changed your surname after marriage, but are still getting mail addressed to your maiden surname, don't forget to have both surnames on the letter box.

If there's a parcel or a registered letter for you and you're not at home, the postman may leave them with a neighbour or at the nearest post office. Either way, you will find a slip of paper in your letter box telling you where your parcel is. If you're collecting them from the post office, you need to bring some form of identification with you. Parcels not collected within seven working days are returned to sender.

Information Board

At the main entrance to the building, you are likely to find a notice board. The management of the building will post here all information which affects tenants in the building. For example, you're likely to see information on when you have to observe 'quiet time' (when you can't practise on your saxophone or drill a hole to hang up your newly acquired painting). The other important information put up might include when the meter-readers are coming to record individual household's usage of heating and water (*Ablesedienst*), when the major spring-cleaning and polishing of common corridors will take place so that you have to remove the floor mats and potted plants outside your front door, or perhaps a stern lecture on *somebody* having used the rubbish (garbage) bins wrongly. For correct usage of rubbish bins, a special paragraph is dedicated to that below.

The German Window

It may strike you as strange that I should highlight the window. But the German window is often a 'three-way' type of contraption which is not found in many other countries. Many foreigners usually are not aware that apart from closing and opening the window, by twisting the handle (usually upwards), you can get it to tilt, letting in some air but without having to fully open the window.

'Winter Service'

If you live in a house, there is a special task you have to perform during winter. You, as occupier, must ensure that the public walkway just outside your house is free from snow, and properly strewn with *Streugut* (a special mixture of sand and grit which can be bought from DIY stores) if the pavement is icy. If you don't and a pedestrian falls down and gets injured, you can be sued for occupier's liability. The public roads are the responsibility of the BSR (*Berliner Stadtreinigungsbetriebe*—Berlin State cleaning service), but the walkway in front of your house is your responsibility. You can get a *Winterdienst* (winter service) company to do this for you for a fee.

Rubbish Disposal

In Germany, throwing rubbish is a whole science in itself and regulated by law. As apartment dwellers, you will find a number of different coloured bins in an obscure corner at the bottom of your block. You must separate your rubbish into plastics, paper, glass etc and throw them into the correct coloured bins. For organic rubbish, you can actually buy special bags (biodegradable, of course) for them.

Glassware must be taken to the glass bins, which won't be at the bottom of your block, because of the noise they make. These bins are often found in some quiet corner of a neighbourhood. To avoid disturbing the poor people living nearby, there are permitted throwing times which you must observe (see box). Batteries must be disposed off in special bins which can be found outside most supermarkets and drugstores. Any store selling batteries must take used batteries back.

Bulky household items like sofas, tables, cupboards and laundry drying racks, doors and umbrellas are classified as *Sperrmüll*, and these must be disposed off separately. The BSR can collect them from you for a fee. Electronic equipment refuse are classified as *Elektroschrott*, and another team of specialists take care of their disposal.

Christmas trees are not *Spermüll*, though. The BSR troops collect the forlorn-looking discarded trees at specific times after the Christmas season for free from the roadside. The dates for collection are published in the newspapers, usually in January.

The upper platform of the Berlin Hauptbahnhof. Travelling within Berlin and to the other parts of Germany is convenient and fuss-free due to the country's efficient transportation system.

The Staatskapelle Berlin is one of the oldest orchestras in the world with almost 450 years of tradition. This orchestra of the Staatsoper Unter den Linden is under the leadership of Daniel Barenboim, who was voted chief-conductor-for-life in 2000.

Students at the Humboldt-Universität zu Berlin (Humboldt University of Berlin) enjoy some afternoon sun and a chat with friends during their lunch break.

Berlin has a strong 'coffee and cakes' culture, and there are many good cafés all over the city, like this cosy and unpretentious one on Oranienstraße.

Berlin's Carnival of Cultures street party and parade celebrates the capital's multicultural spirit with music and dancing in the Kreuzberg district.

Bins and What They Mean

Household Rubbish

- Yellow bins: plastics, non-refundable beer cans, aluminium foil
- Blue bins: paper, cardboard, magazines
- Brown bins: marked with the word 'BIOGUT', here's where you dump organic stuff like vegetables and other food waste
- Grey bins: non-recyclable rubbish (those that don't belong to the other bins)

Glass

In some quiet street corner around your neighbourhood, you will find a trio of brown, white and green bins. These are for glass only, and your brown, clear and green glass must be thrown into the correct coloured bins.

Throwing times:
Mon to Fri: 8:00 am to 1:00 pm, and 3:00 pm to 6:00 pm
Sat: 8:00 am to 1:00 pm
Sun & Public Holidays: throwing forbidden

If you live in a house, you have to order the bins yourself. The BSR are the people to contact as well. Some of the bins have a slightly different colour, and all these information can be found on the BSR website (German only). They also provide bags for rubbish from your garden, which can be quite a lot in autumn, when all the deciduous trees shed their leaves.

Most of the mineral water (in polyethelene terephthalate or PET) bottles are refundable. When you buy the bottles of water, €0.25 is built into the price of each bottle. The idea is to encourage you to bring the bottles back to the recycling machine to get your money back. You bring the empty bottles back to the supermarket recycling machine (called *Leergut annahme*), pop the bottles into the hole in the machine one by one and then press a green button when finished. A receipt will be printed and you give this receipt to the cashier at the check-out point, who will then give you your

Glass recycling bins: these are usually found in the quiet corners of the neighbourhood and there are permitted times for disposing your glassware.

refund. At some other places, you return the bottles straight to the cashier.

Aldi, Lidl and Plus accept each others' 'house brands' of water, so you can, for example, bring the empty Lidl bottles to Aldi to get a refund. But not all supermarkets accept refundable bottles bought from elsewhere, so you should check before lugging all your bottles to the supermarket. By the way, don't crush your bottles to save space, as the machines reject misshapen bottles.

Special Rubbish Disposal

SPERRMÜLL (sofas, beds, cupboards etc)
Berlinstadtreinigungsbetriebe (BSR)
http://www.bsr.de

ELEKTROSCHROTT (computers, toasters, ovens etc)
BRAL Reststoff-Bearbeitungs GmbH
http://www.BRAL.de

Utilities

The main energy suppliers are E.On, RWE, Vattenfall and EnBW. The consumer is free to choose a supplier that offers the best rates.

While it's practical to just take over the supplier that has been providing energy to the apartment you have rented, it's worthwhile to compare the rates when you've settled down in Berlin. You can always change supplier, and German laws protect consumers from being left without energy supplies just because you've given notice you want to change to another supplier.

A very helpful site where you can check which supplier offers the best rates for electricity, gas, and car insurance is http://www.toptarif.de (German only).

Furnishings

Berlin has a wide selection of furnishing shops, including three Ikea megastores (in Spandau, Tempelhof and Waltersdorf). Höffner also has three stores in Berlin (Marzahn, Wedding and Waltersdorf) and like Ikea, they carry not only furniture but all other conceivable household needs. Möbel Kraft is another furniture store. The location of Ikea in Waltersdorf is a convenient place for one stop shopping: there's not only Ikea and Höffner but also toy store Toys'R'Us, an electronic goods store and a DIY store. There are hundreds of free parking lots too. Waltersdorf is theoretically in Brandenburg, but so close to the south eastern 'border' of Berlin, it's often considered part of the city.

Berlin's Water Quality

Tap water is safe to drink, although it's not a German habit to drink straight from the tap. They somehow prefer to lug the heavy crates of mineral water home, as if they were in a third-world country. One of the possible reasons is that in some regions, the water is unpleasantly hard. In Berlin, it's certainly the case. This not only leaves a peculiar taste in your beverage, but also a yellow sheen on your clothes and bathtubs. Limescale-busting (*Antikalk* or *Kalk-Stopp* in German) chemicals are sold in the supermarkets. You can buy

Antikalk liquid or pellets for cleaning bathtubs, sinks, kettles and coffee machines, or for popping into washing machines together with your laundry to prevent limescale build-up. If you're uneasy about using chemicals for your coffee machine, vinegar solution works just as well. You have to run clear water through the machine a couple of times thereafter, though, if you don't want your coffee to taste like lemon tea. You can also buy water filters (the British BRITA brand is available).

If your white clothes turn yellow in spite of all measures taken, bleaching them will often remove the yellow sheen.

SHOPPING

Since November 2006, shopping in Berlin is no longer the stressful one-eye-on-the-clock affair to get errands done before the shops close. The stores and shops may now set their own closing times, and are even allowed to open on ten Sundays each year from 1:00 pm to 8:00 pm. Many shops now close at 8:00 pm from Mondays to Saturdays and mega bookstore Dussman closes only at midnight! Stores and shops take the opportunity to open on Sundays in the four weeks leading up to Christmas. Shops at major railway stations (e.g. Hauptbahnhof, Ostbahnhof) are allowed to open on Sundays.

Supermarkets

There is no shortage of supermarkets, big and small.

At the top of the range are the two consumers' paradise— the food temples of the department stores KaDeWe and Galeries Lafayette. The food (and prices) are not for TV dinners. Both food halls are lovingly decked with gourmet food from different countries (with KaDeWe boasting more than 34,000 different items). They do also carry daily food items, but the prices are higher than in ordinary supermarkets. Kaufhof also has *Feinkost* (gourmet) departments. Although not as attractive as KaDeWe and Galeries Lafayette, Kaufhof has been pumping in money to upgrade itself and offering a wider selection of fine foods.

Middle-of-the-range supermarket chains such as Kaiser's, Edeka and Extra have outlets all over Berlin. These supermarkets carry a comprehensive range of needs, from food for human

KaDeWe celebrates Christmas. A top of the range supermarket is located at the popular shopping mall, featuring gourmet food from different countries.

and animals down to stationery and basic haberdashery.

The best prices for basic needs can be found at the discount stores. Aldi, Lidl, and Plus are the market leaders, competing hard for this segment of consumers. Most Germans have a misplaced distrust of these discounters; many are embarassed to admit to shopping at any one of them. Once, a customer 'caught' by a TV crew doing a special programme on discounters hurriedly explained that he normally did not go to Aldi's; he just happened to have popped in on this fateful morning on his way to work to pick up some coffee for the office. A newspaper interview of unemployed Germans on social welfare had many mournfully stating that they ate unhealthily, as they could only afford buying from Aldi and Lidl. It's a very strange perception because these discounters have as fresh products as any other supermarket, healthy low-fat or sugar-free products and even exotic goat's cheese imported from France and tender lamb steaks from New Zealand. The main differences compared to the middle-range supermarkets are that they don't have such a wide range of products, and the shopping experience is one of no-frills self-service. Since we know by now that the average German service is basically robotic at best, customers are not missing much.

When going to any supermarket, arm yourselves with a €1 coin and shopping bags or baskets. You need the coin to unlock a trolley. When buying fresh vegetables and fruits in loose form, you may need to weigh them and get them priced before going to the cashier. Look around you and if you see a weighing machine or two around, with pictures of fruits and vegetables and numbers pasted on a panel, they need to be weighed in advance. There will be free freezer bags on a roller around the products. Take however much you need of the, say, apples, and note the number on the tray of apples. This helps you to identify which button you need to press on the weighing machine. Put your tied bag of fruits on the machine, press the number (or the picture of apples) and a price tag will be printed. Stick this on your bag of apples. If you forget to weigh and price your purchases, the cashier will have to run to the machine to do it for you, leaving you standing there with a queue of people fuming at you for holding everyone up.

Most of the products which are already packed in styrofoam packages usually do not need weighing, as this is already stated on the package. The disadvantage of styrofoam and cling-film packs is that you can't check the underside of the products. They can already be mouldy due to condensation. This is especially a problem in winter when the products come in from the cold into the heated supermarkets.

Butter Lindner

Although not a supermarket, the Butter Lindner chain of shops must be mentioned, as it's a Berlin institution. A cross between corner shop and delicatessen, what started out in Spandau in the 1950s as a small stall selling butter, cheese and milk has grown into a chain of shops all over Berlin and Hamburg. The shops are small but interesting, not least for the butter that is still sold cut from a big block.

At the check out, you unload all your purchases onto the conveyor belt and collect them after they have passed through the cashier. At the check-out counters, customers have to bag their groceries themselves. The cashiers are there only to collect payment, period.

Ideally, the Germans prefer you to be very environmentally

conscious by your bringing your own reusable cotton bags or baskets for your purchases. If you didn't bring any, you can buy the cotton or plastic bags at the check-out point.

Open-air Markets

Practically every district has an open-air market or at least, some stalls. Sometimes, it's just a hand-made sign stuck on a lamppost telling you that there is fresh fish for that day round the corner, or someone with fresh mushrooms just picked from the forest that morning.

The open-air markets tend to have fresher produce than the supermarkets, as you would expect. Probably the most well-known open-air market is the Maybachufer Türkischer Markt in Neukölln (on Tuesdays and Fridays), selling a wide range of things from fresh fruits and vegetables to clothing. Another popular market is the Winterfeldtplatz Markt in Schöneberg (Wednesdays and Saturdays).

Flea Markets

There are also many flea markets around Berlin, the most famous one being the Kunst and Trödelmarkt on Straße des 17 Juni (Saturdays and Sundays).

Find interesting knick-knacks at one of the many flea markets around Berlin.

Electronic Goods

Electronic goods chains, like Media Markt and Saturn, have stores all over Berlin. They carry electronic goods (TV, videos, car Hifi, computers), all kinds of accessories and 'wellness' equipment.

Shopping Malls and Pounding the Streets

Berlin may not yet be the undisputed fashion capital of Germany, but it certainly is the shopping-mall capital. By the end of 2007, it had a whopping 57 shopping malls (see http://shoppingmall-berlin.de for full list). Hamburg has 41, Cologne eight, Frankfurt seven and Munich, only three. The largest, Gropiuspassagen in Neukölln, occupies 85,000 sq m (914,600 sq ft). The second largest, Alexa, with 54,000 sq m (581,040 sq ft) and a pink facade, opened in September 2007. The anchor tenants of shopping malls tend to be the usual suspects, such as electronics store Media Markt and clothing stores Hennes & Mauritz and C & A. One advantage of this boring repetition of the same stores means that you don't really have to travel across the city just to get to a particular store—there's bound to be one in a nearby mall.

The recently opened Alexa is the second largest shopping centre in Berlin.

The purchasing power of Berliners may not warrant such a rash of shopping malls, but this is balanced out by the high population density and large number of tourists.

Berlin has a number of shopping meccas. Kurfürstendamm (affectionately called Ku'damm) is quite a workout, stretching for 3.5km (2 miles). The fame of this street rests in its being the showcase of Western capitalism during the Cold War. It is still a popular shopping area today. The area between Uhlandstrasse and Adenauerplatz is Gucci and Versace territory. Fasanenstrasse, at right angles to Ku'damm is for those with deep pockets. An elegant street filled with top designer boutiques, it's worth taking a stroll through even if just to soak up the ambience. At the junction where the Kaiser-Wilhelm-Gedächtnis Kirche is, Ku'damm merges into Tauentzienstrasse. Here's where the largest department store in Europe, KaDeWe, resides. This street is also filled with restaurants, cafes, a MacDonald's, Peek & Cloppenburg (an old-timer from the early 1900s), and lots of 'High Street' fashion shops. Esprit, Spanish chain Zara and Swedish chain Hennes & Mauritz are all here. The shops here won't exactly break your bank, so this street tends to be more crowded than Ku'damm.

Clothing Sizes Rough Guide

Women's dresses, skirts, pants

US	8	10	12
UK	10	12	14
Europe	40	42	44

Men's suits, coats, sweaters

US/UK	38	40	42
Europe	48	50	52

Note: we all know there are plenty of discrepancies in clothing sizes, so the above is just a rough guide. Sizes differ throughout Europe too; as a rule of thumb, German clothes are cut larger than Italian, French or Spanish, so you would need a (hurrah!) smaller size.

Ku'damm, Berlin's famed shopping stretch, now faces competition from other trendy shopping areas such as Friedrichstrasse and Prenzlauer Berg.

Since unification, Ku'damm and cousin Tauentzienstrasse have faced competition from eastern compatriots such as Friedrichstrasse and Hackescher Markt. The shoppers' paradise on Friedrichstrassse is concentrated around the ultra-chic Friedrichstadtpassagen, a series of passages with luxury shops, offices and apartments. French Galeries Lafayette is here, as are fashion nobility like Jean Paul Gaultier, Donna Karan, Gucci and Versace. Hackescher Markt is more for young, alternative fashion. The other trendy place for thirty-ish folks is Prenzlauer Berg, especially around Kastanianallee and Szredzkistraße. For more staid fashion, Kaufhof (at Alexanderplatz and Ostbahnhof) and C & A (many branches) are the places to go. The spanking new giant, Alexa is also out east, a few hundred metres away from Kaufhof Alexanderplatz.

When Trying Out Footwear....

When trying out shoes or other footwear, you may notice a box of disposal socks on the shelves. If these socks are available, use them. They are there to prevent customers passing on or picking up athlete's foot.

Special Dietary Needs: Vegan, Organic, Kosher and Halal

Traditional German food is focused on meat, especially pork, which is often served in a manner that leaves you in no doubt that it's part of an animal. *Eisbein* (pig's trotters) comes to you as they are; the obvious amputated legs of the poor animal. There are few vegetarians among Germans. Eating out for vegetarians would therefore involve careful scrutiny, as the vegetable soup you order would probably come garnished with bacon bits or had used meat stock to give the soup some zest.

For lacto-ovo vegetarians, there is a wide variety of cheeses from all over Europe, apart from the fruits and vegetables. Germans are good with dairy products, and the yoghurt comes in countless flavours and different percentages of fat. German cheese has also improved in quality and variety, compared to decades ago.

For vegans, the choice is not too limited either. As more and more people become lactose-intolerant, soya-based products are seeing a boom. Soya curds, soya milk (sugar-free or with flavours like banana, strawberry and chocolate), 'soghurt' and even soya-based crème fraiche can be found in supermarkets. The supermarkets and organic food shops also carry a wide range of nuts.

Once limited to the organic food shops, organic produce are making inroads into supermarkets, and they can be identified by the word Bio. But if you need to potter around a real organic products shop, there are many in Berlin. Germans are particularly wary of genetically modified (GM) foods; some 66 per cent of Germans, according to an article in *Der Spiegel* online in 2008, think GM foods are unhealthy.

With the large number of Turks in Berlin, getting *halal* food is a breeze. The Maybachufer Türkischer Markt is certainly the place to head to for *halal* meats. Other *halal* foodstuff can be obtained from the numerous Turkish shops in Berlin.

There are numerous *kosher* cafes, restaurants and grocery shops in Berlin. The grocery shops have a wide variety of products catering to the Jewish community, from cooked meals, baked items and frozen meats to non-food items like

Kosher food can be found easily at the grocery stores catering to the Jewish community.

Sabbath candles, books and Israeli cosmetics. There is also a wine store with an international selection of *kosher* wine.

American and British Food

There are a number of British food shops catering to home-sick palates. Heinz baked beans, frozen Irish sausages and the must-have Christmas pudding and mince pies can be found in these shops.

For people across the Pond, apart from Dunkin' Donuts and McDonald's, goodies like Snapples, Root Beer, Marshmallow, Betty Crocker's and other American favourites can be found in American Lifestyle, a shop in Tempelhof.

DIY Stores

One thing you will notice very quickly is that Germany is a nation of DIY-ers. There are plenty of cavernous DIY stores all over Berlin, selling everything from the tiniest of screws to home swimming pools. Hornbach, OBI and Toom are the big players, and even if you're not going to build anything, it's worth just looking around one of these stores. You won't believe what you might find in a DIY store. I was bowled over by the selection of yummy-looking nuts, banana chips and some sort of muesli mix, all nicely laid out like in a candy store in Hornbach; and these were 'only' pet food.

These stores are manned by knowledgeable service staff, who are able to advise customers on the right product. If you need pieces of planks of a certain dimension, you can have it sawn down to size there as well.

Haberdashery
Departmental stores like Wertheim and Kaufhof have all your basic sewing needs. For unusual buttons, check out Knöpfe von Paul Knopf (http://paulknopf.de) , and for fabrics, have a look at Stoffhaus (http://stoffland.de).

For the Myopic
There is a mixture of optical shop chains and smaller individual shops around Berlin. Fielmann, with about 23 shops, is probably the largest. Other chains are Apollo Optik and Bursche Brillen.

If you know your prescription and simply need to order a fresh stock of disposable lenses, there are some internet companies where you get them at better rates than from an optical shop, such as http://contactlinsen-man.de and http://onlens.de.

COMMUNICATIONS
Telephones and Internet
There is a mind-boggling list of service providers offering simple land lines, DSL/ISDN connections and all-in-one packages (telephone and Internet) with catchy names in English like 'Call and Surf Comfort'. Many of them offer flat rates, and they are really good value for money if you surf or phone a lot. The competition is very keen; one of them even has Brad Pitt in their commercials to woo customers.

If you feel uncertain about grappling with all these technical things in German, TKS Telepost Kabel-Service GmbH & Co. KG is probably the best place to start. This Germany based company specialises in providing English language communication services (including cable TV), and

Google Mail

Google mail users access their inbox by going to mail.google. com and not gmail.com, when in Germany.

they even bill in English. Having supplied English language radio and television channels to U.S. military communities in Germany for over a decade, they are familiar with the needs of the English-speaking community.

Some Service Providers

- Alice
  http://www.alice-dsl.de
- Arcor
  http://www.arcor.de
- 1 & 1
  http://www.1und1.de
- T-Home
  http://www.t-home.de
- Telepost Kabel-Service GmbH & Co. KG
  http://www.tkscable.com
- Vodafone
  http://www.vodafone.de

Public Phones

Public phone booths are easily recognised by the magenta and grey colour of Deutsche Telekom. Most of the public phones are card-operated phones, and rarely will you find a coin-operated one nowadays. You can buy phone cards from post offices and some newsagents. Some public phones accept credit cards as well. These are mostly to be found in areas frequented by tourists and in the main train stations.

At some public phones (indicated by a ringing bell symbol), you can also take calls.

If you're staying in a hotel, the telephone rates are often a king's ransom. It's worthwhile to run out to a public phone to make that international call. International call rates are also much cheaper outside of office hours (after 9:00 pm and before 8:00 am).

Mobile Phones

German mobile phone networks operate on GSM technology, as does most of the world's (around 73 per cent, say some experts). For most foreigners, your mobile phone should be able to roam in Berlin, if you activate this feature. Most American and Canadian mobile phones use the CDMA technology, though, so they may not work in Berlin.

Roaming charges often cost an arm and a leg, so it's more practical to buy a prepaid SIM card, rent a mobile phone (see http://edicom-online.com) or get a new mobile phone altogether when you get to Berlin. If you intend to buy a prepaid card to use on your existing mobile phone, make sure that your network operator has not 'locked' your mobile phone such that you are restricted to using only their network. This often happens when you buy one of those packages which throws in a free handphone with your subscription. The 'locked' phone can be unlocked for a fee.

BANKING

The banks in Berlin range from the local ones like Berliner Bank, Berliner Volksbank and Berliner Sparkasse to more international ones like Dresdner Bank, Commerzbank and (American banks) GE Money and Citibank.

In Germany, the use of cheques is as rare as spotting the Abominable Snowman. Payments into and out of current accounts are usually done by *Überweisungen* (bank transfers/giros). Your salary will be credited directly to your account and you can pay your utilities bills by bank transfers.

ATM machines can be found even in the less central parts of Berlin. Most of the ATM machines accept credit cards and foreign debit cards. Just look for the Cirrus, Plus or Maestro signs on the machines. A withdrawal fee is charged.

Even if you have an ATM card from a Berlin bank, note that when you withdraw money from another bank's ATM, you may be charged a service fee (about €3). Check with your bank which bank's ATMs you can use without incurring this fee, which is quite a hefty sum if you withdraw often.

Banking hours vary from bank to bank. Some are open 9:00 am to 1:00 pm, and 2:00 pm to 6:00 pm from Mondays to Thursdays, and up to 4:00 pm on Fridays; others are open from 1:00 pm to 4:00 pm on Mondays, Wednesdays and Fridays, and 10:00 am to 7:00 pm on Tuesdays and Thursdays. Some branches are open on Saturdays from 10:00 am to 2:00 pm, others are closed. You will notice that it's very common in Berlin for banks and healthcare professionals to have this awkward different opening times on different days of the week, which makes it difficult for service users to remember.

If you're Internet savvy, thankfully Internet banking is widely available. For additional security, German banks also have a TAN (transaction authentication number) system. The TANs may be issued to you as a printed list of numbers which you choose at random whenever you have a transaction, or instructions may appear as a 'watermark' on your computer screen after you have keyed in your transaction details, telling you which TAN you should use. Different banks have different systems, but they all now have some additional security feature apart from passwords.

DEBIT AND CREDIT CARDS

Credit cards are not so widely accepted as they are in American major cities. Although most department stores and higher-end restaurants accept credit cards, the smaller shops may take only debit cards or cash. In some stores, like Peek & Cloppenburg, only American Express is accepted, and not Visa or Mastercard.

POSTAL SERVICES

Post offices and mail boxes can be easily spotted by their bright, canary yellow colour.

Note that true to the German instinct for orderliness, the cost of postage is not only according to weight, but the size and shape matter too. The postal staff are armed with templates which will confirm whether an odd-shaped envelope fits into the regulated size and shape or not. If you have a quirky Valentine's Day card that isn't quite the standardised format, you will end up paying a lot more euros than the weight warrants.

Post offices sell the relevant stationery as well such as packing boxes, bubble-wrap, strings and marker pens. As mentioned above, telephone cards are also available here.

Mail boxes have two slots; the right is for *Region Berlin/ Brandenburg* (postal codes 10000 to 16999), and the left for *Andere Postleitzahlen* (other postal codes), so make sure you pop your mail into the right slot. If there's a red dot on the mail-box, it means that there are collections later in the day and on Sundays as well.

Sending by DHL

If you're sending a parcel within Germany, you may want to consider sending it by DHL (which has been bought over by Deutsche Post). A DHL Paket weighing not more than 10 kg costs €6.90 (price in August 2008) and promises next-day delivery.

Stamps and phone cards can also be bought at vending machines, which are also in the same yellow colour.

Deutsche Post incidentally no longer has a monopoly of the postal market. Private companies, such as the Berlin PIN AG, now provide competition, with their own shops and mail boxes.

KNOWING THE QUALITY OF A PRODUCT

The Stiftung Warentest (Foundation for Testing Products) is an independent institution founded as long ago as 1964. They test the quality of all sorts of product and services at their discretion, from face creams to tyres to insurance. They publish their results in a magazine which you can buy at most newsagents. Their website is http://test.de (German only). You need to have a grasp of German to capitalise on their research, but even those who can't understand German can benefit from the institution's findings in a limited way. Many companies, once any of their products has been found to be well-rated by the foundation, will make sure consumers know this by printing the results on the product packaging. If you see *Stiftung Warentest-Sehr Gut* 2008 on the packaging of, say, a face cream, it means the product has been tested in the year specified and found to be very good.

This foundation faces competition from *Öko Test*, a similar product tester, but which is said to have a more commercial bent.

TRANSPORT

Berlin is located quite smack in the middle of Europe, so it's well connected by road and rail to most European cities. There are also good flight connections to North America and Asia. Currently, Frankfurt is still Germany's airport with the busiest international traffic, so not a few flights to outside Europe go via Frankfurt. Once the new Berlin/Brandenburg International Airport (BBI) at Berlin-Schönefeld is ready (targeted 2011), it's expected that international flights will take off directly from there.

The German autobahn is legendary. It is well maintained and there are only a few stretches that have speed limits. During the holiday season, there are often ghastly jams, but otherwise drivers can try to emulate Formula One drivers on them. The Berliner Ring is an autobahn that, as its name suggests, surrounds the city. There are exits that lead you onto the autobahn to other German cities, and there are well-posted signs to guide drivers.

Travelling within Berlin itself is convenient, as the city has an efficient public transport network of S and U-Bahn, bus and (only in east Berlin) tram services. The public transport system runs like clockwork, unless there's an accident or a strike, and reaches even the farthest corner of Berlin. Buying a ticket entitles you to the use of all of the abovementioned modes of public transport, limited only by the type of ticket you buy as further explained below.

Driving within the city with its 5,334 km (3,314 miles) of well-maintained roads present few problems except for traffic jams.

Airports

At the time of writing, Berlin has only two functioning airports, at Tegel and Schönefeld. Tempelhof closed in

Berlin has an efficient public transport network and it is convenient to get around the city.

October 2008, in spite of lobbying against its closure. For many, this was sacrilegious, given that this was the location where the Berlin airlift took place during the blockade by the Russians in the late 1940s. The Berlin parliament and the federal government opted for closing both Tempelhof and Tegel and to have just the BBI airport serving the city, not least because the maintenance cost is a drain on the already strained city budget.

Tegel and Schönefeld can't hold a candle to Frankurt at the moment. Although efficient enough, they are much smaller than Frankfurt, not to mention grand ones like Schiphol.

Tegel
Although small, hexagon-shaped Tegel is chock-a-block with shops. Food (including Burger King), souvenir, duty free and fashion shops are open 365 days a year, most from 7:00 am to 9:00 pm. Some like Burger King and Market Place are open for hungry travellers from 4:30 am and 5:00 am respectively. The post office here has longer opening hours than most in the city.

Though Tegel is not too far away from the city centre (8 km /5 miles), it is not served by a connecting S or U-Bahn. Travellers have to take taxis (about €15 for a trip to Ku'damm) or the buses, which take you to central places like Bahnhof Zoo or Unter den Linden (about a 30-minute ride). The taxi stands and bus stops are just outside the main hall. Bus tickets can be bought from a ticket machine or directly from the bus driver. If you want to connect to the S and U-Bahn system without travelling all the way to the city centre, you can take the TXL bus to Beusselstrasse, or the X9 or 109 to Jungfernheide, to connect to the S-Bahn; or bus no.128 to U-Bahn Kurt-Schumacher-Platz.

Schönefeld

Schönefeld currently serves mainly budget airlines. But this will change when it becomes the spanking new BBI. Schönefeld is about 20 km (12 miles) south of the city centre. Taking a taxi from Schönefeld to the city centre might be too costly for budget travellers, so a more economical way is to catch a train into town from Schönefeld S-Bahn station. It will be much more convenient in the future when the BBI Bahnhof is completed. Do note that since 1 April 2008, Schönefeld is in Zone C (formerly B), so if using the train, you need a ticket that is valid for that zone.

Trains

The Deutsche Bahn (German Railways) provides efficient and comfortable rail transport such as the high speed ICE (Intercity Express) which goes at 300 km (186 miles) per hour, the EuroCity and the InterCity. In 2008, the German parliament approved the partial privatisation of the state-owned railway.

Deutsche Bahn

For detailed information (various languages available), see their website: http://www.bahn.de

---

Hauptbahnhof (reopened in May 2006 after a massive makeover) is the crème de la crème of Berlin's train stations. The main station for all regional and intercity trains, the cavernous glass building has a shopping mall, shower facilities, a post office and practically anything that a traveller might need.

Bahnhof Zoo (west Berlin) and Ostbahnhof (east Berlin) cater more for local and regional trains.

The three train stations are better than the airports in terms of transport connection, as they are connected to the S-Bahn lines.

Coaches

A cheaper, but less comfortable way of travelling long distances is by coach. The main coach station is the Zentraler Busbahnhof, near the Funkturm. Apart from other German cities, coaches also go to some European cities.

S-Bahn and U-Bahn

The size of Berlin should not deter you from exploring all corners of the city, as it is well-served by the public transport system. It makes sense to use the public transport to get to the city centre, too, as it's congested and finding a parking space is like finding the proverbial needle in a haystack. And if you should be so lucky, the cost of parking is off-puttingly astronomical.

Although the system looks complicated at first, you can navigate your way around like a pro once you are familiar where the end stations of the lines are and after a few practice runs. You can get hold of a plan of the network (*S and U-Bahn Netz*) from any ticket counter. The different lines are helpfully marked in different colours.

The S-Bahn is mainly overground, while the U-Bahn is mostly underground, although it does surface on certain stretches of some lines. The S-Bahn is run by an independent company, S-Bahn Berlin GmbH (a subsidiary of Deutsche Bahn AG) and the U-Bahn, buses and trams are run by the BVG. But all transport systems are seamlessly integrated.

Berlin is divided into three zones, in concentric rings. Zone A is the city centre area circumscribed by the Ring lines

(S41 and S42), Zone B is the area of Berlin outside the Ring line, and Zone C is the area of Brandenburg. Tickets can be bought for travel to a combination of different zones (AB, BC, or ABC), and on single-trip, one day, seven-day, monthly or yearly basis. There are also reduced rate (*Ermässigungstarif*) tickets for children under 14, and special tickets, like the Welcome Card and the City Tour card, which are useful for short-term visitors. The Welcome Card entitles you to three days of unlimited travel around all three zones. The City Tour card is for 48 or 72-hour unlimited travel within the AB zones. Both cards offer discounts to selected tourist sites.

The tickets can be used for S-Bahn, U-Bahn, buses and trams. Tickets can be bought from ticket counters manned by personnel or ticket machines at train stations. Tickets must be validated before starting your journey (for longer term tickets, on the first day you use it) by getting it punched at a small red or yellow machine on platforms or on the bus. Tickets bought on trams and buses are automatically validated.

The single ticket entitles you to get from point A to point B (with any amount of train changes) within two hours. But you cannot use it to return from point B to point A, even if it's within the two-hour limit. The station is printed on your ticket when you validate it.

There is a cheaper version of the single ticket: the *Kurzstrecke*. This can be used only for three stops on trains or six stops on buses/trams and you cannot change trains or buses.

Ticket type	Zone AB €	Zone BC €	Zone ABC €
Single	2.10	2.50	2.80
Four-trip ticket	8.00	-	-
One Day	6.10	6.30	6.50
7 Day	26.20	27.00	32.30
One month	72.00	73.00	88.50
Prices as at August 2008			

Passengers don't need to go through a turnstile when entering the stations. But before anyone gets tempted into not buying a ticket, don't. Many plain-clothes inspectors check tickets frequently and the fine for not having a valid ticket is €40. Not to mention the embarrassment of being caught. The inspectors often work in pairs and start from the doors towards the centre of the carriage only after the train has started moving, effectively blocking off any escape route. Incidentally, you're not supposed to be on a train platform if you don't have a ticket. Although checks are rare, I've actually experienced it once. So if a ticket inspector stops you on the platform and asks to see your ticket, don't think it's someone trying to be funny. They won't be in uniform, but should be carrying identification cards.

The most common announcements you will hear when on the platform are '*Einsteigen bitte*' (please board) and '*Zurückbleiben bitte*' (literally 'please stay back', it means 'door closing, do not board'). To make sure you're getting onto a train taking you in the correct direction, you should always check not only the number but the end station displayed on the front of the train.

The more modern S-Bahn trains have an electronic screen which shows the next few stations. On the U-Bahn, you will also hear automatic announcements before each station that goes something like this: '*Mehringdamm. Übergang zum U1, U2 und Metrobus*', which tells you the name of the next station (Mehringdamm), and that you can connect to (*Übergang*) the lines U1, U2 and the Metrobus. Just before some stations, such as Spittelmarkt, you will hear '*Bitte beachten Sie die Lücke zwischen Zug und Bahnsteigrand.*' This mouthful means basically 'Mind the gap'; you should take care not to step into the space between the train and the platform.

Train doors are opened by pushing a button or turning a lever on the door.

Though it doesn't happen very often, sometimes you have to make an impromptu change of train. An announcement in German may tell you to take the train across the platform instead. If you don't understand German, should you hear an announcement followed by the passengers all getting out of the train, you should ask someone who hopefully speaks English what's happening. On other occasions, especially in the more outlying areas of Berlin, only the first three carriages will continue the journey, due to the lack of passengers. Similarly an announcement will come on, followed by all passengers getting out, so you should check with someone what the announcement is about. Outside of the city centre, the station staff may not speak English, so you have to get the help of someone who can.

For travellers who are not so mobile, you can look at the S and U Bahn plan to see which stations have lifts/elevators (indicated with a lift symbol) to plan your trip.

Uncle Tom's Cabin
There's a train station called Onkel Toms Hütte (Uncle Tom's Cabin). Germans are familiar with the novel, *Uncle Tom's Cabin*, but not aware of the negative racial stereotyping associated with the book. The station's name is therefore not intended to be offensive to African-Americans.

Trams and Buses

The buses and trams complement the S-Bahn and U-Bahn to take you to the places not covered by the trains. Trams are found primarily in the eastern parts of the city. Some of the buses and trams have special low platforms to make it easier to board for those in wheelchairs or with prams. If you haven't bought a ticket, you can do so from the bus driver, or from the ticket machine (but not the tram driver) on a tram. The ticket machines on trams take only coins, and is quite complicated with the different types of tickets available.

The buses and trams run frequently on weekdays, but slightly less so on weekends. There are also express buses, marked with an 'X', which make lesser stops. The day buses stop running before midnight, and the service is replaced by night buses, marked by the letter 'N' in front of the numbers. They don't cover the same routes as the daytime buses, and you can get a map of the Nachtliniennetz from any BVG information counter.

A bus stop with an electronic bus schedule and ticket machine.

All bus and tram stops have a detailed time table on display.

For buses, you have to board at the front to show the driver your ticket. For trams, you can board through any door.

Buses 100 and 200 are double decker buses passing through interesting sites in the city. It's a nice way way to sight-see if you're newly arrived or have guests in town.

Information for BVG Services

Available from :

- BVG pavilion on Hardenbergplatz (near Bahnhof Zoo)
  Website: http://www.bvg.de

Taxis

Taxis are an expensive way of getting around but they are very reliable. All taxis (often a Mercedes) are cream coloured with a 'TAXI' sign on the roof. You can hail a taxi on the road, call for one by phone or go to a taxi-stand.

If you hail a taxi on the streets and are travelling only a short distance (less than 2km/1¼ miles), you can tell the driver you'd like to use the *Kurzstrecketarif*. The ride will cost only a flat rate of €3.

There are around 6,000 taxis in Berlin.

Calling a Taxi
- City-Funk: 21 02 02
- Taxi-Funk: 44 33 22
- Würfelfunk: 0800 22 22 255

The taxi drivers know their way around, and many taxis are equipped with a GPS, too.

It's common to round up the fare or even add another 10 per cent as a tip.

Water Transport

While not exactly Venice, Berlin does make use of water transport, some taking you from the city centre to other parts of the city, such as Spandau and Müggelsee and farther to Potsdam. There are many water tour companies and you can make trips all the way to Szczecin in Poland. Apart from

Explore Berlin on a river cruise.

water tours, some ferries run by BVG provide public transport across lakes. You can use the normal BVG or S-Bahn tickets for these ferries.

Driving

If you're driving into Berlin, alll the highways will connect with the Berliner Ring (A10). From there, the signs will direct you to the various districts of Berlin. One thing to remember is that Berlin has two city centres, a hangover from the days when the city was divided. Mitte, although it sounds like the city centre, will lead you to the district 'Mitte', which is the city centre of the east (the area around Friedrichstrasse). The city centre of the west is around Ku'damm, which is about a 15-minute drive away.

For citizens of the UK, Australia, New Zealand and most of the countries of the Commonwealth of Nations, some adjustments are required to your automatic reflexes in driving. In Germany, vehicles drive on the right, and the driver's seat is on the left-hand side of the car.

Drivers in Germany are on the whole not reckless and comply with all traffic rules, unless they've had too much to drink. The police are strict, and violation of traffic rules may result in the driver getting not only a fine, but also violation points. When a maximum of 18 points is reached, the driver loses his/her driving licence. The points are recorded in *Kraftfahrt Bundesamt* (federal department of vehicles) in Flensburg (a city on the border with Denmark). Drivers can apply to the authority to see the number of points accummulated. Points can be reduced by attending a special course.

Kraftfahrt Bundesamt

For more information, see http://www.kba.de

(English information available)

The legal age for driving is 18 years. Drivers must have their driving licence, car registration and ownership papers and insurance documents with them whenever they drive. All cars must carry certain essentials as well (see box).

Things You Must Have in the Car

- Driving licence,vehicle registration and insurance documents
- First aid kit
- A warning triangle
- Reflective safety vests
- A spare tyre and tools to change it
- Windscreen sticker if you're driving into the Umwelt Zone (Environmental Zone)

Some of the rules that drivers must observe:
- All front and back passengers must use a seatbelt.
- On the autobahn, keep to the right lane unless you're overtaking or driving very fast. Before overtaking, check the rear and side mirrors. Be aware that cars travelling at 200 kmph (124 mph) can come up behind you faster than you think.
- Always give way to traffic coming from the right, unless a sign tells you otherwise (e.g. that you're on a priority road).
- You are on a priority road if you see a diamond-shaped yellow and white sign. Traffic entering priority roads must yield. Note that sometimes priority roads are not apparently one (e.g. a smaller lane going into a larger road).

Here are some important 'no-nos' to note for drivers:
- Using the mobile phone when driving is forbidden, unless it's a 'hands-free' unit.
- Don't drink and drive. The legal blood alcohol limit is 0.5 grams of alcohol per litre of blood.
- Don't overtake on the right.
- Children under three must be in the back seat.
- Children under 12 or shorter than 1.5 m must use a child safety seat if sitting in front, but if there's an air bag, they are not allowed in the front seat.
- When driving through a tunnel, don't use your high beam and don't stop or make a u-turn.

You can purchase your parking ticket at one of the parking ticket machines by the road.

- Don't use your horn or headlights to tell the driver in front to 'get out of your way'.
- Don't sound your horn outside someone's home to signal that you've arrived. Park, and go ring the intercom/doorbell instead.
- Don't wash your car in a public place. Take it to a car wash.

Parking

Some rules about parking:
- Some streets are reserved for residents only, designated by signs (*Anwohnerparken* or *Anliegerfrei*).

- Some lots are reserved for disabled persons (marked with a wheelchair sign).
- Some places require you to display a disc on your dashboard to show the time of arrival, as you are allowed to park for free only for an hour or two. Discs can be obtained from gas stations.
- Always park in the direction of traffic flow to avoid getting fined.

Technical Organisations

Help for vehicle breakdowns is provided by ADAC (the German equivalent of AA) for its members. Vehicle inspections and other technical matters are handled by organisations such as TÜV (*Technischer Überwachungs-Verein*) and DEKRA (*Deutscher Kraftfahrzeug Überwachungs-Verein*).

Driving Licence

Citizens from EU and EEA countries can use their driving licences without further ado. Citizens from other countries can drive for up to six months with an international driving licence. If they intend to stay longer than six months, depending on their nationality, they can either exchange their national driving licence for a German one for a fee, or they have to take a theory test, or even sit for the theory and practical test. For example, all Canadians can simply exchange their licence for a German one, while for US citizens, it depends on their length of stay and which state they come from. If the US citizen can prove that he or she is staying for less than a year, they may drive with their US licence for 364 days after registering with the drivers' registration office. For those staying longer than a year, they must get a German licence. US citizens from some states may simply exchange their licence for a German one, while others must take a written test. US citizens can get detailed information from the websites of the US Embassy or the Residents' and Regulatory Affairs (see box on the next page).

For those who need not sit for a test, they may still be required to attend a one-day first-aid course conducted by the

Red Cross, and get an eye test done. But these requirements are relatively easy to fulfill, compared to those for obtaining a German driving licence from scratch.

To get a German driving licence, enrolling in a driving school (*Fahrschule*) is a must. What is needed for the licence is an application to the local resident's office for a driving licence, the completion of the abovementioned first-aid course, an eye-test certificate from an optician, and the completion of the theory and the practical driving test. The driving lessons are costly and involve practices driving on normal roads, highways and at night.

Berlin State Residents' and Regulatory Affairs
Landesamt für Bürger-und Ordnungsangelegenheiten (LABO)
—Führerscheinbüro—
Puttkamerstr. 16-18
10958 Berlin
Tel: (030) 90269-2300
Fax: (030) 90269-2399
Website: berlin.de/labo/fuehrerschein/dienstleistungen/index.html
For list of countries and requirements, see: http://www.berlin.de/labo/fuehrerschein/dienstleistungen/staatenlisteauslandsfs.html

---

Driving in Winter Conditions

Winters in Berlin can mean very heavy snowfall or slippery, icy roads. Although the BSR does a great job of clearing the snow and spraying anti-skid material on the roads, there is only so much they can do to combat Mother Nature.

All cars must have winter tyres throughout winter. As the weather is unpredictable, it's best to keep your winter tyres on through April. Since Berlin is basically flat, you're unlikely to ever need snow chains. A 50-50 mix of antifreeze and water in the cooling system is recommended in winter. Windscreen washer fluid should be topped up and treated with a proprietary additive (not engine anti-freeze) to reduce the possibility of freezing. Have warm rugs in the car in case your car stalls and you have to wait for help in the cold. Having some food and water in the car makes sense as well.

A bicycle carriage on the S-Bahn; look out for the bicycle symbol!

Cycling

In Berlin, cycling is a serious option of transport, and not just for leisure. Cyclists are well catered for, with separate bicycle lanes (marked with a line, or in brownish pink colour) on most main roads. There are also traffic lights for cyclists at some road junctions. When driving, keep your eyes peeled for bicycle lanes when turning into another road, as often the cyclists have right of way. Many shops have a bicycle rack outside reserved for their *Kunden* (customers).

You can take your bikes on the S and U-Bahn, in certain carriages (denoted with a bicycle symbol), but you have to buy a bike ticket.

On Foot

If using your trusty legs, be careful not to walk on the bicycle lanes. Many cyclists ride like Formula One drivers, and apart from the risk of being hit, many are not shy of glaring at you with murderous looks if you get onto their sacred path.

At pedestrian crossings, you should never cross if the 'red man' is on, even if there's not a single car in sight, as it's illegal.

MEDIA
Print Media
You can get the usual staple of international newspapers and magazines from newsagents at airports, main train stations and in the city centre.

Many of the bigger bookshops (Dussmann and Hugendubel) in the city centre carry a wide selection of English books. There are also smaller English bookshops around Berlin (see Resource Guide).

If you read German, there is a wide range of newspapers and magazines available. The local newspapers are the *Berliner Zeitung*, *Berliner Morgenpost* and *Der Tagesspiegel* and two tabloids, *BZ* and *Berliner Kurier*. For a broader coverage of national and international news, there are the national newspapers like *Frankfurter Allgeimeine Zeitung*, *Handelsblatt*, *Die Welt*, *Süddeutsche Zeitung* and *Welt Kompakt* (a tabloid-format newspaper with shorter text aimed at younger readers), and magazines like (the well-respected) *Der Spiegel* and the lower-brow *Stern* and *Focus*. English-speakers will be pleased to know that *Der Spiegel* has an English site on their online newspaper (http://www.spiegel.de). There is also an explosion of women's magazines, with lots of (often untrue) sensational news about European royalty and film stars peppered with doctored pictures.

There are two popular listings magazine in German, *Zitty* and *Tip*, with articles thrown in. For an English language listings magazine, there is the *Exberliner*. The articles in the *Exberliner* will not appeal to everyone, but hey, it's in English.

TV
There are more TV channels than you probably have time and interest for. There are two national channels, ARD and ZDF, two local channels, TVBerlin and RBB (*Rundfunk Berlin Brandenburg*) and a cornucopia of private channels. Foreign TV is available too. The type of programmes are also diverse: there are political talk shows, a German version of BBC's *Hard Talk*, called *Hart aber Fair* (*Hard but Fair*), amazingly popular folk music shows with an audience clapping along,

matchmaking programmes for lonely farmers, a casting programme—*Germany's Next Top Model*, a generous dose of soap operas that seem to go on forever, German crime movies and love stories, some excellent history movies and documentaries, Hollywood blockbusters and American TV series, like *Desperate Housewives*.

There are also special interest channels like Eurosport and Arte (a French-German channel of quality films/documentaries with a focus on culture).

If you have young children, you'd want to be careful about what movie is being shown on TV. The German nonchalance with nudity means that some shows have very energetic bedroom scenes that threaten to bust the bed springs and leave nothing to the imagination. Some are shown not very late at night either. German popular TV stars would also be the envy of their over-40 American counterparts. American have-beens should consider making a second career in Germany once they see how many not very glamourous quinqagenarians and sexagenarians still have lead roles on German TV, and not cast only as grandparents either.

Foreign language movies are dubbed into German, so it's quite impressive to see Teri Hatcher and Co speak fluent German. Although it takes some getting used to, it's a good way of picking up German.

CNN, BBC World, MTV Europe and NBC provide the English language broadcasts.

Radio

There are more than 30 stations to tune into, mostly pop music and news broadcast in between.

For English-language broadcasts, tune in to BBC World Service (90.2) and US National Public Radio (87.9), or Radio MultiKulti (96.3) which broadcasts in a multitude of languages.

TV and Radio Licence

You must pay licence fees for your TV and radio (including car radio). As soon as you buy a TV or radio, you must register with the GEZ (*Gebühreneinzugszentrale*). Registration forms are available at most banks, *Sparkassen* or post offices, or you can sign up online at http://gez.de. The monthly fees as at mid 2008 are €5.52 for radio, and €17.03 for TV as well as TV and radio combined.

As of 1 January 2007, computers which have Internet connectivity, PDAs and Smartphones which can receive radio or TV over the Internet need to be registered as well.

The GEZ has the reputation of being extremely efficient at catching people who fail to register, by using special devices to detect TV sets and peering into houses, or according to some whispers, paying the *Hausmeister* to spy for them.

TIME
Germany uses the 24-hour system. 1 pm is therefore *13 Uhr* and 2 pm is *14 Uhr*.

The way Germans use the phrase 'half six' is also different from the British usage. When a British person says 'half six', he means half past six or 6.30. When a German says '*halb sechs*' (half six), he means 5.30 (half before six).

The other thing to note about time is that Germany practises daylight saving hours, so there is a one hour difference between summer time and winter time. On the last Sunday in March, the clock goes forward one hour (i.e. at 12 midnight on Saturday, it becomes 1 am on Sunday). On the last Sunday in October, the clock moves back by one hour.

HEALTH MATTERS
Water Quality
You would think tap water is not potable, the way Berliners buy mineral water for home consumption. Berlin's water is hard, so it does taste queer, but it's absolutely safe to drink.

Medical and Dental Services
There are 69 hospitals in Berlin. The medical and dental services in Berlin are of good quality, if expensive. It therefore makes sense to have private insurance. Citizens from EU countries can apply for the European Health Insurance Card before leaving home, which entitles them to healthcare in

Germany. But be aware that it doesn't cover all medical
costs, so do check the finer details. The major hospitals are
the Charité and DRK (German Red Cross) hospitals, both
with several medical centres across Berlin, and St Hedwig
Krankenhaus. The medical personnel and facilities in the
east are of no lesser quality. For example, the DRK Köpenick
hospital has a good reputation, and the medical centre in
Adlershof has doctors with various specialisations. The only
drawback is finding a medical or dental professional who
can speak English fluently in the east.

Pharmacies and Drugstores

Every pharmacy (*Apotheke*) is manned by qualified
pharmacists, who will provide advice and recommend the
appropriate medication for not too serious ailments like
coughs, colds and minor skin problems. Pharmacies can
easily be recognised by a big red letter 'A' (for *Apotheke*)
outside the shop. Doctors in Germany do not provide patients
with medication; they issue prescriptions to patients who
must make that additional trip to the pharmacy before being
able to head home and collapse in bed. Pharmacies often
also sell special herbal teas and medical accessories.

Patients have to purchase their medication from pharmacies, identified by
the large red 'A' sign.

If you need a pharmacy outside of normal shop hours, there should be a list outside all pharmacies indicating which pharmacy in the vicinity is rostered to stay open. If the pharmacy which is supposed to be open looks shuttered up when you get there, don't hesitate to ring the bell. There should be someone in.

Drugstore chains (e.g. Schleckers, Rossmann, DM, Drospa) sell a great variety of things such as vitamins, herbal teas, cleaning chemicals, hygiene products, pet food and make-up, but you can't get any basic medication from drugstores, not even paracetamol, which are usually an over-the-counter drug in other countries.

Psychological Health
Culture Shock
People, especially Europeans, don't think that culture shock will be an issue, coming to Berlin. Berlin is, after all, a major European city, so they don't expect that there are many adjustments to make. Or are there?

The phrase 'culture shock' is, in a way, misleading in that people coming to Berlin think they will never feel anything so bad as a shock, so dismiss it summarily. But culture shock can take the form of mild confusion and disorientation, that can lead a person to feel insecure. The grappling with a new language, getting used to rather curt people and some German ways of doing things that are very different from what one is used to can be frustrating in the beginning.

The sense of disorientation that comes with being in an unfamiliar environment can affect different people in different degrees. First-time as well as seasoned expatriates can suffer from culture shock.

The people in the high-risk groups are the accompanying spouses and children. Often, the spouse has to forgo her (it's usually the wife who is the accompanying person) own career to accompany the husband on the posting, while the children leave their friends behind, to land in totally new surroundings. The slight advantage the husband has is that he's got his job as a focal point and colleagues to ask for information, things which his accompanying family does not have. The feeling of disorientation is therefore often more acutely felt by the family members. The common shock faced by expatriate wives I've met is the loss of identity—reduced to being known only as 'Mr. Grey's wife' or 'Kimberly's mom'.

If you suddenly feel you've become excessively irritable or insecure, lethargic and in need of a lot of sleep, or feel unsociable and prefer to stay at home, find everything about the host country unbearable or cry over the smallest things, then chances are you're encountering culture shock.

Some ways of dealing with culture shock recommended by cross-cultural experts are:

- Learn as much as you can about Berlin and the culture. Your reading this book is already a step forward!
- Avoid people who grumble about Berlin all the time. It'll only make you depressed
- Make friends with locals wherever possible
- Don't try to be perfect. You *are* in a new environment, so be kind to yourself

What's important is to understand that suffering from culture shock is not something to be ashamed of, but rather like having the flu; you feel lousy, but once you recognise the ailment, you know it's not life-threatening and you can do something to get better. Being a foreigner is exactly that; things are foreign to you so there's no need to get everything right on day one. If you make a *faux pas*, shrug it off as part of the learning process. Don't let the passing phase of confusion shatter your self-confidence and identity.

Seasonal Affective Disorder

Dark and cold winters can affect people in an unpleasant way. Berlin's winter can wreak havoc on your well-being. Researchers widely believe that the lack of sunlight in the fall and winter causes seasonal depression. The darker days results in the brain not producing enough serotonin, which results in the symptoms of depression, while overproducing a hormone that regulates sleep, melatonin. That can leave a person feeling down and lethargic or in more serious cases, with impaired social interaction and cognitive ability.

Seasonal Affective Disorder (SAD), or winter blues, as this disorder is called, can be treated with light therapy. The oft-recommended treatment is to have lots of bright light (at least 300 watts) at close range (1 metre/3 feet distance) for an hour and preferably in the mornings.

Exercise, even if it's only a half-hour brisk walk outdoors, is also said to be helpful. If for any reason you are unable to go outdoors, sitting at an open window (wrapped up warmly, of course) for about 20 minutes will also give you a dose of the lux out there.

One other thing: if you're not suffering from culture shock or SAD yourself, but someone you know is, don't dismiss it as whinging or an attention-seeking ploy. Because it isn't. No sufferer wants to be in that position, because it's very debilitating and unpleasant. People who are affected can't help it, so don't tell them to 'Snap out of it!' or 'Get a grip on yourself!' More than anything else, they need the support and understanding of family and friends, as they try to grapple with the disorientation or the lack of sunlight, or both.

PLACES OF LEARNING
German Schools

German children go through 12 years of schooling, from age six to 18. Toddlers may attend kindergartens before that. At age six, children go to a *Grundschule*. From around ten years, they move on to secondary schools, which may be a *Hauptschule*, *Realschule*, *Gesamtschule* or *Gymnasium*. The different types of schools have different foci (general education, comprehensive or academic). To go on to university, students must graduate with an *Abitur* certificate from a *Gymnasium* or *Gesamtschule*.

There is quite a good selection of international schools in Berlin, many teaching in both English and German and from Grade 1 through to Grade 13 (i.e. ages six to 18). There are the Berlin British School, John F. Kennedy School, Berlin International School and State International School, just to name a few.

Tertiary Education

Berlin is an attractive university city, with over 140,000 students registered in the universities, 14 per cent of them foreigners. The main ones have a long history: Humboldt-Universität zu Berlin was founded in 1810, Freie Universität in 1948, and the Technische Universität in 1879. A newer university, the Universität der Künste Berlin (focusing on art, drama, music, fashion design, film and media) was founded in 1975. In October 2002, the European School of Management and Technology was established.

PUBLIC TOILETS

All department stores, shopping malls, major bookstores and restaurants will have toilets which you can use, but often expect you to leave a tip of €0.30 to €0.50 on a plate at the entrance. The norm is to pay after using, although some attendants may wish to collect before you enter. It's worth paying the few cents, as the toilets are kept very clean.

There are also coin-operated, self-flushing 'City Toilets' around with instructions in various languages.

BEGGARS, BUSKERS AND THE HOMELESS

You see a lot of women (often with a clutch of sorry-looking children) begging for money in the city centre. Many of them are Roma (or gypsies) and probably belong to begging syndicates. You'll be surprised at what polyglots they are. They will beg in German and if you don't respond, they'll then ask 'Speak English?' If you look Chinese, they might approach you with a '*Ni Hao*'. They tend to be rather aggressive in their begging, or resort to wailing in a discomfiting way.

In recent years, more and more young Germans are turning to begging. They might approach you for some spare change, sometimes adding plaintively, for 'us', meaning the numerous puppies at his/her feet.

On the streets and on the trains, there will also be hopeful buskers playing some instrument or other.

Another group looking for financial assistance are the homeless selling street newspapers (such as *Motz* and *Strassenfeger*). The sellers get a percentage of each newspaper they sell. I tend to buy these newspapers as I feel that they are at least trying to do something instead of outright begging. Many stand quietly in one corner holding up their newspaper, while quite a few trawl through the S and U-Bahns.

BERLINERS' BEST FRIEND

Berliners love dogs and cats. While walking along the streets or in parks, you have to watch out for the doggy land mines, as Berliners don't clean up after their pooches.

Some 107,355 dogs are registered with the Finance department and in 2007, about €10.7 million of dog taxes was collected. And mind you, not all dog owners register their dogs.

Cats are tax-free, so they are also well-loved as pets.

BERLINERS' WILD NEIGHBOURS

In recent years, wild boars all over Germany have been making trips to cities and towns to forage for food. In spring 2008, a man walking his dog along a street in Köpenick was attacked by two wild boars. Though it doesn't happen too often, wild boars do come out of the forest, and when with their young, are prone to be aggressive, as in this unfortunate case.

I myself have come across a herd of about 15 wild boars while walking in the forest at 2:00 pm. For a spell, wild boars also rampaged in the garden in front of our apartment, cleverly burrowing under the fence to get in. When you do come across wild boars, keep still to avoid making them nervous. And get ready to climb a tree or make an Olympian leap onto a higher place if they charge. Foxes and a racoon have also made their debut in the Chancellery and Hotel Park Inn respectively.

FOOD

CHAPTER 6

'I didn't fight my way to the top of the
food chain to be a vegetarian.'
—Anon

THAT SEEMS TO SUM UP how Germans feel about food. German food may vary across regions, but it mostly features meat, preferably smothered with a rich sauce. Of all meats, pork is the favourite, whether compressed into a sausage or served as a dismembered limb (*Eisbein* and *Schweinshaxe*). In fact, a pig is never slaughtered in vain; almost every organ is eaten, including the blood to make *Blutwurst* (blood sausage), or sometimes called by a euphemism, *Rotwurst* (red sausage).

Other oft-eaten meats, although very distant seconds, are poultry and beef. Chicken is the most common poultry consumed, and goose traditonally appears for Christmas. Germans like game too, such as hare, venison and wild boar.

Although fish doesn't traditionally feature very highly in German food, in Berlin it's more common, considering the many lakes and rivers in the region. Eel, pike-perch and pike are popular and carp is a favourite for the new year. Pickled herring (*Rollmops*) is also common.

From the brief sampling of German fare above, you probably can tell that eating German food is not about savouring some delicate and artistic creation, but about getting your money's worth of a hearty and caloried meal. German gastronomy, like its fashion, has some nice pieces, but no one with discerning taste will think of the country as a food mecca. Berlin has never been associated with

Sausages, ham and cheese—food for the German palate.

gourmet food, not even during the times of monarchy. The Hohenzollerns did love hunting, though, hence Berlin cuisine does include game meat.

But it's not that there's nothing palatable to be had in Berlin. German traditional food may not be *haute cuisine*, but they're tasty. The French Huguenots also exerted an influence on Berlin food culture. After the fall of the Wall, Berlin could count on the fresh produce coming from rural Brandenburg and also a resurgence of Brandenburger specialities. Since becoming the capital of Germany, many five-star restaurants have sprung up, as well as avant-garde eateries. There is now the *Neue Deutsche Küche* (new German cuisine) which is much lighter to consume, but heavier on the pocket.

Like any cosmopolitan city, the immigrant population can be relied upon to bring you on diverse culinary trips such as Turkish, Italian, Greek, Indian, Chinese, Thai, Vietnamese and Mexican.

TYPICAL GERMAN AND BERLIN FOOD
Sausages
The range of delicious sausages available is legendary. Of different sizes, lengths and tastes, it's thought that there are

at least 1,500 different types of sausages in Germany. It's so much a part of German life that many sayings are based on the *Wurst*.

German Sayings and Expressions Featuring Sausages

Jetzt geht es um die Wurst—the moment of truth has come

Alles hat ein Ende, nur die Wurst hat zwei—everything has an end, only the sausage has two

Ein armes Würstchen—a poor soul

Wurstfinger—podgy fingers

In Berlin, it's the *Currywurst* that is the star. Invented by a snack stall owner, Hedwig Müller, just after World War II, the *Currywurst* is jeolously guarded by Berliners as the city's famous child. In 2007, Berliner butchers even filed an application with Germany's Patents and Trade Mark Office to register 'Berliner Currywurst' as a brand, so that only the sausages made in Berlin could be called that. Yes, it's treated

Currywurst, the snack well loved by many Germans, including Gerhard Schröder, the former Chancellor.

as seriously as champagne from Champagne. Berlin has 70 meat processing firms, so there's a lot of support for the little sausage, traditionally served diced, drenched in ketchup and dusted with curry powder, on a cardboard plate. This snack food got an added boost from former Chancellor, Gerhard Schröder, who frequently stopped his limousine in front of Ku'damm 195 (a *Currywurst* shop) on his way home from work. Pictures of him are proudly displayed on a side wall at the front of the modest-sized shop.

Currywurst may come *Mit Darm* or *Ohne Darm*: literally with or without intestines, meaning with or without the sausage skin. A portion apparently has a dizzying 1,000 calories, so be warned.

Boulette
Often sold side by side with different types of sausages, the *Boulette* (from the French word for little ball) is a hamburger-like meat ball and a fast-food favourite. This was introduced into Berlin by the French Huguenots.

Main Courses and Side Dishes

More substantial typically Berlin food are *Kasseler Rippen*, *Brandenburger Landente*, *Berliner Leber* and the famous *Eisbein*. The *Kasseler Rippen* is salted and smoked pork chops served usually with potatoes and sauerkraut. The *Brandenburger Landente* is a duck stuffed with onions, apples and herbs with a crispy skin mostly accompanied by red cabbage and potato dumplings, and the *Berliner Leber* is a chunk of liver perched on a bed of mashed potatoes and topped with onions and apple slices. The *Eisbein* is a sizeable portion of pig's trotter, served with sauerkraut, potatoes and *Erbspuree* (mashed split peas).

Apart from boiled potatoes, a meat dish may also be served with potato dumplings (*Klößen* or *Knödeln*) or French fries (called *Pommes frites*, like in French, or simply *Pommes*).

In the eastern parts of Berlin, you will find dishes like *Soljanka* (a Russian soup) and *Shopska* (Bulgarian tomato, cucumber and white cheese salad) or references to a style of cooking *Nach Böhmischer Art* (in Bohemian style). These are influences from Russia and other east European countries picked up by the east Germans during DDR times when they went on holiday to these countries.

Brandenburger Landente is often served as a tasty main course.

Mushrooms

The abundant forests in and around Berlin are full of mushrooms in late summer and autumn. The *Steinpilze* and *Pfifferlinge* are the chart-toppers and expensive. Many locals pick their own mushrooms, and some actually sell them in street corners. Since some mushrooms are poisonous, if you're no expert yourself, stick to the market stalls and supermarkets.

When in season, many restaurants offer *Pfifferlinge*-themed dishes.

Vegetables

Germans may not traditionally eat too much vegetables, but meat dishes are often accompanied by red cabbage. They (especially the younger generation) are, however, becoming more health (and figure) conscious, so vegetables are gaining popularity. Carrots, beans, cauliflower, spinach and all types of salad leaves are now sold in the supermarkets as well as finding their place in restaurants and other eateries.

One vegetable that is treated with the utmost reverence by Germans is the *Spargel* (asparagus). This prima donna makes a brief appearance between April to June. It's mainly the white asparagus that is received with so much adoration. During the season, restaurants can devote a lot of space on their menus to asparagus, whether as a side dish, a main or a soup. Adventurous types have moved on to asparagus desserts (asparagus mousse, anyone?) as well, and a confectionery in Bayreuth has apparently also created asparagus pralines.

Spices, Herbs and Condiments

Germans don't normally like spicy food, and a mustard marked *scharf* (meaning very spicy) is already considered too spicy by most. *Mittelscharf* (medium spicy) is the most popular, and often eaten with sausages. Garlic 'stinks' too much and you often hear Germans apologising for the smell as they had eaten some garlic the night before!

Parsley, chives, laurels, thyme, cinnamon, caraway and juniper berries are the usual herbs and spices used in German cooking. Basil, sage and oregano have become more common recently with the increased popularity of Italian cuisine.

Apart from mustard, two other rather ubiquitous condiments are mayonnaise and *Remoulade* (mayonnaise with herbs added). Many fish dishes come with *Remoulade*. Mayonnaise is so widely applied to all types of food that I once had mayonnaise slapped on my Spanish omelette. Yuks. *Meerrettich* (horseradish) is another favourite.

Bread

If there's any German food that can rival the variety of sausages, it's bread. Most Germans prefer their bread dark, not the fluffy white bread so loved by the British, although white bread (*Weißbrot*) is available. The bread is often made with rye-wheat flour, wholegrain, multi-grain or sourdough. The rolls (*Brötchen*) very often come topped with pumpkin, sunflower or poppy seeds. *Schrippen* are a type of *Brötchen* in Berlin. They are plain white rolls that are sold very cheaply. The other popular Berlin *Brötchen* is called *Schusterjunge* (cobbler boy), and is made from a wheat and rye flour mix.

Bread is so much a part of German diet that the names of meals refer to it: *Abendbrot* (evening bread) is what Germans call dinner and *Brotzeit* (bread time) is a coffee-break.

Desserts

Walk past any confectionery and you can wave goodbye to your diet. The array of cakes and tarts on display is simply too tempting. The famous Blackforest cherry cake, the *Schwarzwälder Kirschtorte,* loaded with cherries and cream, is really worth the half an hour jogging to work it off. German doughnuts come without a hole in the centre; in other parts of Germany, they call doughnuts *Berliners*, but the Berliners (as in the people) call them *Pfannkuchen*. Elsewhere in Germany, *Pfannkuchen* means pancakes, though.

Another all-time German favourite is *Rote Grütze*, a mixture of different red-coloured berries and currants cooked in its own juice and thickened with cornstarch (traditionally with sago).

WHAT BERLINERS DRINK
Alcoholic Drinks
Beer

Among all alcoholic drinks, Germany is best known for its excellent beer, and for good reason. As long ago as 1516, a German beer purity law, the *Reinheitsgebot*, was passed by Duke Wilhelm IV of Bavaria. It stipulated that only barley, yeast, hops and water were permitted ingredients for brewing beer. Although no longer officially a German law nowadays, many German brewers still faithfully follow the purity traditon.

Like sausages and bread, there is a wide variety of beers (about 4,000) produced in Germany. Lager (*Pilsner*) is popular with Berliners, and the city's breweries produce a variety of *Pilsner* beers, as well as darker beers such as *Schwarzbier* and *Bock*. But Berlin's most famous beer is the *Berliner Weisse mit Schuss*, a light, sour wheat beer sweetened with either raspberry

> To reduce the alcohol content, beer is often mixed with Sprite or lemonade, and this mixed drink is known as *Radlermaß* (or *Radler*) in South Germany and *Alsterwasser* in North Germany.

or woodruff syrup, which turns the beer into a red or green coloured drink respectively. These are served in huge wine glasses rather than beer mugs.

As a beer advertisement stated, beer makes thirst worth it!

Wine

Wine is seeing a surge in popularity, especially in establishments that serve French, Italian and Spanish cuisine. Oenophiles have no problems finding excellent international wine in Berlin. German wine does not enjoy the same reputation as its beer, although there are fans of German white wine, some of which are very good. *Riesling* is king in Germany while *Gewürztraminer* is also popular. German wine mainly comes from the southern and western parts of the country. There are two broad categories of wine: *Tafelwein* (nothing to shout about wine) and *Qualitätswein*. The latter is sub-divided into *Qualitätswein*

eines bestimmten Anbaugebietes and *Qualitätswein mit Prädikat* (the finest).

In winter, especially over the Christmas and New Year period, Germans nation-wide quaff mulled wine (*Glühwein*) by the litres. It's also one of the items that give the Christmas markets their characteristic scent.

The German sparkling wine is called *Sekt* (as the French have a trademark on the name 'Champagne', which can only be used for sparkling wine from the French province with that name). Many German bubblies range from very drinkable to good.

Other Alcoholic Drinks
Other alcoholic drinks which are widely consumed are a vodka-like drink, *Weizendoppelkorn*, and herb liqueurs like *Jägermeister* and *Kümmerling*.

Non-alcoholic Drinks
Coffee, Tea and Chocolate
Coffee is preferred over black tea by many Germans, but the latter is widely available. Germans are also fond of herbal

teas like camomile, peppermint, *Yogi Tee* (a mixed spice tea) and rose-hip. Hot chocolate is a winter favourite.

Other Drinks

Apart from the international soft-drink best-sellers like Coke and Pepsi, *Apfelschorle* (half apple juice and half sparkling water) is also popular throughout Germany. Packaged fruit juices and lemon tea also fly off the shelves quickly. Another mixed drink, *Spezi* (half Cola, half orange) is also quite a hit. It's commonly sold under the brand names *Schwip Schwap* (by Pepsi Co) or *Mezzo Mix* (by Coca Cola company).

Nowadays, healthy drinks like aloe vera and drinking *joghurt* are also quite the rage.

Other popular dairy-based drinks are *Buttermilch* (buttermilk), and *Ayran*, a liquid joghurt with Turkish origins.

Mineral Water

The one thing you will quickly notice is that Germans like their mineral water carbonated, referred to as *Sprudel* or *mit Kohlensäure*. Some of the brands come with varying degrees of carbonation. If you prefer your water non-carbonated, ask for *Stilles Wasser* or *ohne Kohlensäure*.

FOREIGN INFLUENCES

With such a high immigration population, you can expect Berlin to have a Benetton-ad variety of food. Turkish, Greek and Italian food places are omnipresent. There are also Spanish, Mexican, Indian, Thai, Vietnamese, Japanese, Moroccan, Jewish.....really, quite a United Nations representation. Many of them unfortunately tweak their delicious cuisine to suit German palates, so true natives of these countries won't find the food too authentic.

The best example of how an immigrant dish became a national bestseller after being modified to suit German taste is the *Döner Kebap*. In the 1970s, a Turkish immigrant in Kreuzberg added sauce and salad to his dry-ish grilled meat on *pide* (a Turkish bread) to make it more appealing to Germans. The result: the *Döner Kebap* is an extremely popular fast food in Berlin today and comes dangerously close to upstaging the *Currywurst*.

THE DIFFERENT MEALS OF THE DAY
Breakfast (*Frühstück*)

The traditional German breakfast consists of hard-boiled eggs, different types of rolls eaten with cheese, ham and cold cuts, jam and butter, and washed down with juice and coffee. But the average German with a busy schedule nowadays simply down some toast, *müsli* or cornflakes on a weekday, taking no more than a hasty quarter to half an hour for this meal. On weekends, Germans still like to have a drawn-out breakfast, especially if there are house guests. The attention to breakfast can be seen in the special permission for bakeries to open for a few hours on Sunday mornings so that Germans can pick up fresh rolls for breakfast. This picking-up-fresh-rolls ritual is performed as religiously as (or whisper it, even more religiously than) going to church.

It's not uncommon that Germans grab a nibble and coffee in the late morning, to stave off hunger pangs before lunch time; this is the same thing as the British 'elevenses'.

> Hotels in Berlin often serve the full German breakfast. Not a few Americans have been dismayed at the miserly spread of a German breakfast, being used to a larger offering of breakfast buffets. Luckily, buffet brunch is now offered by many hotels and eateries on Sundays in Berlin where hearty eaters can have their fill.

Lunch (*Mittagessen*)

Lunch is traditionally the main meal of the day, although nowadays busy, working people or calorie-counting ones may just grab a sandwich or a light salad. Many big German companies do have their own canteens which serve substantial hot meals to their employees, though. Germans like to lunch at noon sharp.

Tea-time (*Kaffee und Kuchen*)

This 'coffee and cakes' ritual is time-honoured. Working people hardly have the time for this luxury anymore during the work-week, but pensioners and other Germans who can afford the time observe and enjoy it. It's not only about the pot of coffee and the various types of cakes that make *Kaffee und Kuchen* so attractive; it's the *gemütlichkeit* (cosiness) of sitting around with family and/or friends to natter.

Coffee klatsch is, incidentally, derived from the German *Kaffeeklatsch*, which means 'coffee-chat'.

Sometimes, instead of inviting you for dinner, Germans may ask you over for *Kaffee und Kuchen*. This shouldn't be seen as any 'lesser' an invitation, as Germans set great store by this meal.

Dinner/Supper (*Abendessen/Abendbrot*)

In the old German tradition, the evening meal is a light meal of bread and cold cuts. This is why this meal is sometimes referred to as *Abendbrot* (evening bread). But things change with the generations, and as more and more people meet friends in the evening for a meal and drinks, dinner has become an important meal, making *Abendessen* (literally evening eating/food) a more appropriate word.

THE DIFFERENT TYPES OF EATERIES
Snack Kiosks (*Imbissbuden*)

Berlin has a wide range of eateries catering to all budgets, from the easy-on-the pocket *Imbissbuden* to the astronomical fine-dining restaurants.

Two of the most famous snack kiosks are possibly Ku'damm 195 and Konnopke (under U-Bahnhof Eberswalder Straße), said to have the best *Currywurst*. But it's easy to find snack kiosks all over Berlin, selling either sausages and *Bouletten* or *Döner Kebap*. The kiosks often have little standing tables for customers. Some kiosks sell the Middle Eastern favourite, *Falafel* (deep-fried chick pea balls).

There are also vendors who sell just hot-dogs for an affordable €1.50. These are kiosk-less vendors, who simply have the hot-dog 'stand' slung over their necks.

Snack Shops and *Stehcafés*

A little more expensive than kiosks, there are shops which sell all sorts of bread and ready-made sandwiches. Some

even have ready-made salad, pastries and cakes. Many offer a small eating area, where you sort of lean-sit on a wedge but have a table for your food. Kamps Bäckerei is one such popular sandwich place. Others are essentially fish places where you can get fish burger sandwiches, fish fingers or a fish fillet with side-dishes, ranging from €3–8 in the city centre. Nordsee is one of the more popular chains of seafood shop.

The coffee brands, Tchibo and Eduscho, have *Stehcafés* (standing cafes) where you can get a good cafeine injection and cakes. It's mostly standing room only, hence the standing tables. The rest of the space is given to selling their other non-coffee products, from houshold items, leather shoes, clothing to underwear. Not all outlets are *Stehcafés*; some sell only coffee and those tempting products which you don't really need but buy anyway because of the reasonable prices.

American chains like Dunkin' Donuts, McDonald's and McCafe offer mid-priced sandwiches, cakes and pastries, of course.

Eating Places within Shopping Centres and Departmental Stores

Within some shopping centres such as Quartier 205 on Friedrichstraße (next door to Galeries Lafayette at Quartier 207), Das Schloss (in Steglitz-Zehlendorf) and the Arkaden (Potsdamer Platz), you'll find foodcourts offering an array of international cuisine for reasonable prices. The Arkaden has also cafes and bars on the first floor (US second floor) offering bagels, Asian food and a famous gelato place, which are often packed.

KaDeWe has the famous 6th floor filled with gourmet food and many self-service but stylish and pricey snack bars offering even lobsters. The bar stools seem always occupied by some chic-looking person taking a much needed break after an exhausting shopping spree balancing on Manolo Blahniks. On the 7th floor is a spacious self-service restaurant, the Wintergarten.

Foodcourts such as this provide a variety of cuisine at affordable prices and a comfortable place to take a break from your shopping.

A worthy rival to KaDeWe's gourmet floor is the basement of Galeries Lafayette, although the focus here is decidedly French.

Food places are often located in the basement, or right on the top floor of department stores and shopping centres.

Cafés

With such a strong 'coffee and cakes' culture, it's no surprise that there are plenty of good cafés in Berlin. Most cafés serve breakfast as well. Cafe Einstein, one of the popular ones, has a few outlets and the one on Unter den Linden near the Brandenburger Tor is said to be a favourite breakfast meeting place of German politicians and other hangers-on. Also on Unter den Linden, Operncafé im Opernpalais is another revered coffee-and-cake place. Cafe Wintergarten in the Literaturhaus on Fasanenstrasse is another oft-cited café in all Berlin guides.

There are many more cafés in Berlin which are well worth a visit; you'll find them listed in the many Berlin guides or discover them yourself when you start moseying around the city.

If you feel homesick for Starbucks, there are many outlets in Berlin such as on Friedrichstrasse, Ku'damm, and at Potsdamer Platz.

Opernpalais Cafe is a cosy coffee-and-cake place popular with Berliners.

Posh Places

Posh restaurants have sprung up in Berlin since its becoming the capital. Many top restaurants are, but not exclusively, to be found in hotels: examples are Vox (Grand Hyatt), Hugo's (Inter-Continental), Die Quadriga (Brandenburger Hof), First Floor (Hotel Palace Berlin) and Lorenz-Adlon-Gourmet (in Adlon, naturally). Most of them are Michelin-starred. But some of the lauded gourmet restaurants do not belong to any hotel, such as the Facil, Margaux and Vau, all proud owners of Michelin stars as well. The Käfer im Bundestag, a restaurant perched on the Reichstag rooftop also provides a dining experience not easily forgotten.

Berlin today has countless *avant garde* restaurants or historic heavyweights (Borchardt, Lutter & Wegner) and gourmands will never be short of places to go.

Tipping

Although service and tax is already included in restaurant bills, the norm is to round up the bill. If the bill amount is high, or it's an expensive restaurant, a 10 per cent tip is added.

Tips should not be left on the table. You should give the tip directly to the waiter/waitress.

Example 1: your total bill is €37 and you wish to round it up to €40. You have only a €50 note. Give the €50 to the waiter and say '40'. S(he) will then give you back €10.

Example 2: your total bill is €37, you wish to round it up to €40, and have exactly €40. Give the €40 to the waiter and say '*Das stimmt so*' (It's ok like that).

Caution!

Example 3: Your bill is €20 and you have only a €50 note. NEVER say '*Danke*' or murmur 'Here's €50' when handing the note over! The waiter will think you're Bill Gates and wish to give a tip of €30. Say specifically how much you wish to pay e.g. '25' when handing the waiter the €50 note.

Operating Hours

If cafés and restaurants open for breakfast, they do so usually at 9:00 am. Others will start at noon and end only at

Enjoy a unique dining experience at this floating restaurant on Müggelspree.

midnight or in the early hours of the next morning. Since this is Berlin we're talking about, the city is true to the reputation it acquired since the Roaring Twenties. Many bars and clubs let their customers party all Saturday night through to Sunday morning, with some edgy ones even until the sun rises.

The party scene is so attractive that many Brits are heading to Berlin in droves for their stag parties, not least because drinks cost so much less than in the UK. Some even come replete with costumes (e.g. Superman, Batman and Robin), drink themselves under the table, then hop onto a cheap flight home the next day.

Smoking

Since January 2008, smoking indoors is banned. But no smoker Berliner worth his cigarettes was going to take that lying down. One angry Berliner actually punched a hapless waiter trying to get him to smoke outside. From January to July 2008, bar and café owners could decide whether to allow smoking on their premises, and many put the ashtrays back on the table after angry reactions from Berliners. Many thought up ways of allowing smoking without breaking the rules. One built a cigarette smoke outlet where a customer could thrust his uppermost torso outside to smoke without having to leave the place. Inner courtyard smoking places for patrons became successful flirting venues. Other not-so-lucky establishments had customers go outside apparently for a smoke, but never came back to pay the bill.

Table Sharing

Germans have a practical habit of sharing tables with complete strangers. This doesn't happen in posh restaurants, but when it's really crowded at ordinary restaurants and cafés, people may come up to you and ask if they could sit at your table when they spot the empty seats. It's basically churlish to refuse, even if you're not used to it. But you shouldn't worry that they'll try to chat you up, because it's not done. They will simply thank you, sit down and mind their own business, and you don't have any obligation to be friendly to them either. When either you or they leave, a polite '*Auf Wiedersehen*' is said, but no other exchanges are expected.

Splitting the Bill

When dining with a group of German friends, it's not unusual for everyone to pay for his/her own bill separately and directly to the waiter. German waiters are used to this, that's why they always ask when you call for the bill, '*Zusammen oder getrennt?*' (together or separate?).

The waiters don't bat an eyelid when they have to go round the whole table of 12 persons, and having individuals say 'I'm paying for me and my wife over there....' and the waiter will just add up all the food and drinks consumed by this couple, before moving on to the next person. It's not often that one person first pays for the entire group, then splits up the bill among the friends later.

WATERING HOLES

Drinking can be done at different types of places running the gamut from bars, Irish pubs, wine bars and *Kneipen* (a sort of pub), although it's not easy to distinguish between the different types sometimes. Unaccompanied women might want to avoid some of the traditional *Kneipen* in working class districts, which are filled with beer guzzling testosterone-fueled customers. Try instead the charming Zum Nussbaum (in Nikolaiviertel), Zur Kneipe (Rankestraße 9), Zur Letzten Instanz (Waisenstraße14-16), or Ratskeller Köpenick (basement of the Rathaus Köpenick in the old city centre of Köpenick) for a rustic ambience.

There are plenty of trendy bars, and as they tend to cluster in popular places like Prenzlauer Berg, one can just bar hop through the evening. 'Afterhour-Partys', as the Berliners call them, are also becoming hot-spots. At these places (e.g. Bar

The charming Zum Nussbaum is an ideal place to experience a *Kneipe* atmosphere.

25, Delicious Doughnuts, Weekend, Berghain), the party goes on till the sun rises or at some, even throughout the weekend till Monday morning.

If you like the Oktoberfest type of environment (beer drinking in the open air) then a *Biergarten* would fit the bill.

Beach bars are also popular in summer. A very popular one is the Strandbar Mitte (next to Bode Museum. See http://www.strandbar-mitte.de), where one can drink lounging on deck-chairs and *Strandkörbe* (German sofa-like beach chairs) among imported palm trees. There's no swimming possibilities here, though. In the east, there's the Gestrandet on the shores of the Müggelsee, next to the Spreetunnel (see http://www.gestrandet-am-mueggelsee.de).

Berlin has lots of gay and lesbian bars, some of which are for men or for women only.

ENJOYING FREIZEIT
IN BERLIN

CHAPTER 7

'Berlin is poor, but sexy.'
—Klaus Wowereit, mayor of Berlin, when making Berlin's
case to Germany's highest court for increased federal aid to
help cover the additional costs of being Germany's capital.

THIS FAMOUS QUIP OF WOWEREIT just about sums up the city. Although financially in dire straits, the city manages to maintain three opera houses, more than 300 theatre stages, some 174 museums and a comprehensive cultural programme, with events even in the dead of winter. The city practically has double of everything, as a legacy of the division of the city. Add on the fact that Berlin has always been a magnet for the creative types, the result is the wealth of cultural venues you see today. Apart from higher-brow entertainment, there are many other leisure pursuits available: indoors or outdoors, sedentary or sporty, young or old, there's something for everyone.

There's not only plenty to do in Berlin, but also plenty of time to do it.

Most Germans enjoy an entitlement of 30 working days of holiday a year, that is, six entire weeks dedicated to *Freizeit* (leisure time). Berliners have nine official public holidays, so if you add these to the holiday entitlement, each Berliner has about 50 days off a year. We've heard how serious Germans are about everything they undertake; it obviously includes holidays.

The summer vacation for schoolchildren in Berlin is a seven-week long stretch, usually in July and August. The exact vacation dates change each year, to stagger with school vacation in other states. So July and August are traditionally the months when Berliners (especially those with school-going children) scoot off on vacation, usually to somewhere where they can work on the sun-tan. Berliners also enjoy spending their summers in the *Schrebergarten*.

Schrebergarten

If you look out of the S-Bahn window, you might see a congested plot of land with many tiny houses packed close together like sardines, just below the train tracks. It's not a Berlin slum, but a *Schrebergarten*—a garden colony. Berliners rent a small piece of the land and put their green fingers to work on their Lilliputian plot. BBQs and sun-tanning also often take place here in summer. The garden colonies are all subject to rules and regulations with a formal leadership structure in place. This is Germany, remember?

The idea came from Dr. Daniel Gottlieb Moritz Schreber, a 19th century physician, who wanted children in Leipzig to have more exercise in the fresh air. He died before it could be implemented, but his son-in-law put the idea into practice, and the leasing out of small garden plots started from there.

The gardens came in handy during the hard times of World War I and II, as they were practical places to grow fresh fruits and vegetables, and even to live in after homes were destroyed in the war.

Before looking at the entertainment options, let's first take a peek at what Berliners usually get up to on those official public holidays.

PUBLIC HOLIDAYS

Date	What it Celebrates
1 January	New Year's Day (Neujahr)
Moveable date (usually in March/April)	Good Friday (Karfreitag)
Moveable date (the Monday after Good Friday)	Easter Monday (Ostermontag)
1 May	Labour Day (Tag der Arbeit)
Moveable Date (40 days after Easter)	Ascension (Christi Himmelfahrt)

Moveable Date (in May or June)	Whitsun/Pentacost Monday (Pfingstmontag)
3 October	Day of Germany Unity (Tag der Deutschen Einheit)
25 December	Christmas Day (1. Weihnachtstag)
26 December	Boxing Day (2. Weihnachtstag)

PUBLIC HOLIDAYS
Karfreitag und Ostern (Good Friday and Easter)

Good Friday commemorates the cruxification of Jesus Christ, and the religious attend church services. Non Christians and atheists basically enjoy the day off. Easter is a happier occasion than Good Friday, as it celebrates Christ's resurrection. The faithful go to church, but for the rest, it's just a lovely long weekend. The commercial side of Easter is celebrated with all types of chocolate eggs. Parents of young children organise chocolate egg hunts around the house or garden, which I suspect give them as much pleasure as they do the kids.

Tag der Arbeit (Labour Day)

May Day is often a field day for anti-globalisation, anti-war and anti-whatever protests in many countries. In Berlin, rioting in Kreuzberg is a guaranteed May Day event. It's a tradition that goes back decades to 1987. That year, 900 youths in that district—then a ghetto for the disaffected members of society—clashed with police for 12 hours, looting and setting cars on fire. In the years that followed, police handled the annual May Day riots in Kreuzberg with tough measures; water canons, truncheons and arrests. Realising that such measures were not working, they changed tactics around 2005, adopting a conflict management approach, and banning glass bottles and cans at street parties. The riots, which have since spilled over to some parts of Friedrichshain and Prenzlauer Berg, seem to be less violent in recent years. But that's speaking in relative terms; in 2008, 138 rioters were arrested and 90 policemen injured.

Christi Himmelfahrt (Ascension)

The date for Ascension is also moveable, falling 40 days after Easter. This feast celebrates the ascension of Christ to heaven. For the not-so-religious, this day is also celebrated as Father's Day. Father's Day is like a stag party in Germany; the men go out boozing and celebrating together, rather than spend it with the family.

Pfingsten (Whitsun/Pentacost)

This is yet another moveable religious holiday, observed without too much overt celebration.

Tag der Deutschen Einheit (Day of German Unity)

This day commemorates German reunification. As the breaching of the Berlin Wall was the most powerful symbol of reunification, official celebrations take place around the Brandenburger Tor. Usually some 500,000 congregate along the stretch from Straße des 17. Juni to the Brandenburger Tor for a free concert featuring Germany's top bands and other entertainment.

Weihnachten (Christmas) and 'Weihnukkah'

Christmas is the most celebrated festival, whether the person is a devout Christian or not.

The period from the 1 December to Christmas is the Advent period. The *Adventskranz*, (Advent wreath) with four candles, is brought out and one candle lit on each Sunday. For children, there is the more exciting *Adventskalender*, as each day they get to open a 'window' on the calendar and get a surprise gift such as a piece of chocolate.

The 6th December is St. Nicholas (St. Nikolaus) Day. Children put out their shoes the evening before and hope that St. Nicholas will fill them with candies and chocolates, because they've been good. It's filled with twigs, if they've been naughty, but I don't know of any parent who's so cruel! If it sounds like Santa Claus tradition to you, it's because the St. Nicholas tradition is the pre-cursor to present-day Santa Claus. The St.Nicholas tradition is widely practised in Europe. According to legend, the original St. Nicholas was a bishop in Myra (now a part of Turkey) who used to throw bags of gold through the window of a poor family, so that the three daughters could use them as a dowry to get married. Hence,

Chocolates and candies for the sweet-toothed during the Christmas period.

St. Nicholas is depicted as a bishop-like figure, sometimes holding a staff.

Sweets and chocolates, preferably a chocolate figure of the saint, are also handed out to adults. In the office, the boss usually hands out chocolate St. Nicholas to employees. Some colleagues exchange goodies as well.

One of the highlights of the Christmas season is the *Weihnachtsmärkte* (Christmas markets). There are at least 60 Christmas markets across Berlin, with the most popular ones at Gendarmenmarkt, Opernpalais (just opposite Humboldt University), the old city centre in Spandau, Potsdamer Platz and in the Kulturbrauerei (Prenzlauer Berg). There's also a special Christmas market for children at the Citadel in Spandau. They usually open on 26 November and many carry on till 31 December. The markets have a lovely atmosphere, in spite of the bitter cold. *Glühwein* (mulled wine) will surely warm up any frozen visitor and one quickly forgets the temperature with the different scents wafting around. Typical German Christmas confectionery—*Stollen*

The Opernpalais Christmas market is a lively, festive affair and well loved by both Berliners and tourists.

Stollen, *spekulatius* and *lebkuchen*—enjoy these popular German Christmas confectionery.

(fruit cake), *Lebkuchen* (ginger bread biscuit) and *Spekulatius* (spiced biscuit/cookie)—tempt you at every corner. The famous German marzipan, made into all sorts of shapes, such as fruits, are also popular. Handicraft are also sold in the markets, including the traditonal wooden nutcrakers and pyramids.

Nowadays, all sorts of entrepreneurs sell their crafts at Christmas markets,too, and you might see French cheeses, a Moroccan or an Asian food stall among all the traditionally German offerings.

Baking Christmas biscuits/cookies at home is also a traditional ritual, usually done together with the children.

Christmas is *Das Fest der Liebe* (the Feast of Love) and spent with close family members.

On Christmas eve, shops and offices would close by midday, if they open at all. By the afternoon, you shouldn't be telephoning acquaintances anymore, as it's family time. The tradition was for the children to enter a locked room where the Christmas tree was, upon the ringing of a bell, and then the family sang Christmas carols together. The afternoon

The Christmas tree tradition is said to have originated from Germany and you will find the lavishly decorated trees in homes and shopping malls.

of 24 December is therefore rather sacred, even if modern families don't follow this ritual anymore.

The Christmas tree is traditionally decorated only on Christmas eve, and the children are not allowed to see the tree until fully festooned. The Christmas tree tradition originates in Germany and is said to have been brought to the UK by Prince Albert, the German Consort of Queen Victoria.

Christmas eve dinner traditionally features duck, goose or a roast. Sausages and potato salad are also popular with some Germans, although it seems rather under-festive! After dinner, the presents are exchanged and opened.

The Jewish holiday of Hanukkah (meaning 're-dedication' in Hebrew) celebrates the victory of the Maccabees over the Greco-Syrians in 165 B.C. Known as the 'Festival of Lights', it commemorates the struggles of the early Jews for religious freedom and their reclaiming the Temple of Jerusalem, which Antiochus had ordered the Greco-Syrian soldiers to destroy. The start of Hanukkah (a period of eight days) is calculated according to the Hebrew calendar, so it falls on a different day each year. In some years, it falls in December, so the month becomes a festive one for both German Christians and Jews.

The Jewish Museum lit up in celebration of Hanukkah.

The Jewish Museum in Berlin traces an interesting combined holiday, Weihnukkah (mixing the words *Weihnachten* and *Hanukkah*) to the 19th century, when many middle-class Jewish families in Germany celebrated Christmas as a secular holiday and put up Christmas trees and exchanged gifts, treating it as part of the German culture, rather than of any religious significance.

The Jewish Museum holds a special Hanukkah market in its garden, selling Hanukkah favourites such as *latkes* (potato pancakes) and *sufganiot* (doughnuts), *kosher* food, *menorahs* (special candle holders for Hanukkah), books and crafts. The market stays open pass Hanukkah (e.g. it ended on 12 December in 2007) through till 31 December, and provides a captivating way for non-Jews to get a better insight into the Festival of Lights and Jewish culture over the holiday season.

Neujahr (New Year's Day)

A week or so before the New Year, you will find a bounty of marzipan figures in the form of pigs, pigs with clover and chimney sweeps in the shops, as these are all symbols of luck for the Germans. The few days before the New Year,

Marzipan figures in the forms of pigs and chimney sweeps are sold in shops during the New Year as symbols of luck for the Germans.

it's common for people to wish one another, including sales personnel '*Einen guten Rutsch ins Neue Jahr*' (literally 'Good Slide into the New Year').

Shops and offices close on New Year's Eve (called *Sylvester*) latest by early afternoon, so that everyone can get ready to party the night away. While Christmas is spent huddled with family, New Year is dedicated to friends and partying. The biggest party in Berlin is the one that stretches for 2 km from Brandenburger Tor to Siegessäule (the Victory Column), attracting around a million party-goers each year. Pop bands perform on stage and at midnight, a 10 minute-long fireworks display greets the new year. Those who can't bear the crush at this party turn up at the Wasserturm (Water Tower) in Prenzlauer Berg or the Bowl Arena in Spandau for a smaller party and fireworks display. Others set off their own fireworks (which can be bought even at supermarkets and drugstores shortly before the New Year) at home. On this, please note that fireworks are allowed only over the New Year period.

Some book tickets for glitzy gala dinners as early as in summer. Others head for the countless bars and clubs. The religious head for New Year services in church.

Dinner for One

Apart from the fireworks, there is one other German new year institution: *Dinner for One*. This is not a gala dinner in solitude, but a British short film that plays faithfully every New Year's eve on many German TV channels. The story focuses around aristocrat Miss Sophie and her butler James. Miss Sophie celebrates her 90th birthday with a dinner with friends, and the butler faithfully fills in for the dinner guests, who have all unfortunately passed on, imitating their voices and drinking on their behalf. The punch line in this comedy is the butler's queries before each course: "The same procedure as last year, Miss Sophie?" To which Miss Sophie replies, "The same procedure as EVERY year, James." The last query is made by James just as the sprightly sweetheart heads off to bed (wink, wink). You get the joke. The astounding thing is that this film has never played in the UK, or the US for that matter. It seems like it had only a short run in Australia. But the Germans think this is like *Mr. Bean* or *Monty Python* in the UK, so whenever they meet a Brit, or any native English-speaker, they assume we've all grown up with this comedy. Our blank looks confuse them thoroughly. It's hard for them to understand why any English speaker has never seen this film, while every German can quip the punch line almost without an accent.

Those who opt to bring in the New Year at home will have a nice feast (often carp), and have a hearty laugh over *Dinner for One*. The show also plays at some theatres over the New Year.

Other New Year staples are the *Silversterlauf* or *Neujahrslauf*, which are New Year's Eve or New Year's Day marathons between 2–10 km, taking place in several places around Berlin. Circuses are also a typical New Year feature.

On New Year's Day, some museums are open for about five hours. The Zoo is also open.

OTHER EVENTS

Apart from the celebrations on some public holidays, there are countless other festivals and events, some of which show off a rarely seen side of the Germans—indulging in raucous, raw fun. The repertoire is wide: *mardi gras* type events, jazz festivals, pop concerts, concerts with a classical bent, an international film festival, a music industry event, and even performances by travelling entertainers. Below are some of the more prominent ones:

Rosenmontag Parade (Monday before Ash Wednesday)

The *Karneval* (Carnival) is basically associated with the Rhineland, like *Oktoberfest* is with Bavaria. However, Berliners have started to celebrate this event with gusto. Although the carnival season starts at 11:00 am on 11 November (the focus on 11 is deliberate), the festivities really pick up only in spring, especially just before Ash Wednesday (when it ends).

There are parties in Berlin clubs where guests should come in costumes. On Rosenmontag, the Monday before Ash Wednesday, the *Karneval* parade is a tradition. In Berlin, a parade of about 60 floats go down Ku'damm, with about a million people lining the streets to join in the fun and grab the sweets raining down on them.

Karneval der Kulturen (around Pentacost/Whitsunday)

This carnival of cultures celebrates Berlin's cultural diversity. A parade of floats, street festivals and parties turn Berlin Kreuzberg into a mini United Nations pulsating with music from different lands.

Waldbühne Open Air Concert (June)

The Berlin Philharmonic Orchestra ends its season traditionally with an open-air concert in the Waldbühne, a huge outdoor venue in a natural valley. The ambience is deliberately relaxed, with people leaving their finery behind and bringing instead their children, champagne, caviar and other picnic essentials (including insect repellent). Starting at 8:15 pm, candles are lit when it gets dark, creating a romantic atmosphere. The conductor (currently Sir Simon Rattle), musicians and guest performers all dress down as well.

The last piece is always the Berlin classic, '*Berliner Luft*', and everyone sings his or her lungs out, off-key or on, creating an incredible rapport between orchestra and audience.

Open Air Classic (July)

The beautiful square, Gendarmenmarkt, is the venue for this concert.

Love Parade (July)

This parade must be mentioned, although it's seen its last gasp. This techno music parade was so much a part of Berlin and so successful in the 1990s that millions of people, including international visitors, came to join in the fun, dancing and partying as the floats drive by with skimpily dressed people gyrating on them. The parade is no longer held in Berlin.

Christopher Street Day Parade (July)

The openly gay mayor of Berlin always joins in the festivities with his partner. If you still don't believe that Teutonic folks can let their hair down, just go to this parade.

Tanz im August (August)

The most awaited dance event in Berlin, this dance festival takes place over three weeks mainly at HAU (short for Hebbel am Ufer, Kreuzberg) and Sophiensäle (Mitte).

International Berlin Beer Festival (August)

Touted as the longest beer garden in the world, this 2 km (1.2 miles) long stretch of beer offers attracts 800,000 drinkers each year to sample beers from different countries. In 2008, 260 breweries from 86 countries offered 1,800 beer specialities. *Prost!*

Berlin Marathon (September)

The participants include the disabled and inline-skaters. There is always a huge crowd cheering the competitors on as well. The huge mass of people brings traffic to a standstill for several hours.

Internationale Grüne Woche (January)

This 'International Green Week' is ten days of exhibition of the food industry, agriculture and horticulture from Germany and the world. The attraction for ordinary Berliners is the chance to sample all the free food and drinks for a €12 day ticket, or €25 season ticket.

Popkomm (Sept/October)

This is the pop festival of Europe, where stars and talents are presented in over 25 clubs. It's a summit for record labels, artistes and their management and fans.

Berlinale-Berlin International Film Festival (February)

It must be the Berliner humour. Why else would anyone want to have a film festival in the dead of winter? Female stars or female partners of stars are forced to brave the Berlin sub-zero temperatures as they pose on the red carpet in their décolleté-d Dior or Versace.

The festival attracts international film stars, and in turn attracts throngs of people to Potsdamer Platz, where the festival is held.

Listings Magazines

German Language

- *Tip*
- *Zitty*

English Language

- *Exberliner*

LEISURE PURSUITS

There is no dearth of possible activities to suit different tastes. As is obvious from the events listed above, classical or contemporary tastes are all catered for. So are indoor and outdoor preferences.

Classical Music

The Berliner Philharmoniker (better known as Berlin Philharmonic Orchestra internationally) is world famous, and was especially popular during the 35 years when Herbert von Karajan was its conductor. Currently under the baton of Briton, Sir Simon Rattle, the orchestra continues to enjoy immense respect. Other orchestras include the Deutsches Symphonie Orchester, the Rundfunk Sinfonieorchester Berlin and the Konzerthausorchester Berlin (formerly Berliner Sinfonieorchester). The classical concerts are mostly held in the grand dame, Philharmonie, and the Konzerthaus Berlin. Sometimes, they are held in the Universität der Künste, in one of the palaces or even in the open air. There are also numerous chamber orchestras such as the Ensemble Oriol and the Kammerorchester. For ambience, nothing beats the dinner and concert (performed by the Berlin Palace Orchestra) special in the baroque surroundings of the Grand Orangery, Schloss Charlottenburg.

Classical music recitals also take place in churches big and small all over Berlin.

Operas

There are three major opera houses: the Staatsoper Unter den Linden, Komische Oper and Deutsche Oper Berlin. The Staatsoper is under the leadership of Daniel Barenboim, famous not only as a conductor, but also for his role in promoting harmony among Arabs and Israelis. He co-founded with the late Palestinian-American intellectual, Edward Said, an orchestra of young Arab and Jewish musicians, based in Seville, Spain, called the West-Eastern Divan Orchestra. The Komische Oper's website (http://www.komische-oper-berlin. de) has short videos of the operas to let you sample them before you decide which to attend.

Theatres

Berlin's theatre scene was well known even way back in the 1920s. Theatre was crushed under the Nazis, but rose from the ashes after World War II ended. This development is best personified by Bertolt Brecht, one of the leading figures of Berlin theatre during the Weimar period, who fled Berlin and returned after the war to revive the Berliner Ensemble theatre and ran the place from 1948 to 1956 (then in communist East Berlin).

Apart from Berliner Ensemble, there are many other theatres in Berlin such as Deutsches Theater, HAU and Renaissance. The problem is that they are mainly in Deutsch, so those who are still struggling with the

German language will have to turn to the few which have performances in English. The most popular one is the English Theatre Berlin (formally called Friends of Italian Opera) at Fidicinstraße 40, Kreuzberg. Platypus Theater caters to the younger audience and is at Markgrafenstraße 87, in the city centre. Occasionally, English language productions feature in some theatres such as the Brotfabrik and Schaubühne am Lehniner Platz.

Dance
Both classical and modern dance groups in Berlin are of good quality. But dance companies face ever-growing problems with a shrinking state subsidy. The three ballet companies working within the opera houses became reduced to a single Staatsballett Berlin.

HAU, a consolidation of three former theatres- Hebbel Theater, Theater am Halleschen Ufer and Theater am Ufer, is a venue not only for theatre but also for contemporary dance. Another similar multi-faceted venue is the Sophiensäle. Dances can take place in the most unexpected of places too, such as defunct bomb shelters. A calendar of dance performances Germany-wide can be found at http://tanzkalender.de (German) and http://dance-germany.org (German/English).

Museums
If you're a museum buff, Berlin has enough museums to keep you riveted. The most famous main cluster is to be found on Museumsinsel (the name Museum island speaks for itself). Here, there's the Alte Nationalgalerie (19th century art), Altes Museum (it hosts the Egyptian museum until that moves to its renovated home in the Neues Museum around late 2009), Bode Museum (Byzantine art and sculptures and European antique furniture), Pergammon Museum (an archaeological museum, including imposing ancient Babylonian, Hellenistic and Roman architecture as well as beautiful Islamic art) and the Neues Museum (when repairs finish in late 2009, it will be home to the Egyptian museum and the Primeval and Early History collection currently in Charlottenburg).

Free admission

Every Thursday, admission to the state museums is free for the last four hours. There can be long queues, though, as many tour agencies cleverly free-load on the museums' generosity.

The other museum complexes are the Kulturforum, at Dahlem and around Schloss Charlottenburg.

Twice a year (August and January), there's the *Lange Nacht der Museen* (Long Night of the Museums), where some 80 museums open from 6:00 pm to 2:00 am. It's wildly popular, so expect crowds.

The decorum expected of visitors to the museum is very high. If you sit on the floor, lean against the wall, or remove your jacket when it gets too warm, the museum staff will promptly tell you it's forbidden, politely but very firmly. One winter evening, I left my coat at the cloakroom but kept my light cardigan on in case it got chilly. It got stuffy in the museum, and just as I was shrugging my cardigan off, a security guard whispered frantically behind me 'Don't remove it, don't remove it!' as if I had no clothes on under

The Alte Nationalgalerie houses one of the largest collections of 19th century sculptures and paintings in Germany.

An extensive collection of sculptures, Byzantine art and coins and medals can be viewed at the Bode Museum on Museumsinsel.

my cardigan. It was a security concern, not fear that I might be planning to do a striptease. They didn't want visitors walking around with a coat over their arms, as they could be hiding something.

Many museums have exhibits at a lower level, so that younger visitors or those in wheelchairs have no trouble viewing them. Many museums are beautiful buildings themselves, adding on to the pleasure of the visit.

There are museums all over Berlin, too many to list them all here. But just to highlight the diversity, here are a few of them: For German/Berlin history, visit the Deutsches Historisches Museum on Unter den Linden and The Story of Berlin on Ku'damm. The latter is filled with multi-media exhibits, so is particularly good for younger visitors who get fidgety in a traditional museum. The Museum Haus am Checkpoint Charlie focuses on the history of the Wall and the different means of escape attempted by desperate East Berliners. Some people rate it as a jumbled, rambling collection and not quite the 'harrowing experience' as they expected. But what the East Berliners experienced as documented cannot fail to move visitors.

The Jewish Museum (Kreuzberg), designed by Daniel Libeskind, features zig-zagging turns, slopes and voids, to evoke disorientation and loss and the destruction of Jewish life. The museum has a large collection of artefacts that tell the story of the Jews. The Kunstgewerbemuseum (Museum of Arts and Crafts) at the Kulturforum has a collection that makes it one of Europe's finest arts and crafts museums. A 'branch' of this, Schloss Köpenick's Kunstgewerbemuseum, has a smaller but still sumptious collection of interior decorations from the 16th to 18th centuries. The Schlossinsel, an island where the museum is situated, is itself worth the visit; an oasis of quiet on the River Dahme, it's perfect for reflection or for a a spot of lunch or kaffee und kuchen at the restaurant on the water's edge. In Dahlem, there's the museum complex, housing museums of ethnology, Indian art, East Asian art and European cultures.

A number of museums are also child-friendly. More on these under 'Berlin for Young and Young at Heart'.

The Jewish Museum designed by Daniel Libeskind is an unsual work of art and has a large collection of artefacts that provides insight into the history and lives of the Jews in Germany.

Art

At the Kulturforum, a cultural centre near Potsdamer Platz, there's the Gemäldegalerie (Picture Gallery) and the Neue Nationalgalerie (New National Gallery). Feast your eyes on the breathtaking, comprehensive collection of all European schools of painting at the Gemäldegalerie and the superb collection of modern art (20th century) at the Neue Nationalgalerie. A selected, but fine collection of paintings can also be marvelled at the Sammlung Berggruen (Berggruen's Collection) in Charlottenburg. Picasso fans must make it a point to visit this museum of Heinz Berggruen's collection, which has over 100 of Picasso's works. There are also more than 60 of Paul Klee's work and some 20 by Henri Matisse. Nicolas Berggruen, the son and heir of Heinz who passed away in 2007, has indicated the family's intention to expand the museum, as well as the likelihood of showing some of his own more contemporary collection, such as works by Andy Warhol, Damien Hirst and Jeff Koons.

For those preferring modern works, the Hamburger Bahnhof has works by Andy Warhol, Cy Twombly, Robert Rauschenberg, Roy Lichtenstein, Anselm Kiefer and Joseph Beuys. Here, you can also find exhibits from the Flick collection.

There are also many private galleries, for example around Charlottenburg and Sheunenviertel.

Contemporary and International Music

Some top jazz, rock and pop bands come by Berlin when they tour Europe. There are also festivals such as Jazzfest Berlin and Music Biennale Berlin (on alternate years). The Café Global at the Haus der Kulturen der Welt and the Werkstatt der Kulturen are the places to go for a taste of world music.

Clubbing and Other Nightlife

Berlin was known as a wild child during the Weimar days. Today, it's still famous for its partying nightlife. Nightlife in Berlin should perhaps be dubbed 'Night Alive'. There are clubs which continue till sunrise, and clubs whose clientele are very dressed down, or not dressed, to be precise (check out KitKatClub). Kreuzberg and Prenzlauer Berg are the current hot spots. Whatever your taste in music—techno, jazz, punk, hip hop—there's sure to be a joint somewhere where you can get your fill.

Clubs in Berlin are not so exclusive and expensive as they are in London and New York; one reason why many Brits leg it over to the German capital.

Film

Berlin is closely associated with the film industry. It was, after all, in Berlin that the Skladanowsky brothers showed the first moving picture to a paying audience in 1895.

There are many cinemas in Berlin, but it's the multiplexes that draw the crowds, showing mostly Hollywood blockbusters. The CinemaxX Potsdamer Platz and the Cinestar Sony Center are where you have the best chance of seeing films in their original version. Films shown elsewhere tend to be dubbed into German.

The highlight is, of course, the Berlinale (Germany's Oscar Night), which attracts big names from the industry to Potsdamer Platz, where the event is held.

Listings magazines *Tip* and *Zitty* are where you check what is playing where, and in what language.

Classification of Film Languages

- OF or OV (*Originalfassung*)—Original version
- OmU (*Originalfassung mit Untertiteln*)—Original version with German subtitles
- OmE (*Originalfassung mit Englischen Untertiteln*)—Foreign film with English subtitles

---

SPORTS AND FITNESS

Berlin is the sports capital of Germany, and major sporting events are held in this city, such as the football/soccer finals of the German Football Association (Deutscher Fußball Bund), the ISTAF Athletics Meeting and the international horse-jumping event (Internationales Reitturnier). The FIFA World Cup Final 2006 was also played in Berlin at the Olympic Stadium.

Berliners are very much into sports. Take running, for example; apart from the Berlin Marathon (September) and Berlin Half Marathon (April) which attract a large number of participants, there are the Berliner Neujahrslauf (New Year's run) on 1 January and 'Burn off the Christmas Goose' run on Boxing Day. If not participating themselves, they are enthusiastic spectators.

The State Sports Association Berlin (Landessportbund Berlin) provides information (in German) on the different types of sports and clubs available (http://www.lsb-berlin.org).

Participatory Sports
Jogging and Nordic Walking
The sheer number of parks and woods means avid joggers and walkers are spoilt for choice. Berliners are so fond of sports that you'll find some going through their paces even in sub-zero temperatures during winter. For the competitive runners, there are the organised marathons and runs.

Cycling
Cycling is part mode of transport and part sport for Berliners. You can get the free *Rad & Touren* programme guide from the Allgemeiner Deutscher Fahrrad Club (http://adfc.de) which

Explore Berlin on bike!

features some 580 one-day or longer guided cycling trips. Cycling route maps are also available. Make sure you lock your bikes when left unattended; in 2007, some 20,000 bikes were stolen in Berlin.

If you don't have your own bike, you can rent one from the German Railway company's 'Call a Bike' service or from the many private bicycle rental companies around town (e.g. Fahrradstation and Prenzl'berger Orange Bikes).

Guided bike-tours are also available (see http://berlinonbike. de). If you're not keen to use your own leg-power, you can hop onto a bike-taxi and be taken for a city tour by a 'driver'.

In-line Skating

In-line skating is also popular. Skaters have the same status as pedestrians, so they are legally not allowed to skate on the roads, although some do. Apart from skating on whatever paths they can find, there are also organised skate nights, where skaters are allowed onto the roads. Skate Night Berlin takes place every Sunday evening (7:30 pm to 12:00 midnight) from May to September. The event is not just purely for the fun of skating, but also as a protest to try to get better conditions and rights for skaters.

For more information, see http://skatespots.de.

Ice-skating and Other Winter Sports

In winter, you can have a go at ice-skating. There are indoor facilities (e.g. Horst-Dohm-Stadion in Wilmersdorf and Eisbahn Lankwitz in Steglitz) as well as two popular outdoor rinks at Potsdamer Platz and Bebelplatz (opposite the Humboldt University).

Potsdamer Platz also has a sort of toboggan run, where you can have rides on rubber rings. Tobogganing can also be done on any of Berlin's hill slopes if there is sufficient snow cover.

There's also the 'Gletscher', touted as the longest indoor piste in the world in Pankow (http://der-gletscher.de) for skiing and snowboarding.

Golf

Golf is quite established in Berlin and there are driving ranges and golf courses, such as Berliner Golf Club Gatow (Spandau), Global Golf Club (Tiergarten), Golf-Zentrum (Mitte) and Golf und Land Club Berlin-Wannsee.

Many golf courses can be found in Brandenburg, too, including the worldclass Sandy Lyle course at the Golfclub Schloß Wilkendorf bei Strausberg.

Ice-skating is a popular sport during winter and there are indoor and outdoor rinks available.

Tennis

For a nation with tennis stars like Steffi Graf and Boris Becker, it's no surprise that tennis has a sizeable following. For the tennis clubs (often also offering squash courts) in Berlin, see http://tvbb.de, which is the website of the Tennis Verband Berlin Brandenburg.

Fitness Centres

There is no shortage of gyms and fitness centres in Berlin. Some are branches of chains such as Kieser, Gold's and Jopp Frauen Fitness, the latter for women only.

Swimming

There are 39 outdoor and 62 indoor pools in Berlin, so there's bound to be one near where you live. Check the opening times, though, as the poor financial health of the city means more limited opening hours. Some cater to the handicapped as well (e.g. Fischerinsel Swimming Pool). Many are open in winter and keep the pools heated at a pleasant 28°C (82.4°F). Information on public pools can be found at http://berlinerbaederbetriebe.de.

Swimming in the many lakes is also possible, and not only in summer. There is a group of hardy (or nutty, some may say) Berliners who go swimming in the lakes in winter. If you're keen to try it out, check out http://www.berliner-seehunde.de to find the folks with anti-freeze in their blood. They say it takes training, so please don't leap into a lake on your own in winter without further ado.

There are also special beaches (called *Strandbad* or *Freibad*) where you have to pay entrance fees. Two of the popular ones are Freibad Müggelsee and Strandbad Wannsee. The latter also has water slides and a beer garden.

The *Strandkorb* is the German's favourite beach chair. It's a sofa-like wicker chair with a hood which protects users from gusts of cold wind. Most fee-paying beaches offer these chairs.

An unusual pool experience can be had at the Badeschiff Berlin. A barge turned into a pool and floating on the Spree, it's part of a complex with a restaurant, beer garden and concert venue. It's also in service in winter; the pool gets a cover and massage and sauna are also offered.

The Wannsee lake is a well-known bathing and recreation spot.

Beach Volleyball

Very popular with the younger crowd, Berlin also hosts tournaments. For facilities, see the website of Volleyball Verband Berlin (http://vvb-online.de).

Water Sports

With so many lakes, Berlin is a water-sport lover's paradise. Kayaking, sailing, rowing, windsurfing and cruising on boats are some available options. For junior sailors, Optimist boats are available at some clubs.

Horse Riding

There are a number of horse riding ranches like Reiterverein Onkel Toms Hütte, Reitsportzentrum Heiligensee and Preußenhof for equestrian enthusiasts.

Spectator Sports
Football (Soccer)

Germany is a football nation, so this game attracts huge crowds. Those who don't make it to the stadiums follow the matches on TV avidly. Berlin's top club is the first division Hertha BSC which has its base in the gigantic 76,000-seat

Olympiastadion. Since Germany's hosting of the men's FIFA World Cup 2006 (with the team coming in third), the men's team becoming runner-up in Euro 2008, and the women's team winning the FIFA World Cup in 2003 and 2007, interest in football has shot up even more. The Olympiastadion also hosts the finals of the German Cup for both the men and women's teams.

Another Berlin club, FC Union Berlin, plays in the second division.

American Football

Germany is not thronging with American football fanatics, but it does have a professional league. The Berlin Adler is an amateur team and has its home base in the Friedrich Ludwig Jahn Sportpark, while the professional team Berlin Thunder plays at the Olympiastadion.

The Berlin Adler's players are mostly native Berliners, because of the amateur league rules, but Berlin Thunder's players are predominantly Americans.

Qatar Telecom German Open

Held in May on the grounds of the LTTC Rot-Weiss in Grunewald, this is Berlin's Wimbledon. The tournament attracts many top players like Serena Williams, Maria Sharapova, Justine Henin and Svetlana Kuznetsova.

Handball

After Germany hosted and also won the World Men's Handball Chamionships in 2007, interest in handball has picked up substantially. More information can be found at the handball association's site at http://www.hvberlin-online.de (German only).

Ice Hockey

EHC Eisbären Berlin is the Berlin team. A former East German team, it actually beat all the odds to win the German Ice Hockey league in 2005, 2006 and 2008. It has a loyal fan base, made up mostly of East Berliners. After playing home games for years in the Wellblechpalast, the team's new home since autumn 2008 is the spanking new arena, O^2 World, at Ostbahnhof, which has a capacity of 17,000.

Horse Racing

Horse racing tracks aren't just for that chance of getting a windfall. In June, the Galopprennbahn Berlin-Hoppegarten, one of the biggest in Germany, has attractions for the whole family. Apart from watching the races and 'having a flutter', there is a beer garden in the shade of some old lime trees to just enjoy the atmosphere. At the Trabrennbahn Karlshorst, there's the Great Chariot Race—the Legend of Ben Hur in September, a great way to spend the day for the entire family. The highlight is the chariot race featuring 30 horse-drawn chariots, although there are other activities available, such as pony rides and spear-throwing, all in a Ben Hur atmosphere.

GREEN OASES

For those who aren't exactly looking for a specific activity and just want some Zen-time, Berlin has plenty of lovely parks and forested areas to just chill out. A list of them can be found at http://www.gruen-berlin.de. Below are some of the city's best:

Tiergarten

The largest park in Berlin with an area of 200 hectares (495 acres), Tiergarten started life in 1527 as a hunting reserve for the Elector. Frederick the Great later converted this into a public park. In the 19th century, landscape designer and royal gardener Peter Joseph Lenné turned it into an English-style landscaped park. The trees were cut down after the war by starving Berliners in order to grow potatoes and turnips. By 1949, the then mayor, Ernst Reuter, took steps to revert the place back to a green area. Today, it's a well-loved park with footpaths lined with statues of German poets and composers, ponds and a café.

Schlosspark Charlottenburg

The palace park of Schloss Charlottenburg is a favourite of tourists and Berliners alike. Largely reconstructed after being

The beautifully landscaped Charlottenburg park and palace are a major visitor attraction and a wonderful respite from the bustle of the city.

severely damaged in the war by faithfully following historic prints, the park is breathtakingly beautiful. Just behind the Schloss is the manicured French-style park, which from an aerial view resembles an exquisite carpet. Farther away is an English-style landscaped garden.

Botanischer Garten

Laid out between 1897 and 1903, the Botanical Garden has some 18,000 species of plants. There is also a Tropics House with carefully preserved tropical temperature and humidity for the bamboos, orchids and water lilies.

Erholungspark, Marzahn

Situated in the troubled district of Marzahn with high unemployment and tendency to violence is the charming Erholungspark (relaxation park). This park lives up to its name, and the most attractive parts within it are the exotic Chinese Garden, Japanese Garden and Balinese Garden. The latter is like a hothouse; the temperatures are kept to an authentic tropical hot and humid level for the sake of the tropical plants, but is a nice refuge for humans on cold Berlin days, if only for a brief spell.

Pfaueninsel

The name means Peacock Island, and is called that because there are really peacocks strolling freely around this 98 hectare (242 acre) nature reserve. This park has again the fingerprints of Peter Joseph Lenné. No vehicles are allowed on the island, so visitors have to take a short ferry ride across the Havel.

There are some interesting structures on the island amidst all the soothing greenery. The quirky white Schloss was built in 1794 by Friedrich Wilhelm II for his mistress, Wilhemine Encke, but before he could cuddle up with her in the palace, the poor man died, leaving the enjoyment of it to his successor and wife. There's also the Cavalier's House and a copy of a Roman Temple. But the real treat of being on the island is the feeling of being truly 'far from the madding crowd', to borrow from Thomas Hardy.

NIKE YOU'RE FASTER THAN YOU THINK YOU'RE FAS

Cycling is part mode of transport and part sport
for Berliners, and cyclists have separate bicycle
lanes on most main roads and many shops have a
bicycle rack outside reserved for their customers.

Berlin has an exciting nightlife, and trendy pubs and other nightspots can be found in popular areas such as Prenzlauer Berg.

Enjoy a dip at the Badeschiff, or bathing ship, a floating swimming pool on the Spree River fashioned from an old shipping barge.

A visitor contemplates the works of art at the Alte Nationalgalerie. If you are a museum buff, Berlin will keep you occupied with its large numbers of excellent museums, with the most famous cluster to be found on Museumsinsel.

Christmas is the most celebrated festival in Berlin and the streets are lit up beautifully. Visit the Weihnachtsmärkte (Christmas markets), which have a lovely atmosphere and delicious Christmas confectionery at every corner.

FOR THE YOUNG AND YOUNG AT HEART

While Berlin's partying image precedes it when it comes to leisure pursuits, the younger residents are not left with nothing to occupy them. Berlin is actually quite child-friendly, from the special rates on public transport to the many activities available.

Zoos

The city's former division into east and west has also left the city with not one, but two gigantic zoos. The Berlin Zoo is where the world-famous polar bear Knut was born and bred by hand, after his mother rejected him shortly after birth. Although for about a year after his birth on 5 December 2006, visitors seemed to congregate only in front of his enclosure, there are more than 14,000 animals including a once much oggled panda, Bao Bao, before Knut stole the limelight. Next door is a magnificent aquarium, and you can buy a combined ticket to visit both zoo and aquarium.

Knut

This polar bear was born in the Berlin Zoo on 5 December 2006. His mother rejected him at birth, and Knut was raised by his devoted keeper, Thomas Dörflein, who bottle fed him round the clock. Knut's fame came about after an animal rights activist was quoted in a German tabloid that Knut should have been left to die. Worldwide uproar followed swiftly and Knut (and Dörflein) became stars.

Knut single-handedly raised the zoo's revenues, with worldwide fans and media regularly standing in front of his enclosure. When Knut turned one, he weighed a hefty 112 kg (246 lbs), and was no longer the cute, white 'teddy bear'. In the course of 2008, the poor bear's stardom faded somewhat.

Like Hollywood stars, Knut started losing many of his fickle fans as he aged. However, Dörflein's sudden death in September 2008 brought back a rush of sympathy for Knut, as he was now 'orphaned'.

The other zoo, the Tierpark, is one of the largest in Europe. Many of the animals enjoy spacious enclosures in the open, but some (like the wild cats) are kept in Guantanamo-style enclosures. There is also a palace on the grounds, which is now a museum, with pelicans walking freely in front of it.

Parks and Playgrounds

Apart from the many parks to run around in, most neighbourhoods have a playground or two with slides and roundabouts. The Monbijou Park on Oranienburger Straße even has a wading pool in summer.

Museums

A number of museums like the Deutsches Technikmuseum, (German Museum of Technology), the Ethnologisches Museum (Ethnological Museum) and the Story of Berlin provide opportunities for interaction. At the Museum of Technology, visitors can try their hands at being a news presenter, weaving and printing or learn sailing knots; at the Ethnological Museum, visitors can check out a Tuareg tent and dug-out canoes of the North American Indians; and at the Story of Berlin, the use of multimedia, the original artefacts and the nuclear fallout bunker below the complex are unlikely to bore young visitors.

At the Museum für Naturkunde (Natural History Museum), young and old will be awe-struck by the 12 m (39 ft) high and 23 m (75 ft) long dinosaur skeleton.

The Domäne Dahlem is an open-air museum where visitors can experience farm life and the Museumsdorf Düppel is a reconstructed medieval settlement, where children can try out bread-baking and flax-weaving. Both should be a nice change for city kids.

There are also three children's museums: The Labyrinth Kindermuseum Berlin at Wedding, the Kindermuseum at the FEZ Wuhlheide and the MACHmit! Museum für Kinder in Prenzlauer Berg.

Waxwork museum fans will be delighted with the Madame Tussauds Berlin (on Unter den Linden) which opened in 2008.

Being with Nature
The Naturschutzzentrum Ökowerk (Nature Protection Centre Ecological Works) lets kids learn about Nature and Ecology in a hands-on way. There are courses for children on how to build things with natural material and how to survive in nature (what's edible, how to start a fire, find water etc). More information at http://www.oekowerk.de.

Other Fun Places
There are countless other types of activities, and it's impossible to list all in this chapter. Whether it's 'play, mixed with science' at Kindercity (http://kindercity.de), oggling at miniature trains at Loxx Miniatur Welten Berlin (at ALEXA shopping mall), interactive fun at LEGOLAND discovery centre (http://legolanddiscoverycentre.com/berlin/de), or having a go at trampolines, go-carts and bumper boats at Berlin's biggest (4,000 sq m/43,040 sq.ft) indoor leisure park Jacks Fun World, there's bound to be something to appeal to different youthful interests.

> **Information on Available Activities**
> For details and other information of available activities, check out the Berlin Tourism Board's website: http://www.visitberlin.de

BIRD'S EYE VIEW OF BERLIN
Great Berlin Wheel
Expected to be completed by the end of 2009, the ferris wheel will perform the same function as the London Eye: give people a chance to see Berlin from 185 metres (606 ft) at its highest point (50 metres higher than its London counterpart). The ferris wheel is located near the Berlin Zoo. The project costs an estimated €120 million. The wheel will have 36 air-conditioned cars, each with a capacity of 40 passengers. One rotation will last 35 minutes.

BEYOND BERLIN
As mentioned at the end of Chapter Two, Brandenburg state surrounds Berlin, and with an abundant natural landscape. A

few unpleasant right-wing incidents in some underdeveloped areas have unfortunately given many the wrong impression of the entire state. But if you're going to be living in Berlin for an extended period, it's highly recommended that you explore Brandenburg too. People who are dark-skinned, Asian or look gay should take care to avoid straying into the areas not frequented by tourists, but going to the popular tourist sites especially during the day should not pose any problems.

At risk of sounding like I'm working for the Brandenburg tourism office, Brandenburg does offer a fascinating landscape. With around 3,000 lakes and over 30,000 km (18,642 miles) of waterways, 500 castles and manor houses, 23,000 archaeological sites, idyllic town centres, and some lovely landscaped gardens, it's hard not to gush.

The favourite Brandenburger tourist destination is the capital, Potsdam. Even though Potsdam was devastated by Allied bombings on 14 and 15 April 1945, there are still many attractions: Park and Schloss Sansoucci, Schloss Cecilienhof (venue of Potsdam Conference), the Russian Colony of Alexandrowka, the Holländisches Viertel and the film studios of Babelsberg. Another popular site is the Spreewald, a biosphere reserve with a network of rivers and streams that cater for romantic trips on punting boats, steered with a long sweep oar with the rower standing upright, Venetian gondola-style. The two landscaped parks in Branitz and Bad Muskau of the eccentric Prince Hermann von Pückler-Muskau are also lovely retreats to spend a day.

To whet your appetite further, the site brandenburg-tourism.com has extensive information about Brandenburg and its various sights.

LANGUAGE

CHAPTER 8

'I don't believe there is anything in the whole earth that
you can't learn in Berlin except the German language.'
—Mark Twain

OMINOUS THOUGH THAT SOUNDS, foreigners coming to live in Berlin shouldn't let Twain's tongue-in-cheek comment put them off learning German. It's admittedly complicated, but so essential to living more comfortably in Berlin.

A tourist in Berlin can get by with English, certainly, but a resident needs to have a grasp of enough German to know what *Vorsicht Stufe* means to avoid twisting an ankle just because he didn't know he had to watch his step. There will invariably come a time, too, when you need to communicate with the landlord or understand what the announcement is all about as you wait for the delayed train. Knowledge of German also helps you get rid of that sense of disorientation when new in Berlin—like a three-year-old who has lost his mother in the crowded shopping mall—which often triggers culture shock. And Mark Twain could mock the language only because he had such a good grasp of it.

German in the European Union

German is the most widely-spoken native language in the EU, as about 24 per cent of EU citizens speak it as their first language. French and English come second, each with 16 per cent.

HOW EASY OR HARD?

You might wonder how hard, or easy, learning the language is. For English speakers, the good thing is that you don't have to learn a new alphabet (as you would for Russian, for example). The other piece of good news is that German pronunciation is more consistent vis a vis the spelling than English, so once you've learned the conventions of German orthography, pronunciation is fairly straightforward, unlike foreigners having to grapple with 'Salisbury', 'Edinburgh' and 'plumber'. And you actually know more German words that you think; angst, kindergarten, schadenfreude, baby, hobby, leitmotiv, zeitgeist, dachshund and marketing are derived from or have the same meaning in German.

Sorry to be a wet blanket, but sometimes recognising an English word in a German text can lead you astray, though. There are enough 'false friends' that may trip English speakers up.

German Word	What It Means
Email	Enamel, not electronic mail (which is written as E-Mail)
Gift	Not a present, but poison
Hell	Not the place bad people go to, but bright (light) or light (colour)
Konfektion	Not yummy confectionery, but ready-to-wear clothes (pret-a-porter)
Mist	Nothing to do with the weather, but dung/manure
Pony	Sometimes pony (small horse), sometimes a fringe (US bangs)
Präservativ	Not added to food to prevent it decaying, but a condom
Smoking	Nothing to do with cigarettes, but a dinner jacket/tuxedo

The biggest hurdle for a German-language student is the grammar. For a start, a sentence structure can be complicated.

An example:

A learner trying to find out what '*Es fängt um 6 an*' means would not find the solution by looking up the words '*fängt*', '*um*' and '*an*' in a dictionary. The sentence means 'it starts at 6', but the German infinitive for 'to start'—'*anfangen*'—has been separated and conjugated into '*fängt*' and '*an*'.

While you're still trying to digest that, know also that all German nouns are either male, female or neutral, and they don't necessarily follow the gender assigned by Mother Nature. An example would be *Das Mädchen*, which means a young girl but is a neutral noun. Sexual disorientation started in the German language long before it became acknowledged by society. Additionally, German has four cases, the nominative, genitive, dative and accusative; the words in front of nouns change depending on their function in the sentence.

The Four Cases In German

A dog is '*der Hund*'; a woman is '*die Frau*'; a horse is '*das Pferd*'; now you put that dog in the genitive case, and is he the same dog he was before? No, sir; he is '*des Hundes*'; put him in the dative case and what is he? Why, he is '*dem Hund*'. Now you snatch him into the accusative case and how is it with him? Why, he is '*den Hund*'. But suppose he happens to be twins and you have to pluralize him—what then? Why, they'll swat that twin dog around through the four cases until he'll think he's an entire international dog-show all in his own person. I don't like dogs, but I wouldn't treat a dog like that—I wouldn't even treat a borrowed dog that way. Well, it's just the same with a cat. They start her in at the nominative singular in good health and fair to look upon, and they sweat her through all the four cases and the 16 the's and when she limps out through the accusative plural you wouldn't recognise her for the same being. Yes, sir, once the German language gets hold of a cat, it's goodbye cat. That's about the amount of it.

—Mark Twain

All German nouns start with a capital letter, like proper nouns in English. Some German words are also incredibly long, and you're out of breath even before you finish pronouncing them. Many long German words are actually made up of individual words strung together to form a new word. One rather oft cited example of the longest German word is *Donaudampfschifffahrtsgesellschaftskapitän*, meaning 'Danube steamship company captain'.

The three 'f's you see is not a typographical error. The new German spelling really insists on three 'f's, because of the combination of the two words *schiff* and *fahrt*.

Students of German seem to enjoy trying to find the 'longest German word'. More than most other languages, German tends to string words together to form new words. All languages, including English, do this to some extent, but German really likes to create long words. As Mark Twain said, 'Some German words are so long that they have a perspective'.

German can do this because its grammar allows words to be strung together to form one lengthy term that English and other languages usually break up into several words.

WHERE TO LEARN GERMAN

Goethe Institute (Hackescher Markt area) in Berlin is probably the best place to take German lessons, if the most expensive. But teaching standards are very high, and is certainly worth the expenditure, if it's not too much a strain on your pocket. Otherwise, you can go to a language school (*Sprachschule*). Learning on your own from books is not recommended for beginners, as grappling with pronunciation and a rather complex grammar is easier with a teacher.

THE GERMAN ALPHABET

The German alphabet has the same 26 letters as in English, plus the special letters *ä,ö,ü* and *ß*.

The two dots above the *ä,ö* and *ü* is called *Umlaut*. There is no real equivalent in English for pronunciation guide. On non-German keyboards, *ä,ö, ü* and *ß* can be spelled as ae, oe, ue and ss respectively. You see this very often for websites and email addresses. An example: the website of the Auswärtige Amt (Foreign Service/State Department) is http://www.auswaertiges-amt.de.

The German Alphabet

Letter	Pronunciation*
a	a as in after
b	b as in baby
c	c as in cat
d	d as in dog
e	e as in prey
f	f as in fan
g	g as in good
h	h as in hair
i	e as in she
j	y as in young
k	k as in keep
l	l as in light
m	m as in mother
n	n as in now
o	o as in low
p	p as in pet
q	q as in queen
r	r as in rain
s	s as in sun
t	t as is tea
u	oo as in moon
v	f as in father, or v as in vase
w	v as in vain
x	x as in mix/or as in xylophone
y	y as in yoga
z	ts as in pots
ä	e as in men
ö	o with rounded lips
ü	oo with rounded lips
ß	ss as in stress

*This is only the most basic pronunciation. Pronunciation of a letter does change in some cases.

COLLOQUIALISM AND IMPORTED WORDS

There are many colloquial words and turns of phrases which you aren't likely to learn in a formal language class. Instead of '*Guten Tag*' (Good Day) or '*Guten Appetit*', people (especially working class folks) may greet you with '*Mahlzeit*' (meal time). Instead of '*Haben Sie*', some Germans may slur '*Harm Zer?*' White rolls are called *Schrippen*, and a big cup of coffee is called *Pott Kaffee* (and it doesn't come in a coffee pot). Words like *Hammer!* and *Geil* are used by youngsters to give the thumbs up to something, which are never used in formal situations. Foreigners pick up the slang after living among Germans or watching German movies for a length of time. The High German you learn in the classroom will make you sound like an uptight headmaster if used to chat up a lady in a bar, but you'll pick up (pardon the pun) the argot soon enough, never mind. Before mastering that, it might be easier to get by with the English words like 'Cool'. English words are fashionable at the moment, so younger Germans do say '*Kuhl*' too. Most advertising blurbs are nowadays in English as well, like TV channel Pro 7's slogan: 'We love to entertain you', and Vodafone's 'Make the most of now'.

Many Germans words are also derived from French and these have become part of formal German e.g. *Abonnement*, *Chaussee* and *Chef*. French words retain their French pronunciation.

BERLINERISCH

And then there's Berlinerisch—the dialect of the capital city. The Berlin dialect is, like other German dialects, almost incomprehensible to those who don't know it. For foreigners who are still struggling with High German, Berlinerisch doesn't sound like German at all. It's like listening to a rapper, or to cockney. Berlinerisch is spoken with a sort of drawl, words are truncated, and 'g' is replaced with the German 'j', and sometimes don't follow standard grammar rules.

Some examples of Berlinerisch:	
Berlinerisch	High German
Jutn Tach	*Guten Tag*
Ick	*Ich*
Wat	*Was*
Haste	*Hast du*
Ma	*Mal*
Jejehm	*Gegeben*

Don't weep in despair; you don't have to learn Berlinerisch. It's just good to know that it exists, in case you wonder why on some days the impressive amount of German you have learnt in the past year seems to have deserted you.

PUNCTUATION

The most striking difference between English and German punctuation marks is perhaps the quotation marks. German quotation marks look like English ones reflected in a mirror:

Example:
„Bis bald" sagte er.

Although German also adds the letter 's' to indicate the genitive form of a proper noun, they don't include an apostrophe before the 's'. That's why the children's leisure park, 'Jacks Fun World', is spelled that way, even though the name is actually in English.

German Number Crunching

When writing decimals in German numbers, a comma is used where a point is used in English numbers, and vice versa.

English Decimals	German Decimals
23.46	23,46
10,000.46	10.000,46

This is important to remember when using EXCEL. The German EXCEL programme can't calculate if you put the comma or the point in the 'wrong' place.

Another thing to note is that when handwriting the number 1, Germans include a hook at the top left corner. When written in a hurry, it often looks more like a pictogram of a hill with a very pointed summit.

NON-VERBAL COMMUNICATION

Germans basically don't communicate with their eyes, shoulders or hands. Communication is verbal, and not very voluble, at that. Whatever few gestures they may make are not likely to be misunderstood by an Anglo-Saxon. Just note that Germans count starting with the thumb, so to indicate the number '3', for example, a German shows the thumb, the index and the middle finger. To indicate 'crazy', a German may wave a hand, palm inwards, in front of his face a few times. These are some of the few gestures a (Teutonic) German may make; otherwise, there are no Gaelic shrugs or Italian-style hand gestures.

A Note of Encouragement

If anyone's enthusiasm for learning the language is waning after reading the above, don't. Apart from it being enormously practical to know the language to get around Berlin, you will also then be able to truly enjoy Mark Twain's digs at the language in his *A Tramp Abroad* and *Mark Twain's Notebook*.

BUSINESS IN BERLIN

CHAPTER 9

WORK CLOTHES ARE IN THE BASEMENT WHILE BUSINESS ATTIRE IS ON THE TOP FLOOR

'The Berlin Wall wasn't the only barrier to fall after the collapse of the Soviet Union and the end of the Cold War. Traditional barriers to the flow of money, trade, people and ideas also fell.'
—Fareed Zakaria, editor, International Editions, *Newsweek*

THE ECONOMY

Berlin was once a thriving commercial centre, and profited from its being the Prussian capital. With the Industrial Revolution, Berlin became a hub for the manufacturers of machinery such as locomotives. It also became a financial centre as well. However, the city saw its fortunes plunge with the hyperinflation of the 1920s and the Great Depression of the 1930s. During the Nazi period, the city's fortune saw some recovery as a centre for producing weapons, but lost many entrepreneurs as the core of successful Jewish businessmen fled Germany or were murdered by the Nazis. Berlin, until then the biggest industrial city of Germany, was then bombed to smithereens during World War II.

During the Cold War, West Berlin had to rely on subsidies to survive its geographical isolation, while East Berlin's economy sputtered under the socialist system, as it could not compete on the international stage. Since the fall of the Berlin Wall, the economy of the city has undergone structural changes. With the decision to move the federal government to Berlin, things picked up, not least because of the construction and infrastructure projects needed to turn Berlin into a capital city. Significant funding for development came from the European Structural funds that focused on the economy and infrastructure. Berlin received some €1.3 billion from 2000–2006, and a tranche of about the same amount for 2007 to 2013.

The city has made huge strides since then, but is still very much in the red. In 2007, it had a debt of €57.2 billion, although it was some 3.1 per cent lower than in 2006.

Berlin's private sector, especially the small and medium-sized companies, plays a significant role in the city's economy. Currently, Berlin's economy is very much driven by the service sector, although some manufacturing giants remain headquartered in the city, such as Siemens and Schering. Sectors which are growing fast include information and communication technologies, media and music, advertising and design, biotechnology and environmental services, transportation and medical engineering. The academic and research and development sectors are also growing. Berlin is also one of the leading congress cities in the world.

In 2008, the Financial Times Group's investment publication, *fDi* magazine, awarded Berlin the third position (after London and Paris) in its annual ranking of 'European cities and Regions of the Future'.

Berlin's central location in relation to east and west Europe, its good infrastructure, comparatively low property prices and its increasing vibrancy make it rather attractive for investors. What tends to put foreign investors off is the nation-wide high tax rates, rigid labour laws and tedious regulations. Berlin Partner GmbH and the Investor Service Agency (Zentrale Anlauf-und Koordinierungsstelle für Unternehmen) provide potential investors with assistance.

GERMANY

Germany is Europe's largest economy. It practises what it calls social market economy, which is part capitalism, part welfare and part workers' rights.

The country's political and economic infrastructures are sound. The judiciary is independent and the integrity of the legal system is beyond reproach. Some investors may grumble about the bureaucracy, but the abundant rules and regulations do lend investors a sense of security and stability.

In the Transparency International's Corruption Perception Index 2008, which listed the level of corruption in 180 countries as perceived by business people and analysts,

Germany's economy has been through extreme changes and continues to be resilient in the face of difficulties and pressure.

Germany ranked 14th with a score of 7.9 (10 being the least corrupt). Denmark, New Zealand and Sweden were in pole position, all with the same score of 9.3. Canada and Australia were 9th (8.7), UK 16th (7.7) and US 18th (7.3).

Germany has been rocked by a number of high profile scandals in recent years. In 2008, it emerged that Deutsche Telekom had been sifting through the details of employees' and journalists' telephone calls in a bid to track down leaks of sensitive information to financial journalists. Spying scandals also tainted other big names like Lufthansa and Deutsche Post. Another scandal involved German engineering giant, Siemens, which allegedly used a staggering sum of €1.3 billion for bribes around the world to secure business for the company. There was also the case of Klaus Zumwinkel, then head of Deutsche Post and chairman of the supervisory board of Deutsche Telekom, who allegedly squirreled away money to Liechtenstein to evade taxes. Earlier on, the head honchos of Volkswagen were involved in expense-account sex, where the rates charged by the ladies of the night rivalled those which (ex New York governor) Elliot Spitzer favoured.

If one tries to put a positive spin on these scandals, one can say that at least the German press is free, and that investigations by the authorities immediately got underway once the wrong-doings were uncovered.

The Euro

Germany adopted the Euro as the national currency on 1 January 2002. As it turned six in 2008, a survey by the Association of German Banks found that 34 per cent of the Germans polled would prefer to return to the Deutsche Mark. This was due probably to the Euro being (wrongly) blamed for inflation, as well as a nostalgic yearning for the better times of yesterday

---

THE JOB MARKET

Job seekers from non-EU member countries—and often for those from EU countries which joined only in 2004 and 2007—who come to Berlin in the hope of finding a job will find that it isn't exactly easy. With a stubbornly high unemployment rate of about 16 per cent, jobs are scarce. Unless the person has a very specialised skill, priority is given to Germans and citizens of EU countries. Obviously, most jobs require a rather good command of German.

Many native English-speakers turn to teaching English. There is a high demand for English language teachers (Britons enjoy a special reverence here which may not be commensurate with the person's teaching skills or even standard of English), but the pay is often modest, as there is an abundant supply of teachers.

If you should be applying for jobs in Berlin, make sure you have a very detailed resume, setting out your educational background and work experiences, and supported by educational certificates and letters of reference. A good passport photo should also be included. German job applicants usually have their application letter, resume, copies of certificates and letters of reference elegantly put together in a file, so if you want your application to impress, you should do the same.

WORK ATTITUDE

As mentioned in Chapter Three, the Teutons are serious, disciplined, hardworking and methodical. Anyone who has had to do business with Germans testify to their thoroughness and reliability, as well as the quality of the work. Germans are strong on analysis and conceptualisation, and they spend a lot of time thinking through all the options and possible problem areas before finally making a decision. This is often the bugbear of foreigners who like to close deals quickly; they find the German decision-making process rather plodding. Once the decision is made, it's also pretty much cast in stone; any attempt to try and modify what has been agreed upon is seen by Germans as unreliability.

The Teutonic culture falls somewhere between the individualistic (e.g. American) and the collectivistic (e.g. Japanese) cultures. Germans focus more on individual achievement rather than on the group, but there is a hint of some collectivist traits in the Teutons, as German society is one steeped in social justice and co-determination.

TIME AT AND OFF WORK

Germans start work very early. Business hours are usually from 8:00–9:00 am to 4:00–5:00 pm. Appointments with medical professionals can start even before 8:00 am. The other thing to note about opening hours for some businesses (e.g. medical professionals and banks) is that the they are not uniform throughout the week. Check their specific opening hours before hopping down there.

Hardworking though the Germans may be, they don't spend too much time at work. If you include part-time workers, Germans these days work about 30.3 hours per week, much less than the 41.4 hours in 1960. They also work less than other Europeans and the Americans: A survey of working hours showed that in 2006, Germans worked an average of 192 days in a year, the French 204, the British 217 and the Americans 238.

The Germans also have generous annual leave, maternity and child-rearing leave. Mothers are entitled to 14 weeks of fully paid maternity leave; six weeks before birth and eight weeks after. In addition, a parent is entitled to up to three years of unpaid leave to stay home to look after the child. There is also the *Elterngeld* (Money for Parents) whereby high-earning parents get paid 67 per cent of his/her last-drawn salary (maximum €1,800 per month) for a total duration of 14 months for child-rearing. Employees also have up to six weeks of paid sick leave. For long-term illnesses, the health insurance kicks in to pay a proportion of the last-drawn salary.

WOMEN AT WORK

Germany may have a female Chancellor in Angela Merkel, and German laws provide for equality of the sexes at work, but in practice, the mindset can be quite different. Women earn about 22 per cent less than their male counterparts, according to findings released by the Institute of Economic and Social Research in 2007. There are very few women in top executive positions.

The interesting phenomenon is that it's not only the men, but also the women, who hold prejudices about working

women. According to an article on what makes Germans tick published in *Der Spiegel* in April 2008, 62 per cent of men and 34 per cent of women feel that a woman should stop work once she has children.

Any woman who juggles motherhood with a career is often derided as a *Rabben Mutter* (raven mum), for letting others look after her kids while she goes to work. The antiquated role model for women, *Kinder, Küche, Kirche* (children, kitchen, church) seems to be still the yardstick for many Germans. Not surprising, really, if one recalls that in West Germany, until 1957, women who wanted to work had to seek the permission of their husbands.

BUSINESS ETIQUETTE
Business Attire
Business attire for the mainstream is conservative. Men wear dark suits and sensible ties and shirts. Women also favour well-cut but conservative suits (including pant suits) and minimal make-up. Loud accessories are a no-no. Of course, people in the creative fields or teaching profession don't dress so conservatively. If you're not sure, err on the side of caution and stick to conservative dressing. You can

always adapt accordingly to what the people in the office wear later.

If it's a particularly hot summer day, don't remove your jacket until the German counterpart suggests doing so. If the Germans keep theirs on, follow suit.

Business suits are also appropriate for attending business dinners and most social events. Some more glamourous events like the opening night of an important concert or opera may require tuxedoes and evening gowns, though.

Meeting and Greeting

You've heard enough by now about how formal Germans are. Business acquaintances should not be addressed by his/her first name, but as Mr. (*Herr*) or Mrs. (*Frau*) followed by the surname. All ladies (whether married or single) are addressed as *Frau. Fräulein* (Miss) is hardly ever used nowadays; if ever, it's only appropriate for young ladies of around ten or so. If the person has a professional title, you must use it. A person with a Ph.D is addressed as *Frau Dr.* (plus surname) or *Herr Dr*. (plus surname). If you have a professional title, you should use it too.

Dates

German dates are written in a day-month-year order. So 03.04.09 is 3 April 2009, not 4 March 2009.

Germans shake hands a lot more than the average Anglo-Saxon. You should always shake hands (including someone you've just met yesterday) when you first arrive and before leaving. A firm (but not knuckle-busting) handshake followed by an exchange of business cards is the norm when you meet the business partners for the first time. Germans have a high regard for education, so your business card should have all your professional qualifications listed. If your company is a venerable one, it's a good idea to indicate the founding date on your name card.

When it comes to job titles, German modesty comes to the fore. Don't think that someone with a title *Projektleiter*

(literally project leader) or *Geschäftsführer* (literally business leader/head) is a member of junior management. These titles could well mean a regional director and CEO respectively. If you're used to the American-style titles such as presidents and vice-presidents, German job titles may sound rather lowly, but they're often senior positions.

Presentations, Negotiations and Other Meetings

If you are giving a presentation to a German audience, make sure you have plenty of facts and figures to support your presentation. Germans are not impressed by hype, but solid data.

Your audience will listen quietly, basically expressionless, while you're presenting. When it's question and answer time, however, you may be bombarded by questions which may sound rather interrogative. If that happens, you have done a good job; Germans ask lots of questions because they're interested, and not because they are trying to tear you down.

Germans may not clap after a speech or presentation, but rap their knuckles on the table (if there's one in front of them).

Don't rely on jokes or irony. It's not in keeping with the German seriousness. Germans also don't display much body language. There are no Gaelic shrugs or expressive hand movements. Germans say what they mean and mean what they say, in exact words. So when dealing with Germans, body and facial movements should be limited. The other thing to avoid is the 'first the good news, then the bad news' type of response. If it's something negative you have to say, just say it factually, but without emotions. Germans see those positive/negative comments as contradictory. In the same light, a German means no offence if he tells you only negative things if you ask him for his opinion. What is not raised as an issue is deemed to be in order, or even positive. That's characteristic of Germans in the workplace; they don't give nor expect to receive compliments.

Appointments for meetings should be made about two weeks ahead. Don't schedule meetings for Friday afternoons. Germans are usually on their way home by 3:00 pm on Fridays. July and August are also not good months to meet business partners, as it's summer holidays and many Germans take their vacation (often four weeks long) during this time.

What you've heard about the fabled punctuality is true. Being late for an appointment gives a very bad impression.

Unlike Middle Eastern or many Asian cultures, business discussions need not be preceded by long, getting-to-know you chats. Germans get down to business quite quickly, as is to be expected of their straightforward nature. They might ask a few polite questions about your flight, and if your hotel is fine, but they don't usually go beyond that. No German will ask about the number of children you have etc. in a business environment.

You might feel as if your German partner is rather cold towards you. Don't think that (s)he dislikes you or is annoyed. Germans charateristically keep their smiles for family and close friends, so business meetings are conducted with an unsmiling demeanour, to convey seriousness. You should do the same, by the way. Germans don't appreciate chuckling, grinning business partners.

When negotiating with Germans, substantiate your ideas and arguments with facts, facts and more facts. Even if you have always been successful with your 'gut feeling', with Germans you have to subtantiate with data and examples.

The decision-making process is protracted, as Germans like to weigh the pros and cons carefully, and input (sometimes even approval) must be obtained from various people in the hierarchy. Avoid trying to contact someone who is more senior than your usual contact person in the hope that s(he) may be able to decide more quickly. It'll offend your contact and embarass the senior person. No one should try to 'chase' for a decision either. The reaction can be quite negative if you constantly call to ask if they've come to a decision yet.

Be Patient

I made this *faux pas* once; after two weeks of not hearing from a lady as to what she thought of the proposal for a project I sent her, I emailed her to ask, but she had not decided. Another two weeks went by, and I asked again. She replied with a German phrase, which roughly translates into my behaving like a bull crashing through and bringing down the front door. Ouch.

Once a decision is made and the contract is signed, no changes to the contract terms will be entertained.

In the Office

Relationships between German colleagues are also more formal than those between Americans. Colleagues rarely go on a first name basis, even after working together for years. The fondness of handshaking extends to colleagues you see every day as well. Don't be suprised if a German colleague shakes your hand every morning when you get to the office, even if it's just quick grasp. Other than the handshake, no other body contact is appreciated. Claps on the back or a friendly squeeze on the arm will cause a German to recoil in horror.

The relationship between bosses and subordinates is even more formal. Management style is top-down and instructions are given clearly. Bosses are unlikely to enquire about a subordinate's personal life (e.g. How was your Italian holiday?) as a form of pleasantry; conversations are about work, and there is no smiling or other niceties added. German bosses do not give praise either, so don't imagine your work is not appreciated just because the boss doesn't say anything approving.

As mentioned earlier, hierarchy is observed. Subordinates reporting upwards should follow the chain of command to the letter. Bypassing an immediate superior to go to a higher level manager is not done.

Working overtime is not necessarily seen as hardworking; on the contrary, it could be seen as inefficiency! Unless other colleagues are also working late to finish a rush job, overtime should be avoided.

One interesting point about the boss-subordinate relationship: According to a report by *Der Spiegel* in 2008, a good 40 per cent of both male and female employees believe that 'sucking up to the boss is necessary to climb the corporate ladder'. So although the relationship between boss and subordinate may be generally formal and distant, employees may try to do some flattering such as telling the boss he saw him on TV last night and it was a superb interview, or remarking in an impressed tone how unique the boss's new handphone is.

As mentioned in Chapter Four, colleagues expect you to lay out a spread on your birthday. You should bring food and drinks to the office on your birthday to celebrate with your colleagues. Colleagues will often get together to buy you a gift.

In some offices, colleagues exchange chocolates and sweets on 6 December (St. Nicholas Day). Bosses may hand out chocolate figures of St. Nicholas to subordinates, too.

On an ordinary working day, where there are no meetings with clients, Germans can be rather casual in their dressing. Backroom employees are often particularly casual with their dress code.

Business over a Meal
German businessmen are unlikely to invite you to their home. The business lunch is the most common business meal, and this will be in a restaurant. Business discussions are usually conducted before, but rarely during, the meal. At the business lunch, the conversation will revolve round more general topics about the industry or some world event.

Business Gifts
Gifts for business associates should be of good quality, but not too expensive. Good quality pens, leather bound stationery or a good bottle (if you come from a country which produces quality wine or other liquor) are appropriate.

Globalisation and Its Effects on Etiquette
While good to know the traditional Teutonic ways in the business environment, they may become less and less pronounced over the years. With globalisation, business people are well travelled. Some have studied or worked overseas and are therefore more international in their business dealings. It shouldn't therefore come as a surprise if your German colleagues, especially the younger ones, prefer to adopt a first-name basis and like to go out for drinks together after work.

CLASH OF THE CLASSES
Germany doesn't have the class distinction based on blood line per se prevalent in England. There is, however, the usual tension between have and have nots. Hierarchy exists, but it is based on organisational structure, and not on who one's forebears were. There isn't much affection between management and the rank and file. Opinion polls have found that 85 per cent of Germans think managers are overpaid, leading populist politicans to suggest ceilings for executive pay. There is little trust of the people at the top, and this only worsened when it came to light in 2008 that many leading companies such as Lidl, Deutsche Telekom and Lufthansa were spying on their staff or on journalists. American style 'golden parachutes' paid to departing top management cause

convulsions among the average German and any downfall of a wealthy person is often received with gleeful *Schadenfreude*.

The phrase much bandied about in Germany is '*Soziale Gerechtigkeit*' (social justice). The socialists and left parties compete with one another to show their *Soziale Gerechtigkeit* credentials. The idea that the wealth of those fat cats up there should be re-distributed among all Germans is widely promoted by them. What this translates into in practical terms is that taxes are incorrigibly high, with earners in the top bracket paying a personal income tax rate of 42 per cent, prompting the really wealthy to be domiciled in other countries or try to evade taxes.

DIFFERENT TYPES OF ORGANISATIONS

> For a detailed description of the different types of organisations available in Germany, see:
> - http://www.invest-in-germany.com
>   Click on '10 reasons to choose Germany', then 'Business Guide to Germany'. (Information in English)

Companies
Corporate laws are similar to those in Anglo-Saxon countries. Companies are legal entities, and therefore can sue and be sued. To incorporate a company, a minimum share capital is required. Companies are held to a higher standard of accounting than partnerships.

There are basically three forms of corporations:
- The GmbH (*Gesellschaft mit beschränkter Haftung*)—limited liability company
- The AG (*Aktiengesellschaft*)—stock corporation
- The KGaA (*Kommanditgesellschaft auf Aktien*)—partnership limited by shares

GmbH (Limited Liability Company)
You would have noticed that GmbH is a common legal form for German companies. It's not very complicated to incorporate a GmbH, and it has relatively few obligations.

To start a GmbH, a deed of formation and articles of association are signed by the founding shareholders before a notary. The GmbH must be registered in the commercial register.

AG (Stock Corporation)

The advantages of a stock corporation are that shares can be easily transferred, and it can be listed on the stock exchange, making raising equity easier. But this type of company is subjected to a lot more regulations than a GmbH. It's also more costly and complicated to establish. A minimum share capital of €50,000 is required. The AG must be registered in the commercial register.

The founding shareholders must appoint the first auditors and supervisory board (*Aufsichtsrat*). The latter then appoints a management board (*Vorstand*).

German law prescribes a dual board system for stock corporations: a management board and a supervisory board. The day-to-day management of the company is the responsibility of the management board, while the supervisory board advises and supervises the management board. The members of the supervisory board are elected by the shareholders at the General Meeting. For companies with more than 500 employees, one-third of the supervisory board must comprise employees. The employee representation goes up to one half if the company has more than 2000 employees.

Partnerships

Partnerships are also relatively easy to set up, requiring only at least two partners. The accounting and disclosure requirements are less stringent than for companies. Its disadvantage is the unlimited liability of the partners. There are different types of partnerships:

- Civil Law Partnership
- General Commercial Partnership
- Limited Partnership
- Partnership Company
- Corporate Partnership

Sole Proprietorships

Sole proprietorships (*Einzelunternehmer*) can be set up by just one natural person, making it suitable for small businesses. If the sole proprietorship's business is trading, it must register with the trade office. Registration in the commercial register is only necessary if the annual turnover is more than €250,000 and it has a profit margin of at least €25,000.

Branches

A foreign company can open a branch office, which will not be a separate legal entity. It remains part of the head office and is thus subject to the laws governing the head office.

UNIONS AND WORKS COUNCILS

Worker representation in German companies is achieved through the unions and the works councils (*Betriebsrat*).

Even though membership is at an all-time low, the unions remain a force to be reckoned with, with the ability to call for crippling strikes to push for higher pay and better conditions. Not only workers in the manufacturing sector join unions; there is a powerful service sector union, Ver.di and a just as muscular doctors' union, Marburger Bund. Union representatives are elected by union members. The trade unions conclude regional collective agreements for each industry and decide on any industrial action.

The German policy of co-determination (*Mitbestimmung*) is best illustrated by the existence of works councils. A works council may be established in any company that has five or more employees. Works councillors are elected by the employees within a company to serve a four-year term. The councillors cannot be removed by the company; only by the labour court. The works council must be consulted for things like working hours, hiring and firing policies, vacation schedules, safety issues, welfare, hiring, and transfers within the company.

In companies with 200 or more employees, one employee must be released from his work and become a full-time works councillor. The number of full-time councillors increases with the number of employees in the company. The employer has the duty of providing the works council with meeting rooms, telephones and other office needs.

BERLIN AT A GLANCE

CHAPTER 10

'Berlin combines the culture of New York,
the traffic system of Tokyo, the nature of Seattle,
and the historical treasures of, well, Berlin.'
—Hiroshi Motomura, US law professor

Official Name
Berlin

Berlin Flag
Three horizontal stripes in red-white-red in the ratio of 1:3:1. On the white portion is a black bear standing on its hind legs.

Berlin Coat of Arms
Permitted for use only by officialdom, the coat of arms also features an upright standing black bear, but with a red tongue and a gold crown, and on a silver background.

German National Anthem
The lyrics of the German national anthem is the third verse of the *Lied der Deutschen* or the *Deutschlandlied* (Song of the Germans) written in 1841 by Heinrich Hoffmann von Fallersleben (1798–1874), sung to the melody of the second movement of the Emperor Quartet by Joseph Haydn (1732–1809).

Time
One hour ahead of Greenwich Mean Time (GMT + 1). During summer (March to October), it's GMT + 2. Germany practises daylight saving hours.

Telephone Country Code
Country code for Germany: 49
Area code for Berlin: 030

Climate
Typical continental European, with hot summers and icy winters. The hottest months are July and August, with temperatures anywhere between 23°C (73.4°F) to 30°C (86°F). Rain is not unexpected in summer. From December to February, the temperatures are usually around minus 2°C (36°F) to 7°C (44°F).

Land
Total area: 892 sq km (344.4 sq miles)
Lakes and waterways: 59.7 sq km (23 sq miles)

Highest Point
Müggelberg and Teufelsberg (both 115 m / 377.3 ft)

Major Rivers
Spree and Havel

Population
3.4 million

Ethnic Groups
Although a predominantly Teutonic population, 14 per cent are foreigners (from 184 nationalities). 25.7 per cent have immigrant backgrounds. The Turks form the largest ethnic group after the Teutons.

Religion
A large swathe of the population is secular. The main religious groups are Protestants, Catholics, Muslims and Jews.

Language
The official language is German. There is a Berlin dialect, called Berlinerisch.

Government

Berlin is governed by the Senate (comprising the mayor and maximium of eight senators). The Senate is elected by the House of Representatives (i.e. the parliament) which has at least 130 members. These parliamentarians are elected by Berliners.

The main German political parties are the Christian Democratic Union (CDU); its sister party, the Christian Social Union (CSU) ; Social Democratic Party of Germany (SPD); the Free Democratic Party (FDP); the Left Party; and the Greens. At the time of writing, Berlin is governed by a 'red-red' coalition: the SPD and the Left Party.

Administrative Divisions

Berlin has 12 boroughs (*Bezirke*): Charlottenburg-Wilmersdorf, Friedrichshain-Kreuzberg, Lichtenberg, Marzahn-Hellersdorf, Mitte, Neukölln, Pankow, Reinickendorf, Spandau, Steglitz-Zehlendorf, Tempelhof-Schöneberg, Treptow-Köpenick.

Currency

Euros

Gross Domestic Product (GDP)

€83.55 billion (2007 est.)

Industries

The traditionally strong sectors are electrical engineering, food products, chemicals, mechanical engineering and motor-vehicle manufacturing. In recent years, however, the service industry has overtaken the manufacturing industries in importance. The city is also focusing on forward-looking sectors and promoting cooperation between businesses and science. Transportation technology, biotechnology, medical technology, infotechnology and media are all being nurtured.

Berlin is also the top German venue for congresses and trade fairs, and a seat of film production companies and TV stations.

Exports
Vehicles, chemicals, machinery, foodstuffs

Ports
Berlin's largest port is the Westhafen with an area of 173,000 sq m (1,861,480 sq ft). The second largest, the Südhafen covers an area of about 103,000 sq m (1,108,280 sq ft). Two other ports are the Osthafen with an area of 57,500 sq m (618,700 sq ft) and the Hafen Neukölln, with 19,000 sq m (204,440 sq ft).

Airports
Berlin has currently two functioning airports, Tegel and Schönefeld. Schönefeld is expected to become the Berlin-Brandenburg International by 2011, a development which is about the size of 2,000 football (soccer) fields. Tempelhof closed in October 2008.

FAMOUS BERLINERS
The list below includes those not born in Berlin, but have a close relationship with the city.

Creative Fields
Marlene Dietrich
Born Marie Magdalene Dietrich in 1901 in the district of Schöneberg, Dietrich is hailed as the first German actress to find success in Hollywood.

In the 1920s, she worked as a cabaret singer, chorus girl and actress in Berlin before moving to Hollywood in the 1930s. Her talent for re-inventing herself led her to become a 20th century icon in the entertainment world by the end of her career. Dietrich died in 1992 and her final resting place is at the Städtischen Friedhof III in Berlin.

Helmut Newton
Another ex Schöneberger, this famous fashion photographer renowned for his nude pictures of women was born Helmut Neustädter. Born to a German-Jewish father and an American mother, Newton fled Germany in 1938 to

avoid Nazi persecution. He worked briefly in Singapore as a photographer for the *Straits Times* before settling in Melbourne, Australia, and taking Australian nationality. He also lived in London, Paris, Monte Carlo and Los Angeles.

Newton donated a huge photo collection to the Prussian Cultural Heritage Foundation in his beloved Berlin. The collection can be seen at the Museum of Photography. He died in 2004 and his ashes are buried next to Marlene Dietrich.

Max Liebermann

This famous artist was born in 1847, and is one of the leading German impressionists and painter of portraits. In 1920, he became President of the Academy of Fine Arts, but was sacked in 1933 as he was a Jew. He died in 1934 in isolation in his Berlin apartment.

On 30 April 2006, the Max Liebermann Society opened a permanent museum in the Liebermann family home in Berlin-Wansee, a bitter-sweet development, as it was here that Liebermann's wife committed suicide in 1943, to avoid being sent to a concentration camp.

Käthe Kollwitz

Käthe Schmidt Kollwitz worked with various art forms, but focused on portraying human suffering. A copy of her sculpture, *Mother and Dead Son*, fittingly sits in the Neue Wache, a memorial to victims of war and tyranny. Born in 1867 in what is now Kaliningrad in Russia, she studied in an art school in Berlin. In 1891, she married Karl Kollwitz, a doctor who worked with the poor in Berlin. This proximity to the poor was to influence her work substantially.

Kollwitzplatz in Prenzlauer Berg is named after her, as here was where she lived for much of her life.

Heinrich Zille

Heinrich Zille was born in 1858 in Radeburg near Dresden. He is famous for his satirical illustrations of ordinary people, especially Berliners. His vivid portrayal of the desperately poor residents of the Berlin tenement blocks has become a record of Berlin in the early 1900s. The Zille museum is at the Nikolaiviertel.

Skladanowsky Brothers

Max and Emil Skladanowsky invented the Bioskop, an early movie projector they used to display the first moving picture show to a paying audience on 1 November 1895, in the same year of the public debut of the Lumière Brothers' technically superior Cinématographe. The Bioskop could project 16 frames per second, a speed sufficient to create the illusion of movement.

Heinz Berggruen

Born in Berlin, this Jewish art collector fled Nazi Germany in 1936. He first went to the United States and then to Paris, where he established a reputation as a gallery owner and as a specialist on the works of artists such as Van Gogh, Cézanne, Matisse and Paul Klee. In 1949, he was introduced to Picasso and that was the start of a firm friendship that placed Berggruen in a privileged position to acquire works by the famous artist.

His is one of the most important private collections of modern art in the world. In 1996, he brought his extensive modern art collection back to his birthplace. In 2000, he sold it to the city for a price way below its market value, an extraordinary gesture of reconciliation. The collection is now housed in the Berggruen Museum.

Berggruen died in Paris in February 2007 at the age of 93.

Cherno Jobatey

Jobatey is one of the rare black success stories in Germany. Born in Berlin in 1965, the son of a Gambian and a piano teacher from Berlin worked with talent and persistence to become a top TV presenter. Since 1992, he has been presenting the morning news magazine *ZDF-Morgenmagazin*. Before that, he presented a number of shows including a quiz show, regional news for Berlin-Brandenburg and his own talk show.

Jobatey read politics and music at the Free University in Berlin and won a one-year scholarship to UCLA with the German student exchange programme, DAAD. It was in California that he decided on his career goals. A talk he held on Jesse Jackson also caught the attention of a Berlin radio station which paved the way for his career in radio, before he switched to TV.

He is also the author of a fitness book, *Fit wie ein Turnschuh* (Fit as a fiddle).

Wladimir Kaminer

Kaminer is one of the many Russian Jews who have made Berlin their new home. Born in Moscow, he came to the then East Berlin as a 23-year-old. Enterprising and multi-talented, he has found success as a columnist, an author and a DJ (of the famous Russendisko). Kaffee Burger, a place where creative upstarts can showcase their talents, is also his brainchild.

His books, such as *Schönhauser Allee* and *Ich bin kein Berliner* are humorous reflections of the Soviet Union and everyday life in Berlin, including the occasional prejudices he faced as a Russian immigrant. But Kaminer is guilty of some stereotyping himself, e.g. his all too frequent reference to 'Thai prostitutes' in *Ich bin kein Berliner*, as if all prostitutes came only from Thailand.

The Sciences
Gerhard Ertl

Born in Stuttgart in 1936, Ertl won the 2007 Nobel Prize in Chemistry. He is a Professor Emeritus at the Department of Physical Chemistry, Fritz-Haber-Institut der Max-Planck-Gesellschaft (affectionately called 'Fritz') in Berlin. He was director of the Fritz from 1986 to 2004. Ertl currently lives in Berlin.

Architecture

Many architects left a legacy of breathtaking buildings in Berlin:

Karl Friedrich Schinkel

Schinkel moulded much of the face of Berlin. Many of the city's historical buildings were designed by this talented architect of neoclassicism such as the Neue Wache, the Altes Museum, the Konzerthaus and the Friedrichswerdersche Kirche. He oversaw the Prussian building commission and turned the then unremarkable Berlin into one which still draws tourists to oggle at his beautiful designs today. One of his 'babies', the Friedrichswerdersche Kirche, is today a Schinkel museum. Schinkel was also a painter, mostly of architectural fantasies.

Georg Wenzeslaus von Knobelsdorff

Knobelsdorff was both an architect and a painter. His most famous work is the Schloss Sanssouci in Potsdam, although other no less important works include the original design of St. Hedwigs Kathedrale and the Staatsoper Unter den Linden.

Carl Gotthard Langhans

Langhans designed the Brandenburger Tor (although the Quadriga on top is by famous sculptor Johann Gottfried Schadow). Other works include the dome on top of Marienkirche (added in 1790), the Museum für Vor und Frühgeschichte and the oval banquet hall of Schloss Bellevue (the official residence of Germany's president).

Andreas Schlüter

Schlüter designed the now demolished (but to be reconstructed) Stadtschloss. The other work he was most famous for was the concept and design of the Amber Room, first installed in Schloss Charlottenburg, but later given to Tsar Peter the Great to cement the Prussian-Russian relationship. The Amber room was looted by the Nazis and the present whereabouts remain a mystery. An alabaster pulpit in Marienkirche is also Schlüter's design, as are the masks of dying warriors in the inner courtyard of the Deutsches Historisches Museum and the imposing bronze equestrian statue of the Great Elector in Schloss Charlottenburg.

Eduard Knoblauch

A member of Knoblauch family with the family home, Knoblauchhaus, in Nikolaiviertel, Eduard Knoblauch's most important work was the New Synagogue on Oranienburger Straße which started in 1858, but was only completed after his death in 1866. He also designed the first Russian Embassy in Berlin.

Philosophy, Pedagogy and Natural Sciences
Humboldt Brothers

These two brothers are arguably the most well-known Berliners. The elder, Friedrich Wilhelm Christian Karl Ferdinand Freiherr von Humboldt (born in 1767) was the founder of the Friedrich-Wilhelms-Universität (now Humboldt University), which changed university teaching by making it research-intensive and initiated the 'science revolution' of the 19th and 20th centuries. He is also famous for his contributions to the science of language, and the theory and practice of education. His brother Alexander von Humboldt, called the scientific discoverer of Latin America, worked with other scientists, notably Aimé Bonpland, with whom he conducted many of his explorations. He contributed enormously to the development of science in Germany and Europe.

Moses Mendelssohn

The philosopher Moses Mendelssohn was born in Dessau and came to Berlin in 1743. Mendelssohn is considered the father of *Haskalah* (Jewish Enlightenment).

In 1763, he was awarded the first prize (the second prize went to Immanuel Kant) by the Royal Academy of Sciences for his treatise on Evidence in the Metaphysical Sciences. Mendelssohn was never accepted as a member of the Academy, however, because he was a Jew.

Moses Mendelssohn is the grandfather of the famous conductor and composer, Felix Mendelssohn Bartholdy.

He died on 4 January 1786.

Business
Emil Rathenau

The founder of Allgemeine Elektrizitäts-Gesellschaft (AEG-General Electric Company), Emil Rathenau was born in Berlin in 1838. In 1881, he bought some patented designs from Thomas Edison in order to manufacture products from them and in 1883, founded the German Edison Society for Applied Electricity, which later became AEG in 1887. AEG grew from a supplier of electricity to become one of the few leaders of technical development. He commissioned Peter Behrens to design electrical products for AEG, and Behrens became the father not only of industrial design but of corporate identity as well. He was the first person to create logos and advertising materials with a unified design.

Walther Rathenau, an industrialist and politician during the Weimar years who was assassinated by right-wingers in 1922, is a son of Emil Rathenau.

Sports
Katarina Witt

This famous East German figure skater was born in 1965. At 19, she won her first Olympic gold medal in Sarajevo. At the 1988 Calgary Olympics, she won her second gold. Winner of numerous World and European Championships as well, she was the darling of the GDR. She remains a prominent figure today and is often featured in women's magazines, which busily follows her many luckless love relationships.

Jenny Wolf

Wolf won the Speed Skating World Cup in the 2005/2006 season in the 500 m, and in 2007, at age 28, she broke the world record with 37.04 seconds for the women's 500 m at the ISU World Single Distances Speed Skating Championships in Salt Lake City, Utah.

Civil Courage
Otto Weidt

Weidt was the Oskar Schindler of Berlin. As the owner of a brush and broom factory in one of Berlin's poor towns, he employed some 30 blind and deaf Jews between 1941 and 1943, and managed to prevent their deportation to death camps by bribing Nazi officials. He also hid many other Jews in rented storage rooms.

Otto Weidt died an impoverished man in 1948, aged 66.

Wilhelm Krützfeld

On Kristallnacht (9 November 1938), Nazi thugs tried to set fire to the Neue Synagogue but were prevented from doing so by Wilhelm Krützfeld, the 58-year-old local police chief.

Politics
Klaus Wowereit

Wowereit became mayor of Berlin in 2001 at the relatively youthful age of 48. Although Wowereit is not the only homosexual politician in Germany (for the curious, two others are the Christian Democrat mayor of Hamburg, Ole von Beust, and Free Democrat chairman, Guido Westerwelle), he shook the country by coming out of the closet before he was elected mayor. He famously declared '*Ich bin schwul, und das ist auch gut so.*' (I am gay, and that's okay) at a party convention. He was also the first Social Democrat politician to enter into a coalition with the Party of Democratic Socialism (essentially the former communist party). He was re-elected mayor in 2006.

PLACES OF INTEREST

Frankly, Berlin has so many interesting places that only a guide book dedicated to the city's sights can do all of them justice. The list here is, therefore, not exhaustive.

Free Tours

There is really such a thing. At 11:00 am, 1:00 pm and 4:00 pm daily, well-informed tourist guides wait outside the Starbucks Cafe at Brandenburger Tor to take you on a 3.5 hour tour of Berlin's sights. You give the guide a tip at the end according to your means and level of satisfaction. See http://www.newberlintours.com for further information and the pick-up times for the other meeting point at Bahnhof Zoo.

Unter den Linden

This street is one of the most famous in Berlin and is home to a large number of historic buildings. The Brandenburger Tor is at one end of this long street. The Goddess of Victory on top of this gateway has observed from her vantage point many momentous events in Berlin's history: Napoleon's troops marching through on 27 October 1806, the return of the Kaiser's defeated troops on 10 December 1918, the Nazi's torch parade to celebrate Hitler's becoming Chancellor on 30 January 1933, the fall of the Berlin Wall on 9 November 1989 and nowadays, the parties to honour the national football team after major tournaments.

Nearby is the Hotel Adlon which opened in 1907, where a coterie of international rich and famous stayed. Badly damaged in World War II, it was demolished and a newly rebuilt Adlon opened again in 1997. Past the corner which intersects with Friedrichstraße, there is a concentration of baroque and neo-classical buildings with a long history, albeit mostly rebuilt after being destroyed in World War II. Around Bebelplatz, there is the Alte Bibliothek, Altes Palais, Staatsoper, Kronprinzenpalais and St.-Hedwigs-Kathedrale. The Alte Bibliothek was once the Royal Library, originally built in 1775, and rebuilt after the War from 1967–1969. The Altes Palais was built for Kaiser Wilhelm I when he was still a prince. Built from 1834 to 1837, it was also destroyed during the war and subsequently restored. The Staatsoper was designed by the famous architect, Georg Wenzeslaus von Knobelsdorff, and built from 1741 to 1743. The current building was rebuilt after the original was destroyed during the war.

The Kronprinzenpalais dates back to 1663, but the current building is also one rebuilt after the war, using old engravings as building plans, since it was reduced to ashes during the war. The last German Emperor, Kaiser Wilhelm II, was born here. Another significant piece of history attached to this building is the signing of the Unification Treaty on 31 August 1990, which united the two Germanys. St.-Hedwigs-Kathedrale is now the seat of the archbishopric of Berlin. Built in 1747, it was consecrated in 1773. Its fate during

The glass extension of the Deutsches Historisches Museum.

World War II was similar to the other buildings. The current building was rebuilt between 1952 and 1963. The square, Bebelplatz, was itself the site of an ugly incident in 1933. It was here that the Nazis burned the books they deemed were not in line with Nazi ideology.

Across the road is the Humboldt Universität founded in 1810, an idea conceived by Wilhelm von Humboldt. Nextdoor is the Neue Wache, a fine piece of neo-classical architecture designed by Karl Friedrich Schinkel. In 1993, it became a memorial for all victims of war and tyranny. Inside is an enlarged copy of Käthe Kollwitz's poignant sculpture of a mother holding her dead son. Next to the Neue Wache is the Deutsches Historisches Museum (formerly Zeughaus), built in 1706 as an arsenal. This baroque building had a sleek glass extension added to it in 2003, designed by Japanese-American I M Pei , the same man who designed the glass pyramid at the Louvre in Paris.

Museumsinsel

The Museumsinsel (Museum Island) is aptly named for the impressive museums to be found there: the Altes Museum, the Neues Museum, the Alte Nationalgalerie, the Pergamonmuseum and the Bode Museum. The latter is named after Wilhelm von Bode, head of all museums from 1872 to 1920, who was instrumental in building the collections in these museums into world-class ones. The island was named a UNESCO World Heritage site in 1999.

The island is also where the 'original' Berlin was. In the early 13th century, this area was the twin settlement of Cölln/Berlin.

Other than the museums, other historical buildings on the island are the Berliner Dom (the place of worship and burial place of the royal Hohenzollerns) and the DDR parliament house, the Palast der Republik. The latter stands on the site of the former Stadtschloss (palace), the home of Prussian kings and German kaisers. The communist regime of East Germany tore down the palace in 1950 and built the Palast there. At the time of writing, the Palast was getting its comeuppance; it was being torn down and the former Stadtschloss will be reconstructed there.

Nearby is the Schlossbrücke, a bridge decorated with statues, designed by the renowned Karl Friedrich Schinkel. In front of the Alte Museum is the Lustgarten, a pleasant park to take a break on the park benches and admire the buildings around you. Once the gardens of the royals, it was turned into a military parade ground both by the Prussians and the Nazis, before finally becoming the park of today.

Don't Get Conned!

Around popular tourist sites, you may come across a 'game stall', with a small group of people playing the 'three shell game', also known as *thimblerig*. The game operator places a small pea-sized object under one of three shells (e.g. bottle caps) and then shuffles the three shells around quickly. You then bet which shell the pea is under, and if you guess correctly, you are paid double what you've bet. If you guess wrongly, the operator pockets your money.

No one ever wins, unless the operator intentionally lets you, just to make you bet a higher sum. It's all a sleight of hand; the operator can remove the 'pea' from whichever shell without your ever noticing it. The other gamblers standing around are accomplices, to attract potential victims and act as lookouts for the police. So it's best to stay away from these conmen.

Reichstag

There is always a long line of visitors waiting in front of the Reichstag (the German parliament) building. Designed by Paul Wallot and built between 1884–1894, the building was extensively renovated between 1995–1999 according to a design by Sir Norman Foster who added the distinctive elliptical glass dome with a viewing gallery. Visitors can observe the parliament in session below, which is intended to signify its transparency. From the ground, one can see visitors walk up the spiral staircase to the top. The first sitting of the parliament of a unified Germany took place in the Reichstag on 2 December 1990.

To indulge in a bit of trivial pursuit, the flags flying in front of the Reichstag always look so crisp and new because they are changed every four weeks, or even every three days in inclement weather.

Siegessäule

This Victory Column with a golden Victoria on top commemorates Prussian victory in wars against Denmark (1864), Austria (1866) and France (1871). Originally located in front of the Reichstag, it was moved by the Nazi government to its current location in 1938. This landmark particularly caught American attention on 24 July 2008, when the then Democratic presidential candidate, Barack Obama, made a speech there to an enthusiastic crowd of 200,000.

Gendarmenmarkt

One of the most beautiful squares of Berlin, this 48,000 sq m (516,480 sq ft) was created in the 17th century, and named after the regiment Gens d'Armes who had their barracks and stables here. The square is flanked by the Französischer Dom (French Cathedral) and the Deutscher Dom (German Cathedral), standing at opposite ends of the square. The French Cathedral was built between 1701–1705 for the Protestant Huguenots, who had to flee Catholic France. Today, it houses the Huguenot Museum. The German Cathedral was built in 1708. After burning down in 1945, it was rebuilt in 1993. Between the two cathedrals stands the Konzerthaus,

The majestic Deutscher Dom is located on one of the most beautiful squares of Berlin.

another Schinkel masterpiece built between 1818–1821. The Refugium restaurant is also strategically located on the square. In spite of its very posh looks, the prices are reasonable for such a prime location.

Nikolaiviertel

Nikolaiviertel (Nikolai Quarter) is the eastern part of the early settlement of Cölln/Berlin. It's a favourite haunt of tourists because of the ambience. The oldest church of Berlin, Nikolaikirche, and the taverns and little souvenir shops lend the quarter an air of old Berlin. Nikolaikirche dates back to the 13th century, although the current church is a reconstruction after the original was destroyed in the war. It was from here in 1539 that news of the Reformation spread to the rest of the city.

Although the quarter has real historic significance, most of the buildings are mere replicas of historic buildings. This was the Socialist Disneyland planned by the East German regime. Although some buildings, like the Nikolaikirche, are restored old buildings, many others are reconstructions of buildings that were situated elsewhere in the city. For example, the famous old inn which was frequented by famous people like Heinrich Zille, Zum Nussbaum, used to be on nearby Fischerinsel. It was bombed and destroyed during the war, and the current inn standing there is a well-made copy of the original. The Gerichtslaube opposite is also a reconstruction. For a genuine historical building, the Knoblauchhaus at Poststraße 23 is the perfect example. Built in 1759, it miraculously survived World War II bombings. The house was constructed by master tailor Johann Christian Knoblauch. It was here that Berlin's famous architect Eduard Knoblauch was born. Famous visitors to this house included Mendelssohn and Wilhelm von Humboldt.

Kaiser-Wilhelm-Gedächtnis-Kirche (Kaiser Wilhelm Memorial Church)

What's left of this church has been deliberately left unrestored and pock-marked, after being severely damaged by Allied bombs, as a reminder of the destruction that wars wreak.

The Kaiser Wilhelm Memorial Church is an important reminder of Germany's tumultuous history.

Consecrated in 1895, the remaining tower of the church is now a memorial hall documenting its history. Inside are some intricate original mosaics mostly depicting the royal Hohenzollern family.

A new octagonal church in concrete and blue glass was built in 1961 next to the tower.

Spandau

Spandau is older than Berlin/Cölln, with settlements dating back to the 8th century. There is a medieval ambience in some areas of Spandau and a number of handsome historic buildings are still standing today (although many are restorations): the Zitadelle Spandau (Spandau Citadel), a 16th century fortress; St.-Nikolai-Kirche, a church from the 15th century; the Alte Marienkirche from 1848; the 18th century inn, Gasthof zum Stern; and Das Gotische Haus, the most important secular medieval monument left in Berlin. In the old city centre, it feels as if time had stood still, and is particularly charming when the Christmas market is set up here in the weeks before Christmas.

PALACES
Schloss Charlottenburg and Park

This summer residence of the wife of King Friedrich I, Sophie Charlotte,was first built in 1695 by Johann Arnold Nering, although extensions were added subsequently. The palace's exquisite interior is filled with fine furniture, porcelain collections and paintings. The huge French-style manicured garden and enormous English style park behind the palace give the palace the grandeur that is not easily seen from the front of the palace. Beyond the carp lake is the Belvedere, designed by Carl Gotthard Langhans, and houses a huge collection of the famous KPM porcelain.

The entrance to Schloss Charlottenburg.

Schloss and Park Sanssoucci

Sanssouci means 'without worries' in French, and the massive 287 hectares (709 acres) park located in Potsdam certainly feels very Zen. At the same time, the many splendid palaces and other buildings spread around the vast park give the place splendour, making it easy to appreciate what the expression 'living like a king' means.

Visitors should set aside a whole day, if not two, to truly explore the park and every building.

JEWISH-RELATED PLACES OF INTEREST

Neue Synagoge

Designed by Eduard Knoblauch, the New Synagogue on Oranienburger Straße was completed in 1866. It survived the attacks on all Jewish interests by Nazi thugs on 9 November 1938, thanks to the courage of Wilhelm Krützfeld, only to be destroyed by air raids in 1943. The Moorish style synagogue underwent restoration for seven years, which was completed in 1995. The impressive gilded dome can be seen from kilometres away. The Centrum Judaicum (Jewish Centre) is right next door.

Jüdisches Museum

The Jewish Museum was designed by Polish-American Daniel Libeskind. The building is an unusual lightning shape, to connote a shattered Star of David. The museum's concept is also unusual; the sloping floors, zig zags and empty spaces are intended to evoke a sense of disorientation and the loss following the destruction of Jewish life. The Holocaust Tower, a 24 m (79 ft) high room is left unheated and completely dark except for a small shaft of light coming through a slit near the ceiling. Especially on a cold winter day, the sense of desolation in the Tower is very effective as a commemoration of the Jewish victims of mass murder.

Holocaust-Mahnmal

The Holocaust Memorial, erected to commemorate the murdered European Jews, was designed by American architect Peter Eisenmann. The memorial consists of 2711 concrete slabs of varying heights spread over an area of 19,000 sq m (205,000 sq ft). The floor is undulating and at the centre of this vast area,visitors may experience slight claustrophobia, surrounded by these grim concrete slabs which are at the tallest here. There is also an information centre on the genocide here. The design has its share of admirers and critics, but the open concept does obviously encourage teenagers to play hide-and-seek among the concrete slabs and thoughtless visitors to leave their food packaging and disposal cups on the site. The Dunkin' Donuts outlet nearby actually has a sign on its window telling customers to refrain from eating and drinking at the memorial.

The Bendler Block

This is a historic building complex near the Tiergarten Park. Now the site of the German Resistance Memorial Center, the place is best known as the center of the attempt to overthrow the National Socialist regime on 20 July 1944, led by Colonel Count Claus von Stauffenberg.

The courtyard where the officers who plotted to assassinate Hitler were executed on the night of July 20, 1944 is accessible from Stauffenbergstraße.

There is a permanent exhibition, Resistance to National Socialism, on the second floor of the building. It documents the motives, methods, and goals of the struggle against Hilter and his National Socialists.

COLD WAR RELATED PLACES OF INTEREST
Berlin Wall

Visitors to Germany are often disappointed that there's not much of the Wall left to be seen. The longest stretch of remaining Wall is the East Side Gallery at 1.3 km (0.8 miles) long, just behind the Ostbahnhof Station on the Spree. If you go to the McCafe on the second floor of the food and shopping area of the station, you can enjoy an Arabica and a view of the Wall at the same time. The other places to see the Wall are at the Gedenkstätte Berliner Mauer (Berlin Wall Memorial) at Bernauer Straße 111, the Topographie des Terrors (Topography of Terror, documenting the Nazi reign of terror), in Niederkirchnerstraße (near Potsdamer Platz) and a few panels of the Wall with information in German and English at Potsdamer Platz itself.

The location of the Wall is now demarcated by easily overlooked faint markings, e.g, at Potsdamer Platz and just behind the Brandenburger Tor. Hardly anyone notices them as they stride across nowadays.

Checkpoint Charlie

This checkpoint was the only place where non-Germans could cross between East and West Berlin in the years 1961 to 1990. In 1961, there was a tense stand-off between Russian and American tanks here. Today, the replica checkpoint booth, sandbags and two flag-carrying 'soldiers' smack somewhat of Disney-ish kitsch.

As for the museum, Haus am Checkpoint Charlie, some visitors lament it's rather haphazard, but remember that this is a private museum, without access to state funds. The museum was also more than that during the Cold War;

The replica Checkpoint Charlie is a far cry from the actual checkpoint fraught with tension and danger.

The East Side Gallery is the longest stretch of the Berlin Wall that remains.

through a small window, escape helpers observed all the goings-on at the nearby checkpoint in order to help plan escapes. The museum gives visitors a rundown on the history of the Wall, the ingenious ways of escape that desperate East Germans thought up and include some of the contraptions used as means of escape, donated by escape-helpers who the museum had friendly contact with. You can't help but come away feeling moved by the desperation, successes and tragedies connected to that horrid Wall. The museum sells souvenirs too, of course, and one particularly interesting souvenir (to the author) is a reprint of the 13 August 1961 issue of the Berliner Morgenpost, with pictures of the newly installed barbed-wire fence, the pre-cursor of the Berlin Wall.

Trabi Safari

It's an unusual experience to see Cold War sights in *the* car of former East Germany, the Trabi (short for Trabant). To go on a Trabi-Safari, see their website: http://trabi-safari.de

---

Explore the Cold War sights in a Trabi!

Forschungs & Gedenkstätte Normannenstraße (Stasi Museum)

Formerly part of Stasi headquarters, here's where visitors can look at the spying devices used and other communist paraphernalia.

Gedenkstätte Sachsenhausen

This notorious place started off as a Nazi concentration camp for Jews, gays, communists, gypsies, trade unionists and anyone that the Nazis felt were their enemies or social misfits. During the Cold War, anyone suspected of being against the East German regime were also brought here. This ghastly place is the location where tens of thousands were murdered.

Oberbaumbrücke

This bridge straddled East and West Berlin (Friedrichshain and Kreuzberg to be precise) during the Cold War. This Brandenburg Gothic brick-style bridge was originally built between 1894 and 1896, and Berlin's first underground/subway crossed the Spree over this bridge in 1902. Badly damaged during the war, the bridge was renovated at a mind-blowing cost of €102.3 million and re-opened for traffic in 1994.

Ostel

Want to be totally immersed in East German ambience? Then check into the Ostel (a play on the German words for 'east' and 'hotel') for a few nights. Near Ostbahnhof station, the hotel is in a *Plattenbau* (those communist-era pre-fabricated apartment buildings) and decorated with authentic GDR-era furniture and wallpaper. Don't worry, the mattresses, sheets and plumbing are new. The room rates will please budget travellers, too.

Oberbaumbrücke: the bridge that connected East and West Belin during the Cold War.

ACRONYMS AND ABBREVIATIONS

Political Parties and Politics

Acronym/ Abbrev.	German	English
CDU	Christlich-Demokratische Union	Christian Democratic Union (conservative)
CSU	Christlich-Soziale Union	Christian Social Union. (Bavarian sister party of CDU. CDU and CSU are considered one party in parliament)
SPD	Sozialdemokratische Partei Deutschlands	Social Democratic Party of Germany
FDP	Freie Demokratische Partei	Free Democratic Party
Bündnis 90/ Die Grünen	-	Alliance 90/ the Greens
Die Linke	-	The Left (union of PDS and WASG in 2005)
PDS	Partei des Demokratischen Sozialismus	Party of Democratic Socialism
WASG	Wahlalternative Arbeit und Soziale Gerechtigkeit	Voting Alternative, Work and Social Justice
NPD	Nationaldemokratische Partei Deutschlands	National Democratic Party of Germany

DDR	Deutsche Demokratische Republik	German Democratic Republic (i.e. the former East Germany)
MdB	Mitglied des Bundestages	Member of parliament
MdL	Mitglied des Landtages	Member of state legislature

Business-related

AG	Aktiengesellschaft	Public company
AOK	Allgemeine Ortskrankenkasse	Public health insurance company
DIHK	Deutsche Industrie und Handelskammer	German Chamber of Industry & Commerce
DRK	Deutsches Rotes Kreuz	German Red Cross
e.V	Eingetragener Verein	Registered association
EZB	Europäische Zentral Bank	European Central Bank
GmbH	Gesellschaft mit beschränkter Haftung	Limited liability company
Inh.	Inhaber	Owner/proprietor

Titles

Dipl.-Ing	Diplom –Ingenieur	Qualified engineer
Dipl.-Kfm	Diplom-Kaufmann	Business school graduate

Days of the Week

Mo	Montag	Monday
Di	Dienstag	Tuesday
Mi	Mittwoch	Wednesday
Do	Donnerstag	Thursday
Fr	Freitag	Friday
Sa	Samstag	Saturday
So	Sonntag	Sunday

Letters and Emails

Abs.	Absender	Sender / return address
Adr.	Adresse	Address
Betr.	Betreff	Re / regarding
Beil.	Beilage	Attachments
P.Adr.	Per Adresse	C/o; care of
PLZ	Postleitzahl	Postal / ZIP code

Traffic

ADAC	Allgemeiner Deutscher Automobil Club	Automobile Association (AA)
LKW	Lastkraftwagen	Lorry/truck
PKW	Personenkraftwagen	Car
PS	Pferdestärke	Horsepower
SB	Selbstbedienung	Self-service (at petrol/gas stations)
StVO	Straßenverkehrsordnung	Traffic laws and regulations
TÜV	Technischer Überwachungs-Verein	Product safety organisation, like MOT(UK) / UL and CSA (North America)

Property-related

AR	Abstellraum	Storage room
Bj.	Baujahr	Year of construction
2-Zi.	2-Zimmer	2-bedroomed
2 ZKB	2 Zimmer, Küche und Bad	2 rooms, kitchen & bathroom
EG	Erdgeschoss	Ground floor / 1st floor (US)
1.OG	erstes Obergeschoss	1st floor / 2nd floor (US)

Places

Ku'damm	Kurfürstendamm
KaDeWe	Kaufhaus des Westens
Prenzl'berg	Prenzlauer Berg

CULTURE QUIZ

SITUATION 1

You've just arrived in Berlin and go to the supermarket to pick up some groceries. At the check-out counter, you smile and cheerily say, *"Guten Tag!"* (the few words of German you've learnt) to the cashier. She mumbles *"Tag"* with a grim face, and focuses on scanning your items. Meanwhile, the conveyor belt has transported your groceries to the end of the counter, and she has not bothered to pack your groceries into a bag. You:

Ⓐ Glare at the cashier, and take note of her name to complain to the manager.

Ⓑ Calmly pay and signal to the cashier to pack your groceries.

Ⓒ Not being the confrontational type, you just pay and pack your groceries into your backpack.

Comments

Ⓒ is the right thing to do. In Germany, cashiers have a good life. They're responsible only for collecting the payment. Customers pack their own groceries into, preferably, a reusable cotton bag/basket which they bring from home. Cotton/plastic bags can be bought at the counter, but environmentally conscious people don't do that. And customer service usually does not come with a smile in Germany. So the cashier was not unduly unfriendly; just typically Teutonic.

SITUATION 2

You've just got off the S-Bahn and are walking along the platform when a brown-skinned gentleman (possibly a Turk) stops you and asks to see your train ticket. He's not wearing a uniform, but does seem to have an identification tag slung round his neck. Should you:

Ⓐ Do as you're told; show him your train ticket.

Ⓑ Try to look for a uniformed personnel to complain about the stranger bothering you.

C Ignore him and hurry off. The guy is probably trying to steal your monthly ticket.

Comments
Although you should exercise caution when approached by strangers, plain-clothes S-Bahn personnel do conduct spot checks on passengers, as there is a high incidence of people travelling without valid tickets. So **A** is the correct answer. People should theoretically not be on a train platform (not only on a train) without a valid ticket. And not all Berliners are Teutonic Germans; there are plenty of Turkish-Germans who are train personnel or policemen. You may ask politely to see his/her ID, though, if the person is not wearing any.

SITUATION 3
You've been invited to a dinner party on New Year's Eve, and you're the only native English speaker there. As the host pours out the wine, he asks one of the German guests in English, "The same procedure as last year, Hans?" to which Hans replies in English "The same procedure as every year." Then everyone bursts out laughing and slap their knees. What's going on?

A Since you're the only native English speaker there, they are trying to impress you.

B They're poking fun at you. Never mind, it's New Year's eve after all.

C It's a private joke.

Comments
There's a short British film called *Dinner for One* which plays faithfully every New Year's eve in Germany on TV. The main quips in the film are what the host and Hans have just said. Germans think all English speakers are familiar with this British film, but it actually has never been shown in the UK nor in most English-speaking countries either. Native English speakers are therefore often left mystified when the Germans repeat these quips during the New Year season. Even newspapers make use of these lines.

SITUATION 4

You are having drinks with some German friends and the discussion is about politics and human rights. You've covered topics like the Tibet-China issue, Mugabe's rule of Zimbabwe and Guantanamo. Should you ask aloud how something like the Holocaust could have been allowed to happen in Germany?

Ⓐ It's not a problem, as Germans are straightforward people and these friends are interested in human rights and politics, anyhow.
Ⓑ No, you shouldn't mention the Holocaust.
Ⓒ No, Germans don't discuss the Holocaust.

Comments

Here, Ⓑ is the answer. Germans, especially the older generation, are on the whole very aware (and ashamed) of this part of their history. Many are open to discussing it, at the right time and right place. But this sensitive topic should be left to a German to bring up, if at all, in a social setting. You shouldn't be the one to raise the topic.

SITUATION 5

You've been invited for coffee and cakes with the family of your girlfriend, which includes her grandmother, who speaks no English. Your German is hesitant, but you want to impress your friend's family that you're trying hard. In describing winter in your homeland, you remark that it's often full of mist. Granny looks at you frostily, while your girlfriend shakes with laughter. What happened?

Ⓐ Granny doesn't like misty weather.
Ⓑ You've said something wrong.
Ⓒ It's not what you said; you obviously have something caught between your teeth.

Comments

Unfortunately, it's Ⓑ. There are words in German and English which have exactly the same meaning, and words which are tricky 'false friends'—same word but with entirely different meanings. 'Mist' means animal dropping/dung in German, not moist air. It's good to want to practise your German, but be careful about 'false friends', especially if you're with company you're trying to impress.

SITUATION 6

You and your wife have just finished dinner in a restaurant, and you ask for the bill. The waiter comes, looks at your wife and you and asks, "Together or separated?" Do you:

Ⓐ Retort sarcastically, "We're happily married, thank you."
Ⓑ Ignore the question, and say sternly, "The bill, please."
Ⓒ Say loudly, "It's none of your business."

Comment:

The above answers are all inappropriate. Germans have a habit of paying for meals individually, so the waiter will always ask if the meals should be added together or billed separately. The German phrase is "*Zusammen oder getrennt?*"

SITUATION 7

You are taking a stroll around one of Berlin's lovely lakes. Suddenly you see many naked bodies lying or standing around the edge of the lake. Do you:

Ⓐ Take photos with your mobile phone at this unusual sight.
Ⓑ Assume they are members of PETA or some other animal rights group and ask if you could sign up as it's something you believe in.
Ⓒ Glare in disgust at these exhibitionists, and call the police.
Ⓓ Carry on walking nonchalantly pass them.

Comments

You've just stumbled on Germany's *Freikörperkultur* (Free Body Culture). However you might feel about naturism, it's still practised by a good many Germans. Should you come across FKK practitioners, **Ⓓ** is the correct option to take. Don't oggle or worse, take pictures.

SITUATION 8

After a very fruitful discussion with Dr. Heinemann, a partner of a firm, about a potential project, he suggests you draw up an action plan and send it over to him. You do so. Three weeks pass and you don't get any response. You call Dr. Heinemann and ask him for his feedback. He tells you he and his partners are still studying it and will get back to you as soon as a decision is made. Another two weeks go by and you haven't heard anything. Should you:

Ⓐ Assume the deal is off. This long silence must be their way of saying 'no'.
Ⓑ Wait patiently for Dr. Heinemann to call you when he's ready.
Ⓒ Call Dr. Heinemann again, to nudge him along. This is taking way too long by your standards.
Ⓓ Maybe Dr. Heinemann isn't the most competent of the three partners. Try to get in touch with the other partners.

Comments

Ⓐ, **Ⓒ** and **Ⓓ** would be shooting yourself in the foot. German businessmen take longer than their American/British counterparts to mull over the fundamentals of a project. They like to work through every detail thoroughly at the outset, rather than to 'fire-fight' along the way.

They also don't take kindly to counterparts trying to push them into making decisions before they've finished analysing the proposal. But they're also straightforward to work with. There's no need to guess what an action might mean. They will tell you 'yes' or 'no' clearly when they've decided. And contacting another partner on your own accord will offend Dr. Heinemann, and embarass his other partners.

SITUATION 9

You have just given a presentation to a group of 18 senior executives sitting around a boardroom table. When you finish, they rap their knuckles on the table, instead of clapping. You then invite them to ask questions and one after the other of the executives fire questions at you, often going down to minute details. How should this be interpreted?

Ⓐ The rapping of knuckles on the table instead of clapping must be a sign that they're not convinced. The firing of questions means your presentation was inadequate.

Ⓑ You're done a good job. They're interested enough to ask questions.

Ⓒ The questioning must be a way of trying to test you, since they didn't even bother to clap.

Comments

Germans (especially in academic circles) often rap their knuckles on the table in place of clapping. Remember that Germans don't smile in business settings, so it can be disconcerting when they ask questions with stony faces. But they ask questions only when they're interested enough in the subject. So Ⓑ is the answer.

Just make sure that you have plenty of detailed data and if appropriate, customer references to respond to queries during question time.

DO'S AND DON'TS

DO

- Learn as much German as you can.
- Use public transport. It's efficient, saves on parking fees and is environmentally friendlier.
- Be punctual for appointments.
- Separate your rubbish/garbage.
- Abide by the 'quiet time' rules.
- Watch out for bicycle lanes on sidewalks.
- Remember that Germans are more formal than the average American or Australian.
- Have loose change with you. You'll often need to leave €0.30 to €0.50 as a tip at public toilets.
- Be aware that different lanes of a wider road may have the 'green man' and 'red man' on at the same time.

DON'T

- Be overly friendly with anyone who isn't family or a close friend.
- Gesture too much or be too touchy-feely.
- Be tempted to travel on public transport without a valid ticket. The fine and embarassment are not worth it.
- Bet at 'three shell game/find the lady' stalls, unless you really want to part with your money.
- Try to save money by buying contraband cigarettes. It's illegal both to sell and buy them.
- Hog the far-left lane of the Autobahn.
- Sound your horn unless it's an emergency.
- Cross the road if the 'red man' of the traffic light is on.
- Be intimidated by the seemingly unfriendly Berliners.

GLOSSARY

Here's a starter-kit of words and phrases for a new arrival in Berlin. Some of the phrases are informal rather than classroom German, as you are likely to hear them often in your daily life.

BASIC ESSENTIALS

yes, no	*ja, nein*
please	*bitte*
thank you/ thank you very much	*danke / vielen Dank*
what, why, where, when, who?	*was, warum, wo, wann, wer?*
here, there	*hier, da/dort*
today, tomorrow, yesterday	*heute, morgen, gestern*
morning, afternoon, evening, night	*Morgen, Nachmittag, Abend, Nacht*
At what time?	*Um wievel Uhr?*
Do you speak English?	*Sprechen Sie Englisch?*
I don't speak German	*Ich spreche kein Deutsch*
I don't understand	*Ich verstehe nicht*
left/right/straight on	*links/rechts/geradeaus*

EMERGENCIES AND MEDICAL NEEDS

Help!	*Hilfe!*
Stop!	*Halt!*
Please call: a doctor/the police	*Bitte rufen Sie: einen Arzt/ die Polizei*
Fire!	*Feuer!*
hospital	*Krankenhaus*
ambulance	*Krankenwagen*

dentist	Zahnarzt
pharmacy/chemist	Apotheke
optician	Optiker
painkiller	Schmerzmittel (or 'paracetamol')
allergy	Allergie
diarrhoea	Durchfall

GREETINGS

Good morning	Guten Morgen
Hello (good day)	Guten Tag
Good evening	Guten Abend
Good night	Gute Nacht
Good bye	Auf Wiedersehen/ (informal) Tschüs
How are you?	Wie geht es Ihnen?

AT THE SHOPS

May I help you? (from the shop assistant)	Kann ich Ihnen helfen? Was darf es sein? Kommen (Sie /die Dame /der Herr) zu Recht?
How many/much?	Wie viele/viel?
Anything else?	(informal)Noch ein Wunsch? Außerdem?
large/small	gross/klein
hot/cold/warm	heiss/kalt/warm
How much is that?	Wie viel kostet das?
I would like....	Ich hätte gern..../Ich möchte....
Can I pay with my credit card?	Kann ich mit Kreditkarte bezahlen?

NUMBERS

0	*null*	17	*siebzehn*
1	*eins*	18	*achtzehn*
2	*zwei*	19	*neunzehn*
3	*drei*	20	*zwanzig*
4	*vier*	21	*einundzwanzig*
5	*fünf*	30	*dreißig*
6	*sechs*	40	*vierzig*
7	*sieben*	50	*fünfzig*
8	*acht*	60	*sechzig*
9	*neun*	70	*siebzig*
10	*zehn*	80	*achtzig*
11	*elf*	90	*neunzig*
12	*zwölf*	100	*(ein)hundert*
13	*dreizehn*	210	*zweihundert(und) zehn*
14	*vierzehn*	1,000	*eintausend*
15	*fünfzehn*	1,000,000	*eine Million*
16	*sechzehn*		

FOOD

bread/bread roll	*Brot/Brötchen*
butter	*Butter*
jam	*Marmelade/Konfitüre*
eggs	*Eier*
milk/low fat milk	*Milch/fettarme Milch*
cheese	*Käse*
fish	*Fisch*
meat	*Fleisch*
pork	*Schweinefleisch*
beef	*Rindfleisch*

chicken	Huhn/Hähnchen
turkey	Pute
pepper	Pfeffer
salt	Salz
sugar	Zucker
coffee/tea	Kaffee/Tee
honey	Honig

VITAL SIGNS

Men´s /Ladies´ (toilet)	Herren/Damen or simply H/D
Entrance/Exit	Eingang/Ausgang
'Open'	Auf/Offen/Geöffnet
'Closed'	Zu/ Geschlossen
Careful!	Vorsicht!
Watch your step!	Vorsicht Stufe!
Prohibited	Verboten
Construction works	Baustelle
Road diversion	Umleitung
No smoking	Nicht rauchen/Rauchen verboten
No through road-residents only	Anlieger frei
No admittance	Kein Zutritt/Zutritt Verboten
Counter closed	Nicht besetzt

RESOURCE GUIDE

EMERGENCY NUMBERS
- Police: 110
- Ambulance and Fire Brigade: 112

PHARMACIES AND DRUGSTORES
There is no shortage of pharmacies (*Apotheken*) in every neighbourhood. Look for a huge red 'A' sign. Outside normal opening hours, look up http://www.apothekennotdienst.de or check the list outside any pharmacy, which will indicate the pharmacy near you which is open.

Drugstores are also everywhere. Look for Rossmann or Schleckers, as they have many branches all over Berlin. But note that you can't buy non-prescription drugs (even paracetamol) at drugstores, only in pharmacies.

HELPLINE
- International Helpline Berlin
  6:00 pm–midnight daily (English service)
  Tel: (030) 4401-0607

THE BERLIN POLICE
The police provides a hotline service called *Bürgertelefon* around the clock, which is available to Berliners and guests of the city who seek police non-emergency advice. Call tel: 4664-4664. They also have a website in English offering useful tips: http://www.berlin.de/polizei/english.html

PHONE/FAX
Country code for Germany: 0049
Major City codes: Add prefix '0' if calling from within Germany.
- Berlin: 30
- Bonn: 228
- Bremen: 421
- Cologne (Köln): 221
- Dortmund: 231

- Dresden: 351
- Düsseldorf: 211
- Frankfurt am Main (the financial centre): 69
- Frankfurt an der Oder: 335
- Hamburg: 40
- Hanover: 511
- Leipzig: 341
- Munich (München): 89
- Potsdam: 331
- Stuttgart: 71

Note: if calling from within the same city using a fixed-line phone, you don't need to dial the city code.

Mobile Phone Codes

Note that different mobile phone companies have different mobile codes that precede the phone number e.g. 160, 170, 171, 152, 162 etc. Add '0' before mobile codes when calling from inside Germany.

USEFUL WEBSITES
Berlin in General

- **http://berlin.de**
  This official Berlin website also has a useful information package (in English) called 'Welcome to Berlin' in PDF format which you can download for free. It contains lots of useful information particularly helpful to those intending to live in Berlin. Some of the information needs to be updated, but it still gives a handy overall picture.
- **http://visitberlin.de**
  This is the Berlin Tourism Organisation site.
- **http://berlin.angloinfo.com**
  This site is also very helpful for those intending to live in Berlin.
- **http://berlinfo.com**
  Another great site with sub-sites (worktime, freetime, lifetime, traveltime), loaded with information.
- **http://berlin.barwick.de**
  Yet another good place to trawl through for information.

- **http://timeout.com/berlin**
  This is the *TimeOut* guide site. This site whets your appetite to get the guide book, widely available in bookshops in Berlin.
- **http://inyourpocket.com/germany/city/berlin.html**
  This is the online version of *Berlin In Your Pocket*, a bimonthly city guide.

Maps and Routes
- http://stadtplandienst.de
- http://viamichelin.de
- http://berlin.de/stadtplan/

PUBLIC TRANSPORT
- http://bvg.de
  Very comprehensive site of the Berlin Transport Company, conveniently also in English. You can check the wide range of tickets available and their prices. Note that for some tickets, you can take others with you at specific times (weekends, after 8:00 pm on weekdays etc), so it's worth reading through the site carefully.

Vehicle related
- **ADAC**
  http://adac.de
  This is the main Automobile Association of Germany.
- **TÜV**
  http://tuv.com
  This organisation is for vehicle inspections and technical matters.
- **DEKRA**
  http://dekra.com
  Same function as TÜV.

EVENTS, CINEMAS, RESTAURANTS ETC
- http://zitty.de
  This is the website of Berlin's popular listings magazine, *Zitty*. It's only in German, though.

Jewish Interests
- http://berlin-judentum.de

DIPLOMATIC MISSIONS
- **Australian Embassy**
  Wallstraße 76-79, 10179 Berlin
  Tel: 8800-880
- **British Embassy**
  Wilhelmstr. 70-71, 10117 Berlin
  Tel: 20457-0
- **Canadian Embassy**
  Leipziger Platz 17, 10117 Berlin
  Tel: 20312-0
- **New Zealand Embassy**
  Friedrichstrasse 60, 10117 Berlin
  Tel: 20621-0
- **US Embassy**
  Pariser Platz 2, 10117 Berlin
  Tel: 2385-174

For Visa Appointments & American Citizen Services:
Consular Section, Clayallee 170, 14195 Berlin

The complete list of embassies in Berlin can be found at the German Foreign Service/State Department site at http://auswaertiges-amt.de

HOSPITALS
- **Charité Clinical Centres**
  For full list of Charité clinical centres, see http://charite.de
  - **Campus Charité Mitte**
    Charitéplatz 1, 10117 Berlin
    Tel: 45050
  - **Benjamin Franklin Clinical Centre**
    Hindenburgdamm 30, 12203 Berlin
    Tel: 84450
- **DRK (German Red Cross) Clinical Centres**
  For full list of DRK clinical centres, see http://www.drk-kliniken-berlin.de

- **DRK Kliniken Berlin Mitte**
  Drontheimer Str. 39-40, 13359 Berlin
  Tel: 3035-6000
- **DRK Kliniken Berlin Westend**
  Spandauer Damm 130, 14050 Berlin
  Tel: 3035-0
- **DRK Kliniken Berlin Köpenick** (in East Berlin)
  Salvador-Allende-Straße 2-8, 12559 Berlin
  Tel: 3035-30-00
- **St. Hedwig-Krankenhaus**
  Große Hamburger Straße 5 - 11, 10115 Berlin
  Tel: 23 11 0

DOCTORS

- http://aerzte-berlin.de
  This site (in German) helps you find doctors according to
  their specialisations and the language they speak.

Two general practitioners listed as English-speaking:
- Dr. Christian Kreutzer
  Medical Center Praxisklinik Bogenhaus
  Potsdamer Chaussee 80, 14129 Berlin
  Tel: 8049-0551
- Dr. Sylvia Kollmann
  Holsteinische Str. 6, 10717 Berlin
  Tel: 8738-303

OPTICAL SHOPS

These are two optical shop chains with many branches
throughout Berlin.
- **Fielmann AG**
  http://fielmann.com
- **Apollo Optik**
  http://apollo.de

TELEPHONE BOOK AND YELLOW PAGES

- **Telephone Book**
  http://www2.dastelefonbuch.de
  (Also in English, French, Spanish and Turkish)

- **Yellow Pages**
  http://gelbeseiten.de

ORGANISATIONS TO HELP YOU SETTLE IN AND NETWORK

- **The Berlin International Women's Club e.V. (BIWC)**
  http://biwc.de
  BIWC, founded in 1992, is Berlin's first and only international women's club which is multi-national. The current membership of over 300 comes from 55 nationalities and over 70 professions. The BIWC is nonprofit, apolitical and uses English as a common language. The club has many interest-based sub groups like book and magazine swap, business women/networking and mums and tots. Since Berlin is huge, there are also non-exclusive neighbourhood groups.

- **Connect Berlin e.V**
  http://connectberlin.de
  This is a group of English-speaking 'connectees' who meet for drinks and chats on a weekly basis.

- **English Language Teachers' Association of Berlin-Brandenburg**
  http://eltabb.com
  For English language teachers, ELTABB may be of interest to you. It's a professional association for teachers of English in the Berlin-Brandenburg area. ELTABB is an affiliate of the International Association of Teachers of English as a Foreign Language.

- **Jewish Community in Berlin**
  http://jg-berlin.org
  The Jewish Community in Berlin has a diversified infrastructure to support a Jewish life in Berlin, including social support for members in need.

- **INSSAN e.V**
  http://inssan-ev.de
  '*Inssan*' comes from the Arabic word for 'humans' or 'humanity'. This Muslim association has lots of activities with many focusing on dialogue with other religions and cultures.

INTERNET CAFES

- **Easyinternetcafé**
  They are embedded with Dunkin' Donuts, so there is always a threat to your waistline when using these cafés. The nice thing is that there are many branches:
    - Sony Center (Potsdamer Platz)
    - Hardenbergplatz 2 (next to Zoo station)
    - Kurfürstendamm 224
    - Karl-Marx-Straße 78 (Neukölln)
    - Schloßstraße 102 (Steglitz)

There's also an Internet café in the shopping arcade in Potsdamder Platz on the 1st floor (American 2nd floor). You can't miss it, as the computers are lined up along the 'bridge' connecting both sides of the arcade. You buy online time from a machine installed there.

NEWSPAPERS AND MAGAZINES
There are hardly any German/Berlin newspapers or magazines in English. *Der Spiegel* has an excellent English site (see http://spiegel.de). The *Exberliner* is a monthly English-language magazine with listings, reviews, job offers and some articles.

BOOKSHOPS
International English language newspapers and magazines can be found at newsagents in major train stations (Hauptbahnhof, Friedrichstraße, Ostbahnhof). English language books are available in:

- **Dussmann das KulturKaufhaus**
  Friedrichstraße 90 (Mitte)
  It has Berlin's widest range of books, CD's (pop, jazz, classical music), DVD's, audio books, games, stationery and a cafe within. What's even more astounding, opening hours from Monday to Saturday are from 10:00 am– midnight!
- **Hugendubel**
  Huge bookshop and the Tauentzienstraße branch has a cosy (but often crowded) café, which looks a bit like a

Starbucks. Branches at:
- Tauentzienstraße 13, Charlottenburg
- Potsdamer Platz Arkaden
- Friedrichstraße 83
- Schlossstraße 110, Steglitz

- **Thalia**
  The branch in ALEXA shopping mall has a good selection of English books.
- **U&R Kiepert Buchhandel GmbH**
  Hardenbergstraße 9a (Charlottenburg)
- **Schropp Land & Karte GmbH**
  Potsdamer Straße 129 (Tiergarten)
  They have a great selection of travel guides and maps.

Bookshops with Specifically English Books
- **Another Country**
  Riemannstraße 7 (Kreuzberg)
  http://anothercountry.de
- **Books in Berlin**
  Goethestraße 69 (Charlottenburg)
  http://booksinberlin.de
- **Saint Georges English Bookshop**
  Wörther Straße 27 (Prenzlauer Berg)
  http://saintgeorgesbookshop.com
- **East of Eden**
  Schreinerstraße 10 (Friedrichshain)
  http://www.east-of-eden.de/
- **Storytime Books and Café**
  Schmargendorfer Straße 36/37 (Friedenau)
  http://storytime-books.com
  (This shop specialises in books for children)

SUPERMARKETS
There are plenty of supermarkets and discount stores all over Berlin. You just need to look out for names like Extra, Kaisers, Edeka, Lidl, Plus, Aldi, Norma and Netto. If you need five-star supermarkets, go to KaDeWe and Galeries Lafayette. Two other department stores with supermarkets are Wertheim and Kaufhof.

SPECIAL FOOD SHOPS
American Food
- **American Lifestyle**
  Attilastraße 177 (Tempelhof)
  http://american-style.de

British Food
- **British shop**
  Sophienstraße 10 (Mitte)
  Tel: 285 99307
- **Broken English**
  Körtestraße 10 (Kreuzberg)
  Tel: 691-1227
- **Ye Olde British Shoppe**
  Lindenstraße 18
  Tel: (0331) 505-8792
  (Note: this shop is in Potsdam, for British-foodphiles living there)

Kosher Food
Bakeries
Bäckerei Kädtler
- Danziger Straße 135 (Prenzlauer Berg)
  Tel: 423 3233
- Kastanienallee 88 (Prenzlauer Berg)
  Tel: 4493214
  Sells breads, rolls, cakes and sausages. Delivers to Café Bleibergs (Nürnberger Straße 45a, Schöneberg).

Grocery shops
- **Kolbo**
  Auguststraße 77-78 (Mitte)
  Tel: 281-3135
- **Kosher Deli**
  Goethestraße 61 (Charlottenburg)
  Tel: 3150-9243
- **Pläzl**
  Passauer Straße 4 (Schöneberg)
  Tel: 217 7506

Wine
- **Kosheria**
  Kantstraße 141 (Charlottenburg)
  Tel: 3199-2675

Halal Food
Halal food can be found in Turkish and Arab shops, many of which are concentrated in Neukölln and Kreuzberg. Too many to list, here are just two halal restaurants that also offer catering service:
- **Merhaba Restaurant**
  http://merhaba-restaurant.de
  Wissmannstraße 32, Neukölln
- **Amy's Restaurant**
  http://amys-berlin.de
  Wilmersdorfer Straße 79, Charlottenburg
  Amy's offers something different from the ubiquitous Turkish/Middle Eastern fare. This place offers Malaysian specialities.

Asian Food
Among the Asian food shops, Vinh Loi Asien Supermarkt is probably the most popular with Asians. It stocks food from all over Asia—India, Pakistan, Indonesia, China, Vietnam, Singapore, Japan—as well as fresh vegetables, some Chinese crockery and even joss-sticks! There are two shops where you can mosey around:
- Rheinstraße 45, 12161 Berlin (Steglitz area)
- Ansbacher Straße 16, 10787 Berlin (opposite KaDeWe)

DIY STORES
- **Hornbach**
  http://hornbach.de
- **OBI**
  http://obi.de
- **Toom**
  http://toom.de

SCHOOLS

- **Berlin British School**
  http://berlinbritishschool.de
  Dickensweg 17 -19
  14055 Berlin |
- **Berlin International School**
  http://berlin-international-school.de
  Lentzeallee 8/14
  14195 Berlin
- **John F. Kennedy School**
  http://jfks.de
  Teltower Damm 87–93
  14167 Berlin
- **International School Villa Amalienhof**
  http://is-va.com
  Heerstrasse 465
  13593 Berlin

MANAGEMENT SCHOOL

- **European School of Management and Technology**
  Schlossplatz 1, 10178 Berlin
  http://esmt.org
  The school is backed by German big guns such as Allianz, Axel Springer, BMW, Bayer, Bosch, Siemens and ThyssenKrupp.

PLACES OF WORSHIP

There are places of worship for many diverse religions and denominations, though not all cater to English-speaking worshippers. Below are some churches with services in English:

- **The American Church in Berlin**
  http://americanchurchberlin.de
  An ecumenical, international church. Place of worship at Luther Church at Dennewitzplatz
  71/72 Bülowstraße
  10783 Berlin

- **Roman Catholic Mission at St. Bernhard**
  http://English-Mission-Berlin.de
  Königin-Luise-Str. 33
  14195 Berlin
- **St. George's Anglican Episcopal Church**
  http://stgeorges.de
  Morning service: St George's Church
  Preußenallee 17-19, 14052 Berlin
  Evening service: Marienkirche
  Karl-Liebknecht-Str 8 (near the Fernsehturm)

FURTHER READING

HISTORY
Berlin: A Short History. Christian Härtel. be.bra verlag GmbH 2006.

- This is a compact (80 pages) but detailed history book of Berlin. It's a nice balance between detailed information and readability.

A Concise History of Germany. Mary Fulbrook. Cambridge University Press, 2004.

- For those who want to know more about German history, this is the book to reach out for.

GERMAN CULTURE
CultureShock! Germany. Richard Lord. Marshall Cavendish Editions, 2006.

- As it's from the same *CultureShock!* series, the format is conveniently the same as the one you're holding in your hand. It gives readers another author's perspective of Germans.

Culture Smart! Germany. Barry Tomalin. Kuperard, 2006.

- Another book on German customs and etiquette, this compact book looks at Germans through yet another author's eyes.

BERLIN CITY GUIDES
There are many excellent city guides which you can find in the bookshops. These guides focus substantially on the sights, accommodation, restaurants and leisure activities, rather than on the practicalities of daily life and customs and etiquette, and are therefore good complements to this book. Below are some recommended ones:

Berlin In Your Pocket. In Your Pocket GmbH.

- *In your Pocket* guides come out once every two months, so the information is very updated. It's a compact booklet that fits, well, in your pocket, but manages to fit in lots of useful information. They can be found at a handful of bookshops (e.g.Berlin Story bookshop), in selected hotels (ask the concierge) and a number of embassies (e.g. UK, US, Canada).

ADAC Travel Guide Berlin. Potsdam and Schloss Sanssouci. ADAC Verlag GmbH, 2006.
- This is the German automobile association's travel guide. A comprehensive guide of Berlin's sights, plus an outline of its history and a travel information section. The photos make it an attractive guide.

DK Eyewitness Travel Berlin. Dorling Kindersley Limited, 2008.
- This guide has detailed descriptions about the sights, the history of Berlin, traveller's needs and a very useful Survival Guide. The photos are also sumptious.

The Rough Guide to Berlin. Rough Guides, 2008.
- What it lacks in attractive coloured photos is more than made up for by the densely packed information and special features. The guide has a more extensive coverage of the less touristy suburban areas.

Time Out Berlin. Time Out Guides Ltd, 2006.
- Another guide packed with information about the sights, where to stay, eat and have fun as well as chapters on history and Resources A-Z. It also has interesting features peppered throughout such as on the Berlin Wall and Currywurst.

SPECIAL INTERESTS
Jewish Berlin. Culture, Religion, Daily Life, Yesterday and Today. Bill Rebiger. Jaron Verlag GmbH, Berlin, 2005.
- This handy pocket-sized book contains information on synagogues, Jewish institutions, memorials, cultural events and listings of kosher shops in Berlin.

Stories of an Exhibition-Two Millennia of German Jewish History. Stiftung Jüdisches Museum Berlin, 2005.
- This publication of the Jewish Museum Foundation Berlin accompanies the Exhibition of the Jewish Museum Berlin. Having this book is a bit like being able to 'visit' the museum anytime from your sofa at home.

Muslims in the EU:Cities Report, Germany. Nina Mühe, 2007.
- This paper was commissioned by the EU Advocacy and Monitoring Program of the Open Society Institute. The researcher for this paper on Muslims in Germany is Nina Mühe, a German cultural anthropologist. The full report can be found at:
  http://www.eumap.org/topics/minority/reports/eumuslims/ background_reports/download/germany/germany.pdf

Past Finder Berlin 1933–1945. Maik Kopleck, Christoph Links Verlag, 2006.
- This book takes those interested in Nazi history to various sites connected to the Nazis. Interesting maps and photos accompany the concise description of the historic events related to the sites.

ABOUT THE AUTHOR

Agnes Sachsenroeder has lived in Cairo, Berlin, Bucharest and Sofia for over a decade. While in these cities, she also travelled extensively to other countries in the neighbourhood. Apart from grappling with the 'culture shock' that came from being dunked in cultures as diverse as Middle Eastern, European and Balkan, she also experienced first-hand the 'trailing spouse shock', as she morphed from being a lawyer to just The Wife of her husband whose job postings took them to different countries.

Sachsenroeder worked as a coordinator for a newcomers' orientation programme in Cairo, helping newcomers adjust to life in Egypt. She is also the author of *CultureShock! Bulgaria*.

During her stint as Trailing Spouse, apart from cross-cultural work, she also taught English to German exccutives in a leading bank and other organisations and worked on projects for non-governmental organisations.

INDEX

A

accommodation 106–124
  after moving in 116–117
  buying/renting a home 114–116
  locating your apartment 117–118
  looking for a home 107–114
  short-term accommodation 106–107
airports 138–140
  Schönefeld 140
  Tegel 139–140
angst 51
art 205–206

B

banking 135–136
basic social norms 80–82
beer 171
beggars 160
Berliner humour 55–56
Berliner *Schnauze* 53–55
Berlin Wall 270–271
birthdays 88
births 87–88
boroughs 38–39
Boulette 167
Brandenburger 13,34,38,108,178,188,194,256,259,260,271
bread 170
Bundestag 2,31,33,179

C

Checkpoint Charlie 271–274
Christmas 189–193
classical music 198–199
clothing sizes 129
coffee 172
communications 133–135
  mobile phones 135
  public phones 134
  telephones and internet 133–134
Currywurst 166,167,174,175

D

dance 200
dates 238
deaths 90–91
debit and credit cards 136
demography 76
Der Spiegel 48,49,57,95,131,153,237,242
desserts 170
dirndl 58
discipline 48–49
discrimination 94,95
districts 107–114
  Charlottenburg-Wilmersdorf 108
  Friedrichshain-Kreuzberg 112–113
  Lichtenberg 113
  Marzahn-Hellersdorf 113
  Mitte 108
  Neukölln 113
  Pankow 112
  Reinickendorf 109,112
  Spandau 108–109,267–268
  Steglitz-Zehlendorf 109
  Tempelhof-Schöneberg 109
  Treptow-Köpenick 113–114
Döner Kebap 173,175

E

eating in public 83
eating places 175–182
  cafés 178
  posh places 179
  shopping centres and departmental stores 177–178
  smoking 181
  snack kiosks 175
  snack shops and *Stehcafés* 175–177
economy 231–232
education 159–160
Euro 234
European Union (EU) 91–92

F

famous Berliners 252–259
fashion 76–77
film 206–207
football 52,57,63,93,207,211,212,252,260
foreigners 62–67,92–96
forms of address 80

Friedrichstrasse 3, 5, 130, 147, 178
furnishings 123

G
Galeries Lafayette 5, 124, 130, 177
Gendarmenmarkt 13, 108, 190, 196,
geography 7–8
German windows 119
gifts 87
government 251
Great Berlin Wheel 219
green oases 213–216
greetings 83–84

H
handshakes 80, 81
history 9–37
  becoming a capital city 31–34
  early beginnings 10
  from 2000 to 2008 34–37
  the carving up of Berlin 23–29
  the Wall falls 29–31
  the Weimar Republic 16–18
  under the Hohenzollerns 10–16
  under the Nazis 19–22
  World War II 22–23
Holocaust Memorial 269
homeless 160–161
homosexual 96–97
hooligans 61
House of Representatives 38

I
information board 119
intercom 118

J
job market 234–235
Jüdisches Museum (Jewish Museum)
193, 205, 269

K
KaDeWe 16, 109, 124, 125, 129, 177,
178, 281
Knut 217
Köpenick 10, 36, 38, 46, 113, 114,
115, 156, 161, 182, 204, 251

L
language 222–229
  Berlinerisch 228

colloquialism and imported
  words 227
  German alphabet 225–226
  non-verbal communication 229
  punctuation 228–229
lederhose 58
letter box 118–119

M
main courses and side dishes 168
marriages 88–90
meals of the day 174–175
medical and dental services 155–
156
mineral water 173
museums 200–204, 218
Museumsinsel 10, 38, 108, 200, 202,
261
mushrooms 169

N
national anthem 249
neighbours 83–85
neo-Nazis 60–61
Neue Synagoge 74, 108, 269
New Year's Day 193–195
nightlife 206
NSDAP 19
nudity 52–53

O
Oberbaumbrücke 275, 277
Oktoberfest 58, 183, 196
operas 199
opticians 133
Ossi 3, 56
other festivals and events 195–198

P
patriotism 51–52
pets 161
pharmacies and drugstores 156–157
phone etiquette 83
places of interest 259–277
postal services 136–137
Potsdamer Platz 14, 18, 26, 39, 41, 1
08, 177, 178, 190, 198, 205, 206, 20
9, 271
Prenzlauer Berg 29, 35, 112, 130, 18
2, 188, 190, 194, 206, 218, 253, 281

print media 153
prostitution 97
psychological health 157–159
public holidays 187–195
public toilets 160
punctuality 49–50

R
radio 154
registrations and residence permits 104–106
Reichstag 17,19,20,31,33,37,38, 108,179,263
religion 67–76
  Christians 68
  Jews 70–75
  Muslims 68–70
  Scientologists 75
  Transcendental Meditation 76
Richtfest 91
Rotes Rathaus 15,31
rubbish disposal 120–122

S
same-sex partnerships 90
sausages 165–167
Schloss Charlottenburg 39,108,199, 201,213,213–216,256,268
school 88
Schrebergarten 186
senate 37
shopping 124–133
  DIY stores 132–133
  electronic goods 128
  flea markets 127
  open-air markets 127
  shopping malls 128–130
  special dietary needs 131–132
  supermarkets 124–126
smiling 81
sports and fitness 207–213
Staatsoper 12,199,256,260
summer vacation 185
superstitions 59–60

T
tea 172–173
Teutonic people 46–56
theatres 199–200

the work enviroment 235–243
  business attire 237–238
  business gifts 243
  business meals 243
  presentations, negotiations and other meetings 239–241
  women at work 236–237
  work attitude 235
Tiergarten 213
time 155,236,249
tipping 179
transport 138–152
  coaches 141
  cycling 152
  driving 147–151
  on foot 152
  S-Bahn and U-Bahn 141–144
  taxis 145–146
  trains 140–141
  trams and buses 144–145
  water transport 146–147
TV 153–154
types of companies 244–246

U
unions and works councils 246–247
Unter den Linden 13,21,140,178,1 99,204,218,256,260
utilities 123

V
vegetables 169
violence 61
visas 102–104
visiting 85–87

W
water 123–124,155
watering holes 182–183
weather 9,250
Wessi 3,56
what to bring 100–102
wine 171–172
winter service 119–120

Z
zoos 217–218

Titles in the CultureShock! series:

Argentina	Great Britain	Russia
Australia	Greece	San Francisco
Austria	Hawaii	Saudi Arabia
Bahrain	Hong Kong	Scotland
Beijing	Hungary	Sri Lanka
Belgium	India	Shanghai
Berlin	Ireland	Singapore
Bolivia	Italy	South Africa
Borneo	Jakarta	Spain
Bulgaria	Japan	Sri Lanka
Brazil	Korea	Sweden
Cambodia	Laos	Switzerland
Canada	London	Syria
Chicago	Malaysia	Taiwan
Chile	Mauritius	Thailand
China	Morocco	Tokyo
Costa Rica	Munich	Travel Safe
Cuba	Myanmar	Turkey
Czech Republic	Netherlands	United Arab
Denmark	New Zealand	Emirates
Ecuador	Norway	USA
Egypt	Pakistan	Vancouver
Finland	Paris	Venezuela
France	Philippines	
Germany	Portugal	

For more information about any of these titles, please contact any of our Marshall Cavendish offices around the world (listed on page ii) or visit our website at:

www.marshallcavendish.com/genref